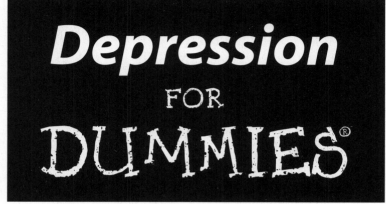

Depression FOR DUMMIES®

**by Laura L. Smith, PhD
and Charles H. Elliott, PhD**

Foreword by Aaron T. Beck, MD

WILEY

Wiley Publishing, Inc.

Depression For Dummies®

Published by
Wiley Publishing, Inc.
111 River St.
Hoboken, NJ 07030
www.wiley.com

Copyright © 2003 by Wiley Publishing, Inc., Indianapolis, Indiana

Published by Wiley Publishing, Inc., Indianapolis, Indiana

Published simultaneously in Canada

No part of this publication may be reproduced, stored in a retrieval system, or transmitted in any form or by any means, electronic, mechanical, photocopying, recording, scanning, or otherwise, except as permitted under Sections 107 or 108 of the 1976 United States Copyright Act, without either the prior written permission of the Publisher, or authorization through payment of the appropriate per-copy fee to the Copyright Clearance Center, 222 Rosewood Drive, Danvers, MA 01923, 978-750-8400, fax 978-646-8700. Requests to the Publisher for permission should be addressed to the Legal Department, Wiley Publishing, Inc., 10475 Crosspoint Blvd., Indianapolis, IN 46256, 317-572-3447, fax 317-572-4447, or e-mail permcoordinator@wiley.com.

Trademarks: Wiley, the Wiley Publishing logo, For Dummies, the Dummies Man logo, A Reference for the Rest of Us!, The Dummies Way, Dummies Daily, The Fun and Easy Way, Dummies.com and related trade dress are trademarks or registered trademarks of John Wiley & Sons, Inc. and/or its affiliates in the United States and other countries, and may not be used without written permission. All other trademarks are the property of their respective owners. Wiley Publishing, Inc., is not associated with any product or vendor mentioned in this book.

For general information on our other products and services or to obtain technical support, please contact our Customer Care Department within the U.S. at 800-762-2974, outside the U.S. at 317-572-3993, or fax 317-572-4002.

Wiley also publishes its books in a variety of electronic formats. Some content that appears in print may not be available in electronic books.

Library of Congress Control Number available from publisher

ISBN: 978-0-7645-3900-8

Manufactured in the United States of America

10 9 8

WILEY   is a trademark of Wiley Publishing, Inc.

Depression For Dummies®

Cheat Sheet

Are You Depressed?

People experience depression in different ways. This symptom checklist can provide you with a rough idea as to whether you're experiencing depression. Check all items that apply to you.

- ❏ I feel worthless.
- ❏ My appetite has changed.
- ❏ I don't feel like seeing other people.
- ❏ I have less energy than usual.
- ❏ I don't look forward to anything.
- ❏ I have more aches and pains lately.
- ❏ I can't concentrate like usual.
- ❏ I feel a lot of guilt.
- ❏ I'm not interested in doing anything.
- ❏ I feel hopeless.
- ❏ I feel sad and empty.
- ❏ I haven't been sleeping well lately.
- ❏ I've been dwelling on thoughts of death lately.
- ❏ I can't make decisions.

Any of these symptoms can indicate that you're not feeling up to par. Merely checking one or two doesn't necessarily mean you're depressed, but the more items you check, the greater the concern of possible depression.

Anyone can have these feelings for a little while. You should mainly be concerned if these symptoms last for more than a week or two. However, if you're having thoughts of suicide or death, get help now. Depression can be deadly. See Chapter 2 for more information about the signs and symptoms of depression.

Getting Help

If you think that you may be depressed, don't despair. Lots of help is available. Here are some sources you can consult:

- ✔ **Your family doctor:** Ask for a complete physical. Sometimes depression is the result of other medical problems.

- ✔ **Mental health professionals:** See one of these professionals after you rule out other physical causes for your low mood. Licensed psychologists, social workers, and counselors can competently diagnose and treat depression.

- ✔ **Psychiatrists:** These physicians have specialized training in the treatment of depression and other mental disorders. They typically focus on the use of medication and other biologically based treatments.

- ✔ **The Internet:** We recommend WebMD (www.webmd.com) and the American Psychological Association (www.apa.org) as especially informative sites with lots of useful, user-friendly information about depression. But remember that the Internet can't replace professional help.

- ✔ **Books about depression:** Start with this book, and then visit your library. You can't read too much about the problem.

For Dummies: Bestselling Book Series for Beginners

Depression For Dummies®

Depression Do's and Don'ts

- **Do get help:** You can start with self-help resources like this book, but you need to see a professional if your depression doesn't lift soon.

- **Don't ignore feelings of hopelessness or suicidal thoughts:** These symptoms are serious! If you have these symptoms, seek help immediately.

- **Do read Depression For Dummies.**

- **Don't think that there's nothing you can do:** Depression is highly treatable.

- **Do keep trying:** If your first attempt to treat depression doesn't work, a variety of ways exist to help you deal with depression.

- **Don't blame yourself:** Depression has many causes, and you certainly didn't ask for your depression.

Dealing with Bad Moods

Everyone experiences bad moods from time to time. A bad mood isn't the same as depression. Bad moods are transient, and they lift after awhile. However, here are a few things you can do for a simple bad mood:

- **Get moving:** Almost any aerobic activity can alleviate a bad mood. Dance, run, or play. Get that heart pounding.

- **Be grateful:** Make a list of what you feel grateful for. Bad moods may make you forget the good things in your life. Spend a few minutes considering life's gifts, from small to large.

- **Don't catastrophize:** Realize that everyone feels a little low once in a while.

- **Help someone:** Focusing on helping someone else is one of the best ways to overcome a lousy mood. It's a great antidote for dwelling on your own misfortune.

Copyright © 2003 Wiley Publishing, Inc. All rights reserved.

Item 3900-0.

For more information about Wiley Publishing, call 1-800-762-2974.

For Dummies: Bestselling Book Series for Beginners

About the Authors

Laura L. Smith, PhD, is a clinical psychologist at Presbyterian Medical Group at the Behavioral Medicine Outpatient Clinic, Albuquerque, New Mexico. At Presbyterian, she specializes in the assessment and treatment of both adults and children with depression and other emotional disorders. In addition, she has presented on new developments in cognitive therapy to both national and international audiences. Dr. Smith is coauthor of *Overcoming Anxiety For Dummies* (Wiley Publishing), *Hollow Kids: Recapturing the Soul of a Generation Lost to the Self-Esteem Myth* (Prima, 2001), and *Why Can't I Be the Parent I Want to Be?* (New Harbinger Publications, 1999).

Charles H. Elliott, PhD, is a clinical psychologist and a member of the faculty at the Fielding Graduate Institute. He is a Founding Fellow in the Academy of Cognitive Therapy, an internationally recognized organization that certifies cognitive therapists for treating depression, anxiety, and other emotional disorders. In addition, he has written many articles and book chapters in the area of cognitive-behavior therapies. He has made numerous presentations nationally and internationally on new developments in assessment and therapy of emotional disorders. He is coauthor of *Overcoming Anxiety For Dummies* (Wiley Publishing), *Why Can't I Get What I Want?* (Davies-Black, 1998; A Behavioral Science Book Club Selection), *Why Can't I Be the Parent I Want to Be?* (New Harbinger Publications, 1999), and *Hollow Kids* (Prima, 2001).

Drs. Elliott and Smith are available for speaking engagements and workshops. You can visit their Web site at www.PsychAuthors.com. Interested readers also can find a list of background literature relevant to *Depression For Dummies* at the site.

Dedication

We dedicate this book to our family: Alli, Brian, Nathan, Sara, and Trevor. And to our parents: William Thomas Smith (1914–1999), Edna Louise Smith, Joe Bond Elliott, and Suzanne Wieder Elliott.

Authors' Acknowledgments

Okay, we broke our promise and wrote another book. We may have to join Authors Anonymous! We thank our family and friends for putting up with our moans and complaints. We send our heartfelt appreciation to the Rodriquez family, especially Melodie and Adriana, who shared their home and table on holidays so we could write until the last second.

Thanks also to our agents, Ed and Elizabeth Knappman, who have supported our writing. We applaud and appreciate the professionalism of our editors at Wiley Publishing; special thanks to Mike Baker, Norm Crampton, Greg Pearson, Jennifer Bingham, Chrissy Guthrie, Esmeralda St. Clair, and Natasha Graf. Thanks to our technical editors, Cory Newman, PhD, and Howard Berger, MD.

We also appreciate Audrey Hite for taking good care of us. And thanks to Scott Love, computer geek extraordinaire, for designing our Web site and keeping our computers up and running. In addition, we thank Diana Montoya-Boyer for keeping us organized, Tracie Antonuk for her optimistic support of our writing, and Karen Villanueva, our personal publicist.

Finally, we're especially grateful to have been invited into the lives of our many clients over the years. We have profited from what they have taught us about the problems they face. They have provided us with a greater understanding of depression as well as their brave struggle.

Publisher's Acknowledgments

We're proud of this book; please send us your comments through our Dummies online registration form located at www.dummies.com/register/.

Some of the people who helped bring this book to market include the following:

Acquisitions, Editorial, and Media Development

Project Editor: Mike Baker

Acquisitions Editor: Natasha Graf

Copy Editors: Jennifer Bingham, Christina Guthrie, and Greg Pearson

Editorial Program Assistant: Holly Gastineau-Grimes

Technical Editors: Howard Berger, MD, and Cory Newman, PhD

Editorial Manager: Jennifer Ehrlich

Editorial Assistant: Elizabeth Rea

Cover Photos: ©Tim Brown/Getty Images/Stone

Cartoons: Rich Tennant, www.the5thwave.com

Production

Project Coordinator: Kristie Rees

Layout and Graphics: Seth Conley, LeAndra Hosier, Lynsey Osborn, Shea Wilson

Proofreaders: Aptara

Indexer: Aptara

Special Help: Chad R. Sievers

Publishing and Editorial for Consumer Dummies

Diane Graves Steele, Vice President and Publisher, Consumer Dummies

Joyce Pepple, Acquisitions Director, Consumer Dummies

Kristin A. Cocks, Product Development Director, Consumer Dummies

Michael Spring, Vice President and Publisher, Travel

Brice Gosnell, Associate Publisher, Travel

Kelly Regan, Editorial Director, Travel

Publishing for Technology Dummies

Andy Cummings, Vice President and Publisher, Dummies Technology/General User

Composition Services

Gerry Fahey, Vice President of Production Services

Debbie Stailey, Director of Composition Services

Contents at a Glance

Table of Contents

Foreword

I'm very pleased that Drs. Charles Elliott and Laura Smith have reviewed and distilled the scientific literature on the treatment of depression for the general public. This book is uniquely comprehensive in that it thoroughly covers the scientifically validated treatments for depression, including behavior therapy, medications, interpersonal therapy, and cognitive therapy. The authors have also included promising ideas based on mindfulness and positive psychology. However, they have chosen to emphasize the importance of cognitive therapy because no other therapy has received as much support as cognitive therapy for the treatment of depression.

Thus, Drs. Elliott and Smith have woven important cognitive-therapy principles into their presentation of the other validated approaches to depression. This decision is appropriate, because research has suggested that some of these other therapies may in fact work due in part to the cognitive-therapy strategies embedded within them.

I believe a word about cognitive therapy is in order. In the late 1950s, I began developing cognitive therapy. At the time, I was dissatisfied with the lack of evidence supporting the value of the prevailing psychotherapy — Freudian psychoanalysis — in treating depression. Cognitive therapy quickly became established as a highly effective treatment for depression, a finding that has been verified in numerous subsequent clinical trials. Over the ensuing decades, cognitive therapy has also demonstrated excellent outcomes in the treatment of problems with anger, anxiety, panic disorder, stress, relationship problems, substance abuse, eating disorders, and, most recently, even schizophrenia. To date, no other psychotherapy has demonstrated such consistent effectiveness across a broad swath of problems. *Depression For Dummies* does a marvelous job of providing readers with the core techniques and principles of cognitive therapy as applied to depression.

I feel it's important to note that *Depression For Dummies* isn't a book for dummies! Rather, this book lays out the principles of cognitive therapy, as well as other validated psychotherapies, in exceptionally clear terms. Drs. Elliott and Smith include fascinating clinical examples and effective exercises within the most reader-friendly, even entertaining, format I've seen in a book of this genre. I have no doubt it will prove to be a powerful self-help resource as well as an adjunct to psychotherapy.

I have known Dr. Elliott since the early 1980s, when he was a highly skillful cognitive therapist serving in a major psychotherapy outcome study. I recall last encountering Drs. Elliott and Smith just a few years ago at an international conference on cognitive therapy in Catania, Italy. They presented at this conference as part of their honeymoon. Such dedication to cognitive therapy!

If you struggle with depression, I strongly recommend *Depression For Dummies.* These authors convey considerable compassion, empathy, and insight in addition to unusual clarity.

Aaron T. Beck, MD
President, The Beck Institute for Cognitive Therapy and Research

Introduction

*D*ecadent luxuries, dazzling technology, and startling new knowledge flood the senses and excite the imagination. What was the domain of science fiction less than a generation ago is now commonplace in many living rooms. Today, cable companies beam recently released movies to inches-thick televisions that hang on walls. All you have to do is press a few buttons on your remote control and your home is a cinema. And, with a couple of mouse clicks, you can order a pizza online that arrives in time for the start of the movie.

In the field of healthcare, advancing knowledge of the immune system promises new cancer treatments that go to the source of the disease. Nanotechnology eventually will allow inconceivably small machines to clean out congested arteries like a plumber's snake. And the human genome project begins to solve the mysteries behind countless inherited diseases.

Truly, life has never been so good and bountiful. What a wonderful time to be alive. Sure, the world still has plenty of problems, but solutions for many of them lie on the horizon.

Yet the World Health Organization paints a less optimistic picture. It estimates that on any given day, 121 million people worldwide suffer from depression. Over the course of a year, almost 6 percent of the world's men and fewer than 10 percent of the women suffer an episode of depression. Depression rates continue to increase. And most experts believe that the increase is real — not just a result of more people seeking help. Today, kids exhibit depression at nearly ten times the rate of previous generations.

Theories abound concerning the alarming increase in depression today. But regardless of the cause, this scourge robs its victims of happiness, joy, and the capacity to give and receive love.

The good news is that more weapons exist for defeating depression than ever before. Clinicians have devised new psychotherapies that have been verified as effective in treating depression and preventing relapse. Furthermore, science is beginning to understand the delicate relationship between mood and brain chemistry. Medications that target specific chemicals provide important additional tools for the alleviation of depression. The vast majority of people no longer need to suffer with long-standing, intractable depression.

A Note to Our Depressed Readers

We're keenly aware of the pain and profound despair you may be experiencing. Likely, your sense of humor is depleted. With this book, we attempt to lighten an exquisitely somber subject with tidbits of humor. Some of you may take offense with our attempts or even feel diminished or discounted by this decision. We can understand that reaction. At the same time, your long-term goals need to include rediscovering laughter. Thus, we hope you can try to take our occasional use of wit in the manner we intend it — as another way to help you lift yourself out of the fog of depression.

In addition, we realize that the title *Depression For Dummies* may seem offensive to some, especially because when people are depressed, they're prone to make negative, personalized interpretations (see Part II for more information on this topic). However, we assure you that the content of this book is as serious and in-depth as any book on depression. The *For Dummies* format simply enables us to present important material in easily digestible segments. We leave it up to you to determine if we succeed in doing so.

Conventions Used in This Book

In this book, we avoid the use of professional jargon as much as possible. When we occasionally find it necessary to use a technical term, we clearly define that term.

We also include numerous stories to illustrate the information and techniques we present. The people you read about aren't real; however, they represent composites of the many wonderful people we've known and worked with over the years. We bold the name of each character the first time it appears to alert you to the fact that we're telling a story.

Finally, if you're reading this book because you want help in defeating your own depression, we recommend that you purchase a spiral notebook. Use that notebook to write out the exercises we present throughout the book. We call these exercises Antidepression Tools and highlight them with an icon. Use your notebook often and reread what you've written from time to time.

About This Book

We have two primary goals in writing this book. First, we want you to understand the nature of depression. Understanding depression makes the idea of dealing with it less frightening. Second, we present what you're probably most interested in discovering — how to overcome your depression or help someone you love who has depression.

We leave no stone unturned in our quest to bring you every possible means for battling depression. We draw strategies for defeating depression from the fields of medicine and psychotherapy. We tell you about the newest arsenal of medications that can combat depression. We show you how focusing on your overall health with exercise and nutrition can pay off. Plus, we extract elements from the psychotherapeutic approaches that have stood up to the tests of rigorous research and been verified as highly effective treatments for depression. These approaches include

- ✔ Cognitive therapy
- ✔ Behavior therapy
- ✔ Interpersonal and relationship therapy

Then we go one step further. We turn to the new field of *positive psychology* for ideas on navigating your way from feeling *good* again to feeling *even better*. We want you to make your life more joyful and more meaningful.

Depression For Dummies offers you the best advice available based on scientific research. We believe that, if you practice the techniques and strategies we provide in this book, you'll very likely feel better. For many people, this book may be a complete guide for defeating mild to moderate depression. Numerous studies show that self-help often works.

However, depression frequently needs more care and attention than you can receive through self-help. If your depression significantly hinders your ability to work or play, you need to get professional help. No book can completely replace therapy. Start by seeing your family doctor. If you're seeing a therapist or counselor, you may find that *Depression For Dummies* can help augment your therapy. Be sure to discuss that possibility with your therapist. Depression can be conquered; please don't give up.

Foolish Assumptions

Who would want to read this book? We assume, perhaps foolishly, that you or someone you love suffers from depression. We also figure that you want to banish depression from your life. Finally, we imagine that you're curious about a variety of helpful strategies that can fit your lifestyle and personality. If these descriptions strike a chord, this book is for you.

How This Book Is Organized

We organize *Depression For Dummies* into 7 parts and 22 chapters. Right now, we're going to tell you a little about each part.

Part I: Discovering Depression and Preparing a Plan

Chapter 1 explores the costs of depression in economic, social, and emotional terms. We describe what depression looks like in various people. Finally, we provide an overview of the best means for treating depression. In Chapter 2, we cover the difference between the various forms of depression. Furthermore, we explain the difference between grief and depression. Chapter 3 shows you how to find the motivation for taking charge of your own depression. And Chapter 4 tells you how to find and get professional help.

Part II: Untwisting Your Thinking: Thought Therapy

More studies support the value of thought therapy (*cognitive therapy*) for the treatment of depression than any other psychotherapy. Part II shows you how certain habitual ways of thinking can be a major contributor to depression. A number of chapters combine to give you a large toolbox of techniques for changing these dark, distorted thoughts into realistic appraisals of yourself, your world, and your future. You can see that this transformation isn't based on rationalization, chicanery, or self-deception. Rather, you discover how to subject your thoughts to reasoned scrutiny based on logic and evidence.

Part III: Taking Action Against Depression: Behavior Therapy

When you feel overwhelmed by depression, you likely find yourself disengaging from everyday life. You start doing less and less as you put off tackling even slightly disagreeable tasks. Of greater concern, previously enjoyable activities seem dull, bland, and devoid of pleasure. Part III shows you how to short-circuit "do-nothingism" and slowly regain confidence and joy. We give you a mental boost to get moving again through exercise and rediscovering healthy pleasures.

Part IV: Rebuilding Connections: Relationship Therapy

Clinical trials of interpersonal therapy demonstrate the value of addressing the relationship side of depression. Depression has a way of disrupting relationships with friends, family, partners, and other loved ones. And relationship problems can worsen depression. Part IV extracts crucial elements from interpersonal therapy and provides additional ideas for handling relationship difficulties that can increase depression. We cover issues such as communicating in healthy ways and coping with loss and grief.

Part V: Fighting the Physical Foe: Biological Therapies

Pharmaceutical companies have invested billions of dollars into developing a wide range of antidepressant medications. We review these medications, from the earliest to the most recent, and give you important information regarding their effectiveness and side effects. We also give you some tools for helping make the decision as to whether or not medications make sense for you and your depression. We also explore the role of herbs, supplements, and nutrition in alleviating depression and review a few alternative physiologically based treatments for depression, such as light therapy.

Part VI: Looking Beyond Depression

We have every reason to believe that the information in the first five parts, perhaps in conjunction with professional help, will lift you out of your depression. But what do you do next? Part VI tells you how to deal with possible relapses in the future. This part tells you how to reduce the likelihood of such slips and how to deal with them if they do occur. Next, we discuss a new approach, called *mindful acceptance* that has recently been found to be very helpful for reducing depression relapse.

Part VI then turns to the field of positive psychology for ideas on how to further enhance your life. We want you to feel better than good again, so we lay out strategies for enhancing your sense of well-being through a sense of purpose and connectedness.

Part VII: The Part of Tens

If you want quick ideas on how to deal with a bad mood, you can find them here. Then we show you ten ways to help your kids if they get

depressed. We conclude with ten ways to help a friend or lover overcome depression.

Icons Used in This Book

Throughout this book, we use icons in the margins to quickly point out different types of information. Here are the icons you'll see and a few words about
what they mean.

This icon alerts you to an exercise you can use to hammer away at or discover more about your depression.

As the name of this icon implies, we don't want you to forget the information
that accompanies it.

This icon emphasizes pieces of practical information or bits of insight that
you can put to work.

This icon appears when you need to be careful or seek professional help.

This piece of art alerts you to information that you may find interesting, but
not reading it won't put you at a disadvantage in the battle against depression.

Where to Go from Here

Most books are written so that you have to start on page one and read straight
through. But we wrote *Depression For Dummies* so that you can use the detailed
Table of Contents to pick and choose what you want to read based on your
individual interests. Don't worry too much about reading chapters and parts in
any particular order. Read whatever chapters apply to your situation. However,
we suggest that you at least skim Part I, because it contains a variety of fascinating facts as well as important ideas for getting started.

In addition, the more severe your depression, the more we urge you to start
with Chapter 3 and continue with Part III. These chapters contain a variety of
ways for overcoming the powerful inertia that keeps severely depressed
people from taking actions. After you read those chapters, feel free to continue picking and choosing what you want to read.

Part I

Discovering Depression and Preparing a Plan

The 5th Wave   By Rich Tennant

"The blues I can handle. Usually, I can express it
with a simple 12-bar guitar lick. Depression,
on the other hand, takes a 3-act opera."

In this part . . .

Discover the symptoms of depression and sort out whether you or someone you care about may be depressed. We tell you about the worldwide depression epidemic. And we explain the different forms of depression.

The task of defeating depression presents numerous obstacles. We show you what these roadblocks are and how to deal with them. In this part, we also give you an overview of the various treatments for depression and how to obtain the best possible help.

Chapter 1

Demystifying and Defeating Depression

*L*ike solitary confinement, depression isolates those who experience it. Alone, fearful, and feeling powerless, sufferers withdraw. Hope, faith, relationships, work, play, and creative pursuits — the very paths to recovery — seem meaningless and inconceivable. A cruel, inhuman punishment, depression incarcerates the body, mind, and soul.

Though depression feels inescapable, we have a set of keys for unlocking the jail cell of depression that confines you or someone you care about. You may find that the first key you try works, but more often than not escape requires a combination of keys. We're here to help — we have a big ol' ring of keys to pass around.

In this chapter, we clarify the difference between sadness and depression; they're not the same. Next, we show you how depression looks among various groups of people. We calculate the costs of depression in terms of health, productivity, and relationships. We tell you about the treatment options for depression. And finally, we offer a glimpse of life beyond depression.

Just Singing the Blues or Depressed?

Life delivers death, divorce, disaster, disease, disorder, disgrace, and distress. Inescapable and inevitable. Even if nothing else goes wrong, you're eventually going to die. Expecting to live a life absent of sharp episodes of sadness, despair, or grief is unrealistic. In fact, without times of sorrow, how would you truly appreciate life's blessings?

Yet, misfortunes and loss need not lead to depression. What's the difference? Sadness and grief lessen in intensity as time passes (see Chapter 2 for more information about grief and types of depression). Sadness and grief may seem fairly overwhelming when they occur. But time does eventually heal.

Unlike episodes of despair, depression involves deep guilt and loss of self-esteem. People suffering from depression feel hopeless, helpless, and unforgiving of themselves. Depression disrupts the body, often impacting sleep, appetite, concentration, energy, and sex. And depression profoundly diminishes the ability to love, laugh, work, and play.

Depression is a mood disorder in which a person feels profoundly sad, joyless, despondent, and unable to experience pleasure. Depression comes in various types that have somewhat different symptoms. We describe these categories of depression in Chapter 2, but all involve a low mood or diminished sense of pleasure.

The Varying Faces of Depression

Depression doesn't discriminate; it can affect anyone regardless of race, social class, or status. Typical symptoms of sadness, loss of energy and interests, low self-esteem, feelings of guilt, and changes in appetite and sleep appear in men, women, children, and the elderly. Such symptoms also manifest themselves across different cultures. However, a depressed preschooler may not exactly look the same as a depressed 80-year-old.

In Chapter 2, we dissect the various categories of depression. In this chapter, we show you how depression looks in different people at different life stages. The cases we present in this chapter, and throughout this book, don't represent real people. However, they're loosely based on the people we've worked with in our collective careers.

Young and depressed

Depression can be found among children of any age, from preschool through young adulthood. Experts agree that the rates of depression in youth have skyrocketed. A recent study among college students at Kansas State University found the percentage of depressed students doubled over a 13-year period.

Kids, depression, and obesity

In a study reported in the September 2002 journal *Pediatrics,* more than 9,000 teens participated in a study on the relationship between depression and obesity. The researchers gave the kids a questionnaire that measured depression and calculated their body mass index (BMI), a measure of obesity. They assessed the kids once again a year later. Kids who were obese and depressed at the first assessment tended to become more obese by the second assessment. Kids who were not obese at the first assessment, but were depressed, had double the risk of becoming obese a year later. Much remains to be discovered about exactly how depression may increase this risk of obesity; however, these findings underscore the importance of addressing depression when it occurs.

The rates of depression in children are likely underreported because parents and professionals often fail to recognize the problem. Children rarely spontaneously report depression to others. Instead, they more typically remain unaware of their feelings, which manifest themselves through changes in their behavior, appetite, and sleep.

Mackenzie's mom surprises her by bringing cupcakes to school on her eighth birthday. The teacher leads the class in singing "Happy Birthday," but Mackenzie barely smiles. After quickly devouring the two overloaded trays of cupcakes, the kids all race out to the playground for recess. Mackenzie trails behind.

Mackenzie's teacher approaches her mother, "I'm concerned about Mackenzie. She seems quiet and less interested in her schoolwork. I often see her alone on the playground. She doesn't raise her hand in class like she used to, either. Is something wrong?"

When children are depressed, they lose interest in activities that they previously enjoyed. If you ask them if they're sad, they may not be able to connect their feelings with words. However, they will show various signs of depression, such as low energy, sleep problems, appetite changes, irritability, and low self-esteem.

Watch children at play for subtle signs of depression. Depressed children may weave themes of death or loss into their play. All children's play includes such themes on occasion, but dark topics show up more often in kids who are depressed. You may need to observe kids over a period of time because their moods change. They may not look as continuously depressed as adults with depression. Their moods may fluctuate throughout the day. Consult a professional if you have any doubts.

Treating depression in old age

Physicians often fail to notice depression in the elderly. Why? They chalk up the signs of depression to the process of normal aging. That's unfortunate, because depression is common — and treatable — in geriatric populations.

Yet sometimes antidepressant medications don't work. A study reported recently in the journal *Psychotherapy and Psychosomatics* found that interpersonal therapy significantly decreased depression in patients over 60 years of age who had previously failed to respond sufficiently to antidepressant medication. This small study supports the idea that dealing with interpersonal issues, such as grief, loss, and transitions, may be particularly useful for people in this age group.

Is grandpa grumpy or depressed?

Some people view old age as inherently depressing. They assume that upon reaching a certain age, quality of life deteriorates. In fact, there is some truth to these assumptions: Old age brings increases in illness and disability and losses of friends, family members, and social support. Therefore, *some* sadness is to be expected.

Nevertheless, depression is absolutely *not* an inevitable consequence of old age. Most symptoms of depression in the elderly mimic those of depression in anyone. However, the elderly are a little more likely to focus on aches and pains rather than feelings of despair. Furthermore, they commonly express regret and remorse about past events in their lives.

Depression interferes with memory. If you notice increased memory problems in grandpa or grandma, you could easily chalk the problem up to the worst-case scenario — Alzheimer's or dementia. However, such memory problems can be the result of depression.

And depression in the elderly increases the chances of death. Yet, if asked about depression, elders may scoff at the idea. Denying depression, the elder person may not get needed treatment.

Elderly men are at particularly high risk of suicide. Men older than 60 are more likely to take their own lives than any other combination of age and gender. If you have any doubts, check the possibility of depression with a doctor or mental health professional.

Real men don't get depressed, or do they?

Most studies show that men get depressed about half as frequently as women. But then again, men tend to cover up and hide their depression;

they feel far more reluctant to talk about weaknesses and vulnerabilities than women do. Why?

Many men have been taught that admitting to any form of mental illness or emotional problem is unmanly. From early childhood experiences, these men learn to cover up negative feelings.

Scott looks forward to retirement from his job as a marketing executive. He can't wait to start traveling and pursuing long-postponed hobbies. Three months after he retires, his wife of 20 years asks for a divorce. Shocked, yet showing little emotion, Scott tells his friends and family, "Life goes on."

Scott starts drinking more heavily than usual. He pursues extreme sports. He pushes his abilities to the limit in rock climbing, hang gliding, and skiing in remote areas. Scott distances himself from family and friends. His normal even temperament turns sour. Yet Scott denies the depression so evident to those who know him well.

Rather than own up to disturbing feelings, men commonly turn to drugs or alcohol in an attempt to cope. Some depressed men express anger and irritation rather than sadness. Others report the physical signs of depression, such as lack of energy, poor sleep, altered appetite, and body aches, but adamantly deny feeling depressed. The cost of not expressing feelings and not getting help may account for the fourfold greater rate of suicide among depressed men than women.

Women and depression

Why do women around the world appear to suffer from depression about twice as often as men? Biological and reproductive factors may play a role. The rate of depression during pregnancy, after childbirth, and prior to menopause is higher than at any other time in women's lives.

However, cultural or social factors likely contribute to women's depression as well. For example, women who have been sexually or physically abused outnumber men with similar experiences, and such abuse increases the likelihood of depression. Furthermore, risk factors, such as low income, stress, and multiple responsibilities like juggling housework, childcare, and a career, occur more frequently among women than men.

Janine gently lays her baby down in the crib. Finally, the baby has fallen asleep. Exhausted after a challenging day at work, she desperately longs to go to bed herself. But, laundry waits, the bills need to be paid, and the house is a disaster. Six months ago, her husband was called to active duty in the Army Reserves and life hasn't been the same since. Janine realizes her overwhelming fatigue and loss of appetite are due to depression setting in.

Depression and miscarriage

The loss of a baby through miscarriage is a devastating event that often causes depression. And new evidence suggests that depression may play a role in inducing miscarriages, as well. Many miscarriages aren't easily explained. However, the mother's immune system may play a role. And we know that depression appears to disrupt the immune system.

A recent study published in the October 2002 issue of the scientific journal *Human*

Reproduction studied the relationship between depression and miscarriage. A group of women who had previously miscarried were given questionnaires to determine whether they had emotional problems. Of the women who then got pregnant, 22 percent miscarried again. What predicted miscarriage? Depression. If you or someone you care about is planning a pregnancy, be sure to get help for any existing depression first. It could save a baby.

Depression and diversity

Everyone experiences depression in unique ways. Attempting to generalize about depression based merely on ethnicity or membership in a certain group can lead to misperceptions. But risk factors for depression include discrimination, social ostracism, poverty, and major losses (like loss of a job or loved one). And unfortunately all these risk factors occur more frequently among minorities. Being different may take the form of race, culture, physical challenge, or sexual orientation.

In addition to these risk factors, many groups face special obstacles when dealing with depression. For example, some ethnic populations have limited access to mental health care because of language differences, embarrassment, economic difficulties, and lack of nearby facilities. More resources designed at helping these groups access care are clearly needed.

Adding Up the Costs of Depression

Depression has existed since the beginning of humankind. But today depression is a worldwide epidemic. No one knows why for sure, but the risk of depression for those born after World War II has mushroomed.

Estimates vary considerably, but today depression appears to occur in 15 to 20 percent of all people over the course of a lifetime. Furthermore, in any given 12-month period, somewhat under 10 percent of the population experiences an episode of significant depression. And at this very moment, an estimated 121 million people are suffering from depression throughout the world. That's an awful lot of people.

Guess what? Estimates on depression are only rough approximations. Because most people with depression fail to seek treatment and many folks with depression don't even realize they're depressed, reliable statistics are few and far between. Whatever the real figures are, huge numbers of people suffer from depression at some point in their lives. And depression has all kinds of costs associated with it.

Counting cash costs of depression

The World Health Organization (WHO) has created a statistic called the Global Burden of Disease (GBD) that puts a number on the worldwide economic cost of various diseases. Depression is now the fifth largest contributor to the GBD. By the year 2020, the WHO predicts that depression will be the second most costly disease.

The financial cost of depression is staggering. In the United States alone, the National Institute of Mental Health pegs the price tag of depression at $43.7 billion per year.

Where do these costs come from? Depressed people miss work more often and get less done when they do work. Parents of depressed kids may have to miss work to get their children to treatment appointments. Treatment also represents part of the total tab, but remember that alleviation of depression increases productivity, reduces absenteeism, and reduces medical costs. (See the section "Detailing depression's physical toll" for more information about medical costs of depression.)

Previewing personal costs of depression

Economic facts and figures do little to describe the human costs of depression. The profound suffering caused by depression affects both the sufferer and those who care. Words can't adequately describe these costs:

- The anguish of a family suffering from the loss of a loved one to suicide
- The excruciating pain experienced by someone with depression
- The diminished quality of relationships suffered both by people with depression and those who care about them
- The loss of purpose and sense of worth suffered by those with depression
- The loss of joy

Detailing depression's physical toll

Depression's destruction radiates beyond personal and economic costs — depression damages the body. Scientists discover new information almost daily about the intricate relationship between mood and health. Today, we know that depression affects:

✔ **Your immune system.** Your body has a complex system for warding off infections and diseases. Various studies have shown that depression changes the way the immune system responds to attack. Depression depletes the immune system and makes people more susceptible to disease.

✔ **Your skeletal system.** Untreated depression increases your chances of getting osteoporosis, though it's unclear exactly how depression may lead to this problem.

✔ **Your heart.** The relationship between depression and cardiovascular health is powerful. Johns Hopkins University studied healthy doctors and found that among those people who developed depression, their risk of heart disease increased twofold. This risk is comparable to the risk posed by smoking.

Another study reported in the October 2000 issue of the journal *Circulation* followed more than 4,000 elderly people who were initially free of heart disease. Researchers found that elderly persons with depression were 40 percent more likely to develop heart disease and 60 percent more likely to die. Intriguingly, they discovered that every increase in depression scores led to even greater increases in heart disease risk. This risk occurred above and beyond the risks posed by smoking, high cholesterol levels, and age.

✔ **Your mind.** Although depression can mimic dementia in terms of causing poor memory and concentration, depression also increases the risk for dementia. We're not sure why, but scientists have discovered that an area in the brain thought to govern memory is smaller in those with chronic depression.

If left untreated, depression can disrupt and possibly damage connections in your brain and may lead to the degeneration and death of brain cells.

✔ **Your experience of pain.** Of course depression inflicts emotional pain. However, depression also contributes to the experience of physical pain. Thus, if you have some type of chronic pain, such as arthritis or back pain, depression may increase the amount of pain you feel. Scientists aren't entirely sure how depression and pain interact, but the effect may be due to disruption of neurotransmitters (see Chapter 15 for more information about neurotransmitters) involved in pain perception. As a matter of fact, many people with depression fail to realize they're depressed and only complain of a variety of physical symptoms such as pain.

Psychotherapy for your heart

If you have heart disease, depression increases your risk of dying from it. How's that for an opening line? Now, the good news. Psychotherapy can improve your chances. A report posted on the American Psychological Association Web site (www.apa.org) indicates that 14 hours of psychotherapy reduces re-hospitalization rates for heart patients by 60 percent. Furthermore, counseling prior to medical procedures leads to shorter stays in the hospital following surgery. Unfortunately, only about 12 percent of hospitals treating heart disease actually offer psychotherapy to their heart patients. We suspect that if a pill came onto the market that reduced re-hospitalization rates by 60 percent, the drug company responsible would have constant commercials extolling the importance of asking your doctor for their new, miracle drug. But there's only so much two authors can do: Just know that if you have heart disease, don't ignore the importance of your emotions.

Depression likely affects the entire way the body functions. For example, altered appetite may lead to obesity or malnourishment and serious weight loss. In addition, depression is associated with disrupted hormonal levels and various other subtle physiological changes. In a sense, depression harms your body, mind, and soul.

Don't let yourself get depressed by all these frightening effects caused by depression. If you're depressed, you can feel better — and we spend the remainder of this book helping you to do so. Effective treatments currently exist and new ones are emerging.

Feeling Good Again

Depression is treatable. With good diagnosis and help, most folks can expect to recover. If you feel a loss of pleasure, reduced energy, a diminished sense of your worth, or unexplained aches and pains, you may be depressed (see Chapter 2 for more information about the symptoms of depression). Please pursue help (see Chapter 4 for ideas on how to find the right help for you).

Many types of help exist for depression. This book is one of them and falls under the category of self-help. Self-help does work for many people. However, self-directed efforts may not be enough for everyone. In the following sections, we briefly outline the different kinds of help that you may find useful.

You don't have to choose only one option. You may need or want to combine a number of these strategies. For example, many people with depression have found the combination of medication and psychotherapy helpful. And combining more than one type of psychotherapy sometimes proves useful as well.

If your depression doesn't start to lift or if you have severe symptoms such as thoughts of suicide, please seek professional assistance.

Thinking therapy

Dr. Aaron T. Beck, who wrote the foreword for this book, developed a system of psychotherapy that he calls cognitive therapy. *Cognitive therapy* is based on the premise that the way you think strongly influences the way you feel. Studies support the value of cognitive therapy above any other approach to the alleviation of depression. Dr. Beck discovered that depressed people

- View themselves in distorted, overly negative ways
- See the world in bleak, dark terms
- Envision a future of continual gloom and doom

Depression causes people to believe that their dark views are completely accurate and correct. Cognitive therapy, which we also refer to as *thought therapy,* helps untangle twisted thinking. You can find out more about this approach in Part II of this book. We encourage you to give thought therapy a try. Research shows that thought therapy even protects you against future recurrences of depression. Skeptical? Try it anyway!

Doing away with depression

Another well-tested approach to the alleviation of depression is what's known as behavior therapy. *Behavior therapy* is based on the premise that changing behavior changes moods. The problem: When you're depressed, you don't feel like doing much of anything. So, in Part III we help you figure out how to take small steps and overcome this mind hurdle using behavior-therapy–based tools. In addition, we tell you how

- Exercise can kick-start your battle with depression.
- You can bring small pleasures back into your life.
- Problem-solving strategies can improve coping.

Reinventing relationships

Depression sometimes follows the loss of a significant relationship and such losses often come in the form of death of a loved one or divorce. But depression can also come on the coattails of other types of relationship losses — like changing a way you relate to the world. For example, retirement requires you to give up (to lose) one role, that of an employee, and take on another. Major life changes or transitions sometimes lead to depression if you don't have a way of dealing with them. So in Chapter 13, we tell you how to handle loss and transitions.

Depression also often causes problems with important current relationships. In Chapter 14, we provide you with various ways of enhancing your relationships. The process of improving your relationships may decrease your depression as well.

Finding biological solutions

Perhaps you think the easiest approach to treating depression is found at the pharmacy or health food store. Simply pop the right potion and voilá, you're cured! If only getting better were so easy!

In Chapter 15, we review the pharmacological therapies. You'll find quite a few to choose from and we help you sort out the options. We also give you strategies for making the complicated decision as to whether anti-depressant medication makes sense for you or if you'd prefer alternative approaches.

In Chapter 16, we discuss the so-called natural way of treating depression. We also bring you information about shock therapy and other not-so-common treatments for depression.

Avoiding help for depression

Researchers at the University of Michigan took a close look at data from national surveys the United States Centers for Disease Control and Prevention gave to teenagers and young adults. The researchers discovered an alarming statistic — 35 percent of the teenagers and 40 percent of the young adults reported having depressive symptoms for longer than two weeks. Of even greater concern is the fact that only 12 percent of both groups reported attempting to find help. In fact, among those who had symptoms that endured for more than two years, only 15 percent informed any type of health professional about the problem.

Given that depression poses a significant risk of suicide, this low rate of help seeking is particularly disturbing. Clearly, much needs to be done to encourage those with depression to seek help.

Feeling Better than Good

After you've overcome your depression, you will likely feel much better. However, you'll want to sustain that improvement. Depression, like the common cold, has a nasty habit of returning. But you can do much to hold off or prevent future depression. We show you how to avoid future bouts in Chapters 17 and 18. Should you catch another round of depression, we also show you how to recover more quickly and keep the symptoms mild.

So, you feel better. You feel good. But guess what? You don't have to settle for good. We want you to feel better than good; perhaps better than you have ever felt in your life. That may sound too good to be true. However, in Chapter 19, we give you ways to add purpose and meaning to your life. In addition, we provide secret keys for unlocking your potential for happiness — those keys probably aren't what you would imagine them to be.

Celebrating Sadness

We begin this book with promises of relief from depression. However, no therapy, behavior, or pill provides a life free from sadness. We're glad that one doesn't exist. And if such a cure existed, we wouldn't take it.

Because without sadness, how could one feel happy? Who would write great plays or create emotionally powerful works of art or songs that sing to the depths of the soul? Human emotions serve a purpose. They distinguish us from computers and give life meaning.

Thus, we write this book wishing you a life of happiness interspersed with moments of pain. To have pain is to live.

Chapter 2

Detecting Depression

● ●

In This Chapter

▶ Looking at the symptoms of depression

▶ Discovering depression's many forms

▶ Understanding the causes of depression

▶ Keeping track of your moods

● ●

Depression appears in diverse demeanors and guises. Sometimes depression slowly and silently possesses the mind and soul. Other times depression explodes, bursting through the door and robbing its victims of joy and pleasure. Some people are unaware that they have depression, although other people fully recognize depression's presence in their lives. Sometimes depression has no obvious cause, often masquerading as a set of physical complaints like fatigue, poor sleep and appetite, and even indigestion.

Depression is a disease of extremes. Its power can destroy the appetite or create insatiable hunger. People with depression may find sleep distressingly evasive; or they may find that fatigue is overwhelming, confining them to bed for days at a time. Depressed people may pace frantically or collapse and hardly move. Depression sometimes takes root and endures for months or years. Other times it blows through like a series of afternoon thunderstorms.

In this chapter, we help you recognize whether you or someone you care about suffers from depression. We do so by categorizing the effects depression has on individuals. We outline the major types of depression and their symptoms. We explore the connections between disease and depression, and we look at the grief/depression link. We delve into the causes of this disorder. And finally, we tell you how you or a loved one can monitor and track your moods if you suspect that you may be battling depression.

Recognizing the Ravages of Depression

Everyone feels down from time to time. Stock market plunges, health problems, loss of a friend, divorce, or failure to reach sales quotas — events like these can make anyone feel sad and upset for awhile. But depression is more than a normal reaction to unpleasant events and losses. Depression deepens and spreads well beyond sadness, disrupting both the mind and the body in serious, sometimes deadly ways.

Depression impacts every aspect of life. In fact, even though a number of types of depression exist (see "The Six Plagues of Depression" later in this chapter), all types of depression affect people in four areas, although each individual may be affected in different ways. Depression disrupts

- Thoughts
- Behaviors
- Relationships
- The body

In the following sections, we touch on the ways that each form of depression affects individuals.

Dwelling on bleak thoughts

When you get depressed, your view of the world changes. The sun shines less brightly, the sky clouds over, people seem cold and distant, and the future looks dark. Your mind may cloud over with recurrent thoughts of worthlessness, self-loathing, and even death. Typically, depressed people complain of difficulty concentrating, remembering, and making decisions.

For **Ellen,** depression emerges about one year after her divorce. She finds herself thinking that all men are jerks. Ellen is quite attractive, although when she looks in the mirror, she only sees the beginning of wrinkles and an occasional blemish. She concludes that even if there are any good men left, they'll be repulsed by her awful looks. She feels tense. Her concentration is shot, and she starts to make careless errors at work. Her boss understands, but she sees her mistakes as proof of incompetence. Although she believes that she's in a dead-end job, she doesn't see herself as capable of doing anything better. She begins to wonder why she bothers to go to work every day.

Does your mind dwell on negative thoughts? If so, you may be suffering from depression. This following "Depressive Thoughts Quiz" gives you a sample of typical thoughts that go along with depression. Check the box preceding each thought that you often have:

❑ Things are getting worse and worse for me.

❑ I think I'm worthless.

❑ No one would miss me if I were dead.

❑ My memory is shot.

❑ I make too many mistakes.

❑ By and large, I think I'm a failure.

❑ Lately, I find it impossible to make decisions.

❑ I don't look forward to much of anything.

❑ The world would be a better place without me.

❑ Basically, I'm extremely pessimistic about things.

❑ I can't think of anything that sounds interesting or enjoyable.

❑ My life is full of regrets.

❑ Lately, I can't concentrate, and I forget what I read.

❑ I don't see my life getting better in the future.

❑ I'm deeply ashamed of myself.

Unlike many of the self-tests you may have seen in magazines or books, no specific score indicates depression here. All the items are typical of depressed thinking. However, merely checking one or two doesn't necessarily mean you're depressed. But, the more items you check, the greater the concern of possible depression. And if you check any of the items related to death or suicide, that's plenty of cause for concern.

If you're having serious suicidal thoughts, you need an immediate evaluation and treatment. If the thoughts include a plan that you believe you may actually carry out now or in the very near future, go to a hospital emergency room. They have trained personnel who can help. If you're not able to get yourself to an emergency room, call 911 for more rapid attention.

For more information about depressive thinking and what you can do about it, see Part II.

Dragging your feet: Depressed behavior

Not everyone who's depressed behaves in the same way. Some people speed up and others slow down. Some folks sleep more than ever, while others complain of a dreadful lack of sleep.

Darryl drags his body out of bed in the morning. Even after ten hours of sleep, he feels depleted of energy. He starts showing up at work late. He uses up his sick leave. He can't make himself go to the gym, an activity he used to enjoy. He reasons that he'll work out again when he gets the energy. His friends ask him what's going on, because he hasn't been spending much time with them. He says that he doesn't really know; he's just tired.

Cheryl, on the other hand, is averaging about three and a half hours of sleep each night. She awakens at about 3 a.m. with racing thoughts. When she gets up, she feels a frantic pressure and can't seem to sit still. Irritable and cranky, she snaps at her friends and coworkers. Unable to sleep at night, she finds herself drinking too much. Sometimes she cries for no apparent reason.

Although everyone is different, certain behaviors tend to go along with depression. Do your actions and behaviors concern you? Depressed people tend to either feel like they're walking in wet cement or running full speed on a treadmill. The following "Depressed Behavior Quiz" can give you an idea as to whether your actions indicate a problem. Check each item that applies:

❑ I've been having unexplained crying spells.

❑ The few times I force myself to go out, I don't have much fun.

❑ I can't make myself exercise like I used to.

❑ I haven't been going out nearly as much as usual.

❑ I've been missing a lot of work lately.

❑ I can't get myself to do much of anything, even important projects.

❑ Lately I've been fidgety and can't sit still.

❑ I'm moving at a slower pace than I usually do, for no good reason.

❑ I haven't been doing things for fun like I usually do.

All these items are typical of depressed behavior or, in some cases, a health problem. On a bad day, anyone might check off a single item. However, the more items you check, the more likely that something's wrong, especially if the problem exists for more than a couple of weeks.

For more information about depressed behavior and what you can do about it, see Part III.

Reflecting upon relationships and depression

Depression damages the way you relate to others. Withdrawal and avoidance are the most common responses to depression. Sometimes depressed people get irritable and critical with the very people they care most about.

Trent trips over a toy left on the living room floor and snaps at his wife Sylvia, "Can't you get the kids to pick up their damn toys for once?" Hurt and surprised by the attack, Sylvia apologizes. Trent fails to acknowledge her apology and turns away. Sylvia quickly picks up the toy and wonders what's been happening to her marriage. Trent hardly talks to her anymore, other than to complain or scold her about something trivial. She can't remember the last time they had sex. She worries that he may be having an affair.

Have you or perhaps someone you care about been responding differently in one or more of your relationships? This "Depression and Relationships Quiz" checklist describes some of the ways in which depression affects relationships. Check the items that fit your situation:

❑ I've been avoiding people more than usual, including friends and family.

❑ I've been having more difficulty than usual talking about my concerns.

❑ I've been unusually irritable with others.

❑ I don't feel like being with anyone.

❑ I feel isolated and alone.

❑ I'm sure that no one cares about or understands me.

❑ I haven't felt like being physically intimate with anyone lately.

❑ I feel like I've been letting down those who are close to me.

❑ I believe that others don't want to be around me.

❑ Lately, I don't seem to care about anyone like I should.

When you're depressed, you turn away from the very people that may have the most support to offer you. Either you feel that they don't care about you, or perhaps you can't muster up positive feelings for them. You may avoid others or find yourself irritated and crabby.

The more items you checked in the previous list, the more likely depression is affecting your relationships. For more information about how depression can affect your relationships and what you can do about it, see Part IV.

Feeling funky: The physical signs of depression

Depression typically includes at least a few physical symptoms. These symptoms include changes in appetite, sleep, and energy. However, for some people, the experience of depression *primarily* consists of these kind of physical symptoms and doesn't consciously include as many other symptoms such as sadness, withdrawal from people, lack of interests, and missed work.

Many folks who experience depression primarily in physical terms are very unaware of their emotional life. Sometimes, that's because they were taught that feelings are unimportant. In other cases, their parents scolded them for crying or showing other appropriate feelings such as excitement or sadness.

When **Carl** was growing up, his father scolded him for crying. He said that big boys tough things out and that Carl should never show weakness. His father also jumped on him for showing too much excitement in anticipation of Christmas. He said that men don't get emotional. Over time, Carl learned to keep his feelings to himself.

After five years of marriage, Carl's wife leaves him; she says that he's an unfeeling and uncaring man. In the ensuing six months, Carl finds his appetite diminished, and food no longer tastes good to him. His energy drains away like oil from an engine when the oil pan plug is removed. He starts to have headaches and frequent bouts of constipation. His blood pressure even rises.

When he goes to the clinic, his doctor asks, "Look Carl, your wife left you just six months ago. Are you sure you aren't depressed?" Carl answers, "Are you kidding? Depression is something women get, I couldn't possibly be depressed." Nonetheless, after an exhaustive work-up, his doctor concludes that depression is causing his physical problems. Nothing else adds up.

Are you experiencing odd changes in your body that you have no explanation for? The following "Depression in the Body Quiz" checklist shows you some of the various ways that depression can show up in your body.

❑ My blood pressure has risen lately for no discernable reason.

❑ I have no appetite lately.

❑ I haven't been sleeping nearly as well as usual.

❑ My diet is the same, but I'm having frequent constipation for no reason.

❑ I often feel sick to my stomach.

❑ I feel lots of aches and pains.

❑ I'm sleeping much more than usual.

❑ I've been ravenous lately for no reason.

❑ My energy has been very low lately.

❑ I've gained (or lost) more than 5 pounds, and I can't figure out why.

Like the other three checklists in this chapter, it really doesn't matter exactly how many of these items apply to you. The more items you checked, the greater the possibility of depression.

If your depression shows up primarily in physical terms, medications or some other physical remedy may seem like the best choice for you. See Part V for more information on physical solutions.

The items in this checklist may be caused by other health-related problems, not just depression. Therefore, if you're experiencing any disturbing physical problems, you need to see your doctor, especially if they last more than a week or two.

The Six Plagues of Depression

In the "Recognizing the Ravages of Depression" section, earlier in this chapter, we outline the four broad ways in which all types of depression can affect an individual. In this section, we turn our attention to the six major types of depression to look out for:

✔ Major depressive disorder

✔ Dysthymic disorder

✔ Adjustment disorder with depressed mood

✔ Bipolar disorder

✔ Seasonal affective disorder

✔ Depression related to hormones

The American Psychiatric Association publishes a book called the *Diagnostic and Statistical Manual of Mental Disorders* (DSM-IV). The DSM-IV describes and categorizes mental disorders. In the following sections, we describe six major types of depression and their symptoms largely based on information contained in DSM-IV. However, we present this information in a condensed format without technical jargon.

Understanding what the forms of depression look like can help you figure out whether you're likely suffering from some type of depression. But don't go so far as to give yourself a formal diagnosis; that's a job for professionals.

If you feel that you have significant signs of any of these types of depression, get help. You can start with the advice in this book, but if you don't feel much better within a couple of months, see your doctor or a mental health professional. Seek help even sooner if your depression includes serious thoughts of suicide or hopelessness.

Major depressive disorder: Can't even get out of bed

As with all types of depression, the symptoms of a major depressive disorder fall into the four areas — thought, behavior, relationships, and the body — we cover in the "Recognizing the Ravages of Depression" section, earlier in this chapter. So what's unique about a major depressive disorder?

Major depressive disorders involve either a seriously low mood or a notable drop in pleasures and interests that unrelentingly continues for two weeks or more. Sometimes depressed people either consciously or unconsciously deny these down feelings and declines in interests. In cases of denial, careful observation by people who know them well usually detects the impairment.

In addition to the low mood and lack of pleasure, in order to qualify as experiencing a major depressive disorder, you generally have to have a wide variety of other symptoms, such as

- Inability to concentrate or make decisions
- Repetitive thoughts of suicide
- Major changes in sleep patterns
- Extreme fatigue
- Clear signs of either revved up agitation or slowed functioning
- Very low sense of personal worth
- Striking changes in appetite or weight (either increased or decreased)
- Intense feelings of guilt and self-condemnation

With major depressive disorders, these symptoms occur almost everyday over a period of at least two weeks or more. Major depressive disorders vary greatly in terms of severity. However, even mild cases need to be treated.

The degree of despondency experienced by those with severe cases of major depressive disorder is difficult to imagine for someone who has never experienced it. A severe, major episode of depression grabs hold of a person's life and insidiously squeezes out all pleasure. But it does far more than obliterate joy; severe depression shoves its victims into a dark hole of utter, unrelenting despair that obscures the capacity to love. People caught in such a web of depression lose the ability to care for life, others, and themselves.

If you suffer from such a severe case of depression, there's reason to hope. Many effective treatments work even with severe depression.

The daily pain of living begins the moment the alarm wakes **Edwin** up. He spends most of the night tossing and turning. He only falls asleep for a few moments before waking up to another day of despair. He forces himself to get ready for work, but the thought of speaking to others feels overwhelming. He can't face the prospect. He knows that he should at least call in sick, but can't lift his hand to pick up the phone. He realizes that he could lose his job, but it doesn't seem to matter. He thinks that he's likely to be dead soon.

He changes out of his work clothes and into sweats; then he goes back to bed. But he doesn't sleep. His mind fills with thoughts of self-loathing — "I'm a failure. I'm no good. There's nothing to live for." He ponders whether he should just end it now. Edwin suffers from a major depressive disorder.

Major depressive disorders generally cause a sharply reduced ability to function at work or deal with other people. In other words, such disorders deplete you of the resources you need for recovery. That's why getting help is so important. If you allow the major depressive disorder to continue, it may result in death from suicide. If you or someone you know *even suspects* the presence of a major depressive disorder, you need to seek help promptly. See Chapter 4 for ideas on how to find professional help for depression.

Major, major depression

Psychosis is a serious symptom of a major depressive disorder in which a person is out of touch with reality. People with depression sometime become so ill that they become psychotic. They may hear voices or see things that aren't really there. In most instances, depression with psychosis requires hospitalization.

People with severe depression also may exhibit paranoid or delusional thinking. *Paranoid thinking* involves feeling extremely suspicious and distrustful — such as believing that other people are out to get you or that someone is trying to poison you. *Delusions* range from the slightly odd to bizarre, but they involve obviously false beliefs such as thinking the television is transmitting signals to your brain. The problems of psychosis, paranoia, and delusional thinking require professional attention and lie outside of the scope of this book. However, we do detail medications commonly prescribed for these symptoms in Chapter 15.

Dysthymic disorder: Chronic, low-level depression

Dysthymic disorder, or *dysthymia,* looks rather similar to major depressive disorder. However, it's generally considered somewhat less severe and tends to be more chronic. With dysthymic disorder, the symptoms occur for at least two years (oftentimes far longer), with the depressed mood appearing on most days for the majority of each day. However, you only need to display two of the following chronic symptoms, in addition to a depressed mood, in order for your condition to qualify as a dysthymic disorder:

- Poor concentration
- Low sense of personal worth
- Guilty feelings
- Thoughts of death or suicide
- Problems making decisions

Compared to major depressive disorder, dysthymic disorder less frequently involves prominent physical symptoms such as difficulties with appetite, weight, sleep, and agitation.

Dysthymic disorder frequently begins in childhood, adolescence, or young adulthood and can easily continue for many years if left untreated. Furthermore, individuals with dysthymic disorder carry an increased risk of developing a major depressive disorder at some point in their lives.

Although individuals with dysthymic disorder don't appear as devastatingly despondent as those with a major depressive disorder, they nonetheless languish, lacking in vigor and joie de vivre. These are the people who you may not identify as being depressed, but they sure seem pessimistic and perhaps cynical and grouchy a good deal of the time.

Charlene doesn't remember ever feeling joy. She's not even sure what the words mean. Her parents worked long hours and seemed cold and distant. Charlene studied hard in school. She hoped to gain approval and attention for her academic accomplishments. Her parents didn't seem to notice.

Today, Charlene leads a life that's envied by her colleagues. She earns a great salary and toils tirelessly in her profession as a mechanical engineer. Yet she senses that she's missing something, feels unsuccessful, and suffers a chronic, uneasy discontent. Charlene has a dysthymic disorder, although *she* wouldn't actually say that she's depressed. She fails to seek help for her problem because she actually has no idea that life can be different.

People with dysthymic disorder often see their problems as merely "just the way they are," and fail to seek treatment. If you suspect that you or someone you care about has dysthymic disorder, get help. You have the right to feel better than you do, and the long-lasting nature of the problem means that it isn't likely to go away on its own. Besides, you certainly don't want to risk developing a major depressive disorder, which is even more debilitating.

Adjustment disorder with depressed mood: When bad things happen

Life isn't a bowl of cherries. Bad things do happen to everyone from time to time. Sometimes people handle their problems without excess emotional upset. Sometimes they don't.

Adjustment disorders are reactions to one or more difficult issues, such as marital problems, financial setbacks, conflict with coworkers, or natural disasters. When a stressful event occurs and your reaction includes a decreased ability to work or participate effectively with others, in combination with symptoms such as a low mood, crying spells, and feelings of worthlessness or hopelessness, you may be experiencing an adjustment disorder with a depressed mood. Adjustment disorder is a much milder problem than a major depressive disorder, but it can still disrupt your life.

James is shocked when his boss tells him that due to downsizing, he's losing his job. He begins a job search but openings in his field are scarce. For the first couple of weeks, he enjoys catching up on sleep, but soon, he starts feeling unusually down. He struggles to open up the newspaper to look for work. He begins to feel worthless and loses hope of finding a job. His appetite and sleep are still okay, but his confidence plummets. He's surprised when tears stream down his face after receiving another rejection letter.

James isn't suffering from a major depressive disorder. James is struggling with what is known as an adjustment disorder with depressed mood.

Bipolar disorder: Ups and downs

Bipolar disorder is considered a mood disorder, just like other forms of depression. However, bipolar disorder is quite different from other depressions because people with a bipolar disorder always experience one or more episodes of unusually euphoric feelings, which are referred to as *mania*.

In bipolar disorder, moods tend to fluctuate between extreme highs and lows. This fact makes the treatment of bipolar disorder different than most depressions. We want you to be familiar with the symptoms so that you can seek professional help if you experience manic episodes with your depression. Self-help isn't sufficient for the treatment of bipolar disorder.

Although individuals with mania may seem quite cheerful and happy, the people who know them can tell that their good mood is a little too good to be true. During manic episodes, people need less sleep, may show signs of unusual creativity, and have more energy and enthusiasm. Sounds like a pretty nice mood to have, doesn't it? Who wouldn't want to feel wonderful and totally on top of the world? Well, hold the phone.

The problem with manic episodes related to bipolar disorder is that the high feelings spin out of control. During these episodes, good judgment goes out the window. People who have this disorder often

- ✔ Spend too much money
- ✔ Gamble excessively
- ✔ Make foolish business decisions
- ✔ Engage in risky sexual escapades
- ✔ Talk fast and furiously
- ✔ Think that they have super-special talents or abilities

Manic episodes can involve mildly foolish decisions and excesses, or they can reach extreme levels. People in manic states can cause ruin for themselves or their families. Their behavior can get so out of control that they end up in the hospital for a period of time.

Most people with bipolar disorder also cycle into episodes of mild to severe depression. They go from feeling great to gruesome, occasionally within the same day. The depressions that follow a manic episode feel especially unexpected and devastating. The contrast from the high to the low is particularly painful. People with untreated bipolar disorder typically feel out of control, hopeless, and helpless. Not surprisingly, the risk of suicide is higher for bipolar disorder than for any of the other types of depression.

Although it's generally chronic, bipolar disorder can be successfully managed. Both medications and psychotherapy, usually in combination, can alleviate many of the most debilitating symptoms. Scientists are continually developing new treatments and medications.

Emily finishes dressing, grabs her keys, and dashes out the door. She feels so excited that she can hardly wait to share her good fortune with her girlfriend, Samantha. "Sam, guess what," she gushes, "I've finally decided to move to L.A. I know that I can make it in the movies. I just have to go. I've quit my job and I'm going. As a matter of fact, I'm leaving today."

When kids go up and down like a yo-yo

In recent years, mental health professionals have begun to realize that bipolar disorders can start in childhood. Nevertheless, many of these children with bipolar disorders continue to receive a variety of other diagnoses, such as conduct disorder (involving problems such as lying and defiance) or, even more frequently, attention deficit hyperactivity disorder. The symptoms of these disorders often resemble each other. But one of the ways that bipolar disorder can be distinguished is by understanding that kids with bipolar disorder typically demonstrate greater amounts of irritability and rage than those with attention deficit disorder.

It's not unusual for pediatricians to prescribe stimulant medication to these kids based on an incorrect diagnosis. When this happens, the stimulant medication can trigger full-blown manic episodes, especially in adolescents.

If your child receives a diagnosis of attention deficit disorder and doesn't respond well to treatment, you may wish to consider getting a referral to a child psychiatrist or psychologist who can explore alternative diagnoses such as bipolar disorder. Treating this problem as early as possible is important in order to avert a poor outcome. Furthermore, these children, as well as adults with bipolar disorder, have an unusually high risk for abusing alcohol or drugs.

Emily's fast talking frightens Samantha. She asks Emily when she decided to move, and what she's going to do about the lease on her apartment; does she have a job offer in L.A. — what is she thinking? This is so sudden.

Emily replies that she hasn't been able to sleep for the past three days. Her thoughts have been racing with ideas. She decided that her life is too boring and she needs a change. She says that her boss can go to hell and so can the apartment manager. She charged the plane ticket and took her last $200 from her bank account. She's going to figure out what to do when she gets to L.A. Emily suffers from a bipolar disorder.

Bipolar disorder is a complicated, serious syndrome. The condition has many subtle variations. If you suspect that you or someone you know has any signs of bipolar disorder, seek professional assistance immediately.

Seasonal affective disorder: Dark depression

Some depressions come and go with the seasons, just like clockwork. People who regularly experience depression during the fall or winter may have *seasonal affective disorder* (SAD). People who have SAD may also experience a few unusual symptoms, such as

✔ Increased appetite

✔ Carbohydrate cravings

✔ Increased sleep

✔ Irritability

✔ A sense of heaviness in the arms and legs

Many mental health professionals believe that the reduced amount of sunlight in the winter triggers this form of depression in vulnerable individuals. Support for this hypothesis comes from the fact that this pattern of depression occurs more frequently among people who live in higher latitudes where light fluctuations from winter to summer are most extreme and darkness prevails for a greater portion of the day during the winter. (We discuss evidence concerning treatment of this disorder using bright lights in Chapter 16.)

What does a bear do to get ready for winter? Bears frantically forage for food, get as fat as they can, and hibernate in a cozy cave. Perhaps it's not a coincidence that people with SAD typically gain weight, crave carbohydrates, have reduced energy, and feel like staying swaddled in bed for the winter.

Premenstrual dysphoric disorder and post-partum depression: Horrible hormones?

Occasional, minor premenstrual changes in mood occur in a majority of women. A smaller percentage of women experience significant and disturbing symptoms known as *premenstrual dysphoric disorder* (PDD). PDD is a more extreme form of the more widely known premenstrual syndrome (PMS).

Although hormones likely play a significant role in PDD, research hasn't yet clarified the causes. Typically, women who suffer from full-blown PDD encounter some of the following symptoms almost every month, during the week prior to menstruation. (These same symptoms can occur — most likely from hormonal fluctuations — over the years leading up to, during, and following menopause.)

✔ Anger

✔ Anxiety

✔ Bloating

✔ Fatigue

✔ Food cravings

✔ Guilt and self-blame

- ✔ Irritability
- ✔ Sadness
- ✔ Tearfulness
- ✔ Withdrawal

Denise drives to the grocery store after work. Impatiently, she pushes her cart through the aisle, only to find another patron blocking her way. She feels a rush of annoyance and clears her throat loudly. The other woman looks up and apologizes. Denise hurriedly works her way around the offending cart, giving it a quick shove as she passes.

Waiting in line, her irascible mood worsens. The man in front of her fumbles around for his checkbook and discovers he has no checks. Then he pulls out a handful of cash and realizes he's a bit short. Next, he starts to search his overstuffed wallet for a credit card. Denise finds herself unable to suppress her raging emotions and snaps, "People don't have all day to stand in line waiting for clods like you! What's wrong with you, anyway?"

The man's face turns bright red and he mutters, "Gosh, I'm sorry lady." The clerk intervenes and says, "Wow ma'am. You don't have to be so mean. It can happen to anybody." Suddenly ashamed, Denise breaks into tears and sobs. She feels like she's going crazy. And this isn't the first time Denise has felt this way. In fact, it happens to her almost on a monthly basis.

Postpartum depression is another type of serious mood disorder that's widely thought to be related to hormonal fluctuations, although no one knows for sure how and why the hormones profoundly affect the moods of some women and not others. This depression occurs within days or weeks after giving birth. The symptoms appear quite similar to those of major depressive disorder. (For a complete discussion of these symptoms, see the "Major depressive disorder: Can't even get out of bed" section earlier in this chapter.)

Carmen had tried unsuccessfully to conceive for the past eight years. She and her husband Shawn feel overwhelmed with joy when at last the home pregnancy test registers positive. Their cheerful, cozy nursery looks like a picture in a baby magazine.

Carmen and Shawn weep with happiness at the sight of their newborn. Carmen feels exhausted, but Shawn assumes that's normal. He takes charge the first day home so that she can rest. Carmen feels the same way the next day, so Shawn continues to take over the responsibilities of caring for the baby. Shawn becomes alarmed when Carmen shows no interest in holding the baby. In fact, she seems irritated by the baby's crying and mentions that maybe she shouldn't have become a mother. At the end of the second week, she tells him that he can't go back to work because she doesn't think that she can take care of the baby. Carmen is suffering from postpartum depression.

Mothers who kill their babies

Occasionally women with severe cases of postpartum depression develop psychoses. *Psychosis* involves serious departures from reality, including *hallucinations* (seeing or hearing things that aren't really there) and *delusional beliefs* (thoughts such as believing that aliens are controlling your mind). *Postpartum psychosis* is psychosis that occurs shortly after giving birth. Psychotic beliefs often focus on the baby and can include thinking that the baby is possessed or would be better off in heaven than living here on earth. The risk of postpartum psychosis increases greatly for any births following an initial diagnosis.

In June of 2001, Texas mother Andrea Yates drowned her five children in the bathtub. Yates suffered from a diagnosed postpartum psychosis after the birth of her fourth child, Luke. After the birth of Luke, and before the birth of her fifth child, she tried to commit suicide twice and was treated with medication. However, against advice of her doctors, she stopped taking her medication.

Yates was found guilty of murder. Had she followed through with adequate treatment at the time of her first diagnosis, it's quite likely that this tragedy could have been prevented.

Most women feel a little bit of postpartum depression, or the "baby blues," shortly after delivery. It's not severe and it usually dissipates in a couple of weeks. However, if you begin to feel like Carmen in the earlier story, you need to get professional help immediately.

Connecting Drugs, Diseases, and Depression

The interaction of depression with illness and disease can be a vicious cycle. Illness and disease (and related medications) can hasten the onset or intensify the effects of depression. And depression can further complicate various diseases. Depression can suppress the immune system, release stress hormones, and impact your body and mind's capacity to cope. Depression may increase whatever pain you have and further rob you of crucial resources. In this section, we focus on the role of medications and illness in the development and worsening of depression.

Depressing drugs

Dealing with an illness is hard enough without having medications make you feel even worse, but some medications actually appear to cause depression.

Of course, sometimes distinguishing whether it's merely being sick or the drug that's causing the depression is difficult. However, in a number of cases, medications do appear to contribute directly to depression.

If you notice inexplicable feelings of sadness shortly after starting a new medication, tell your doctor. The medication could be causing your feelings, and an alternative treatment that won't make you depressed may be available. Table 2-1 lists the most common offending medications.

Table 2-1	Potentially Depressing Drugs
Medication	*Condition Typically Prescribed For*
Antabuse	Alcohol addiction
Anticonvulsants	Seizures
Barbiturates	Seizures and (rarely) anxiety
Benzodiazepines	Anxiety and insomnia
Beta blockers	High blood pressure and heart problems
Calcium channel blockers	High blood pressure and heart problems
Corticosteroids	Inflammation and chronic lung diseases
Hormones	Birth control and menopausal symptoms
Interferon	Hepatitis and certain cancers
Levodopa, amantadine	Parkinson's disease
Statins	High cholesterol
Zovirax	Herpes or shingles

Depressing diseases

Chronic illnesses interfere with life. Some chronic illnesses require lifestyle adjustments, extensive time at the doctor's office, missed work, disrupted relationships, and pain. Feeling upset by such disturbances is normal. But these problems may trigger depression, especially in vulnerable people.

In addition, certain specific diseases seem to disrupt the nervous system in ways that create depression. If you suffer from one of these diseases, talk to your doctor if your mood begins to deteriorate. Diseases that are thought to directly influence depression include

- ✔ AIDS
- ✔ Asthma
- ✔ Cancer
- ✔ Chronic fatigue syndrome
- ✔ Coronary artery disease and heart attacks
- ✔ Diabetes
- ✔ Hepatitis
- ✔ Lupus
- ✔ Multiple sclerosis
- ✔ Parkinson's disease
- ✔ Stroke
- ✔ Ulcerative colitis

Good Grief! Is Depression Ever Normal?

When you lose someone you love, you're likely to feel pain and sadness. You may lose sleep and withdraw from people. The idea of going out and having a good time will probably sound repugnant. Feelings like these can go on for weeks or a few months. Are these the signs of depression? Yes and no.

Although grieving involves many of the same reactions that are associated with depression, the two aren't the same. Depression almost always includes a diminished sense of personal worth or feelings of excessive guilt. Grief, when not accompanied by depression, doesn't typically involve lowered self-esteem and unreasonable self-blame. Furthermore, the intensity of grief usually diminishes slowly (sometimes excruciatingly slowly) but surely over time. Depression, on the other hand, sometimes holds on unrelentingly.

A controversy exists among some mental health professionals concerning how to best deal with grief. Some professionals advocate immediate treatment of any disturbing reactions involving grief; these professionals often advise taking antidepressant medications (see Chapter 15 for more information about antidepressants). Others contend that grief involves a natural healing process that is best dealt with by allowing its natural course to unfold.

When a child dies

The loss of a child may be the most profound loss that anyone ever experiences. The grief following a child's death is thought to be more intense, more complicated, and longer lasting than other profound losses. The anguish and loneliness may seem utterly intolerable. Parents may question the value of living. Others who haven't had such a loss may be sympathetic, but they sometimes fail to understand and appreciate the intensity and duration of this type of grief. At the very least, we suggest that parents who have lost a child consider contacting a support group such as The Compassionate Friends (Internet: www. compassionatefriends.org). This group's mission is to help bereaved parents deal with their loss in a supportive atmosphere.

We tend to agree with this latter group, but if and only if the grief isn't complicated by an accompanying depression. (See Chapter 13 where we talk about getting through loss and grief.) Still, the decision is an individual choice. In either case, a grieving person needs to be aware that depression can superimpose itself on top of grief. If you're dealing with grief, seek treatment if it goes on too long or includes other serious symptoms of depression.

Digging Out the Causes of Depression

There are lots of theories on the cause of depression. Some experts purport that depression is caused by imbalances in brain chemistry. Advocates of this position sometimes believe that those imbalances in chemistry are due to genetics. Other experts emphatically declare that the cause of depression lies in one's childhood. Still other investigators make the claim that depression comes from negative thinking. You can also find professionals who suggest that depression is caused by impoverished environments and/or cultural experiences. Other researchers have implicated learned patterns of behavior as a cause of depression. Finally, some experts have identified problems with relationships as the major culprit.

In one sense, you can probably come to the same conclusion as the dodo bird in *Alice in Wonderland* and declare that "All have won and all must have prizes." In another sense, nobody deserves a prize. Even though you can find evidence to support each of these positions, nobody truly knows how these factors work, which is the most important, and which ones influence other factors in what ways.

The brain's brew

About 100 billion *neurons* (nerve cells) reside in your brain, give or take a few. Busy neurons take in information about the state of the world outside and inside the body. These 100 billion nerve cells don't touch each other. They send information back and forth by spitting out tiny molecules. This communication process involves chemical messengers, called *neurotransmitters* that move through and between the neurons.

Evidence shows that depression is either accompanied or caused by chemical imbalances in the brain. Several theories have been offered to explain the relationship between depression and the chemical messengers.

Many researchers believe that neurotransmitters such as norepinephrine, serotonin, and dopamine play important, interactive roles in mood regulation. Furthermore, these neurotransmitters may interact with other brain chemicals in as yet unknown ways.

What researchers do know is that for some people with depression, the chemical soup may need a dash of salt (one medication), and for others, pepper (a different medication) may be necessary to alleviate the depression. But that doesn't necessarily mean that the depression was caused by a lack of pepper or salt! Experts simply don't know how all this works.

In spite of the indisputable fact that scientists don't yet know exactly how the multitude of depression-related factors function and interact, you may run into doctors, psychologists, and psychiatrists who have strong opinions about what they believe is "the" definitive cause of depression. If you encounter a professional who claims to know the single, definitive cause of depression, question that professional's credibility. Most sophisticated experts in the field of depression research know that a single, definitive cause of depression remains elusive and likely will never be discovered.

Yet the field of mental health isn't clueless when it comes to understanding how depression develops. Strong suggestive evidence supports the fact that learning, thinking, biology, genetics, childhood, and the environment play important roles in the development, maintenance, and potential treatment of depression. All these factors interact in amazing ways.

For example, a growing body of studies has shown that medication alters the physical symptoms of depression such as loss of appetite and energy. And antidepressant medication also improves the negative, pessimistic thinking that accompanies most forms of depression. Perhaps that's not too surprising. (See Chapter 15 for more info about medication.)

Similarly, studies have demonstrated that psychotherapy alone decreases negative, pessimistic thinking (see Chapters 5 through 7), much like medications do. Some scientists are shocked by the fact that other studies now demonstrate that certain psychotherapies, even if delivered without antidepressant medication, also alter brain chemistry.

Taken as a whole, recent studies on the roots of depression fail to support a theory that assigns one specific cause of depression. Rather, they support the idea that physical and psychological factors interact with each other.

Monitoring Mood

You may be pretty sure that you or someone you care about has depression. Now what? Keeping track of how your mood changes from day to day is one important step in recovery. Why?

- ✔ You may discover patterns (perhaps you get very depressed every Monday).
- ✔ You may discover specific triggers for your depressed moods.
- ✔ You can see how your efforts progress over time.
- ✔ You can quickly determine if you're not progressing, which may indicate that you need to seek help.

We suggest that you keep a "Mood Diary" (see Table 2-2). You can profit from tracking your moods and taking notes on relevant incidents, happenings, and thoughts. Try it for a few weeks.

Use a rating scale from 1 to 100 to rate your mood each day (or at multiple times throughout the day). A rating of 100 means that you feel ecstatic. You feel on top of the world, maybe like you just won $80 million or received the Nobel Peace Prize — whatever turns you on. A rating of 50 means just a regular day. Your mood is acceptable — nothing special, nothing bad. A rating of 1 is just about the worst day imaginable. Interestingly, we find that most people without depression rate their average mood at around 70, even though we define 50 as middle range.

In addition to your mood rating, jot down a few notes about your day. Include anything that may relate to your mood such as

- ✔ Clashes with friends, coworkers, or lovers
- ✔ Difficult times of the day
- ✔ Falling in love
- ✔ Financial difficulties
- ✔ Loneliness

✔ Negative thoughts or daydreams floating through your mind

✔ An unexpected promotion

✔ Wonderful weather

✔ Work hassles

John suspects that he may have a problem, so he tracks his mood and finds a few interesting patterns. For an example of one week in John's mood diary, check out Table 2-2.

Table 2-2		Weekly Mood Diary
Day	*Mood Rating*	*Notes (Events or Thoughts, for Example)*
Sunday	20	Not a good day. I hung out and worried about getting my quarterly tax payment together by Thursday. And I felt horribly guilty about letting the lawn go without mowing it.
Monday	30 (a.m.) 45 (p.m.)	The day started miserably. I got stuck in traffic and was late to work. In the afternoon, things seemed to go more smoothly, although I can't say I felt on top of the world.
Tuesday	40	Nothing good, nothing bad today. Just the blahs.
Wednesday	30 (a.m.) 40 (p.m.)	I woke up feeling panicked about the new project deadline. I don't know how I'll ever get it done. By the afternoon I'd made a little progress, but I still worry about it.
Thursday	35 (a.m.) 45 (p.m.)	I was thinking about the fact that the days just seem to drag on. I don't look forward to much. In the evening, I enjoyed a phone conversation with a friend.
Friday	50	Miraculously, I got the project done four hours early. My boss said it was the greatest thing he'd ever seen me do. Of course, he probably doesn't think much about my other work.
Saturday	40	I finally got the grass cut. That felt good, but then I had too much time on my hands and started to worry again.

John studies several weeks of mood diaries. He notices that he usually feels morose on Sunday afternoons. He realizes that, on Sunday, he typically spends time alone and mulls over imagined difficulties of the upcoming week. He also discovers that mornings aren't exactly the best time of the day, because he worries about the rest of the day. Interestingly, he also discovers that his worries often involve catastrophic predictions (like not meeting deadlines) that rarely come true. Finally, his mood improves when he tackles projects he's been putting off, like mowing the lawn.

You can track your progress whether you're working on your own or with a professional. If your progress bogs down, please seek help or discuss the problem with your therapist.

Chapter 3

Breaking Barriers to Change

*A*lex has felt moderately depressed for the past two years. His night shift nurse's job at a nursing home bores him. He has considerable experience in some of the more exciting areas of nursing, such as emergency room work and surgical nursing. But ever since he made an error treating a trauma case two and a half years ago, he has avoided high-risk nursing jobs.

Alex often considers doing something about his depression. He actually tried medication for awhile, but he didn't like the side effects. He thinks that therapy is a tiring, long, drawn-out process. He purchased a self-help book, but it sits on his desk collecting dust. He feels guilty about not reading it, but then he thinks that no book can possibly pull him out of his mind's hazy state. So he ponders his plight and views his situation as hopelessly inescapable. He clings to this belief even though as a nurse he's seen many depressed patients benefit from self-help, medication, and therapy.

Because he's fully aware that effective treatments exist, you may wonder whether Alex actually *wants* to remain depressed. Nothing could be further from the truth. Nobody — and we mean nobody — prefers depression to normal moods.

If nobody prefers being depressed, then why does Alex avoid tackling his depression? Actually, he does so for normal, human reasons. In fact, most people with depression refrain from making a change at least for awhile. And when they do initiate efforts to change their situation, they frequently slip back into inaction for short to prolonged periods of time.

In this chapter, we explain why prospects of change pose such a formidable adversary in people's minds — so much so, that they'll do almost anything to keep clear of the idea. And the mere thought of trying to defeat depression often feels even more frightening, partly because depression, itself, typically goes hand in hand with a sense of hopelessness. We show you the rational fears that fuel procrastination, hopelessness, avoidance, and other self-limiting strategies. And we discuss how certain beliefs, myths, and misconceptions can paralyze people's desire to get to a better place. And, most importantly, we show you how to find out which of these problems may stand in your way and what you can do to push them aside.

Rummaging Through the Reasons for Avoidance

At first blush, it may seem bizarre that you would avoid searching for peace and serenity if you suffer from debilitating depression. After all, you know that depression feels horrible, and the alternative certainly appears more attractive. But we suggest that if you find yourself retreating and delaying when you think about trying to battle your depression, it's for good reasons. We now show you how fear of change, change-blocking beliefs, and myths lie behind this avoidance of taking actions against depression and make far more sense than you may think.

Flushing out the fear of change

Fear stands as the No.1 driving force behind inaction and avoidance. We can understand why you may find yourself avoiding, procrastinating, and feeling hopeless about working on your depression. Do we think that you should stay on the sidelines feeling hopeless and avoid the scariness of change? No.

However, you need to fully appreciate the magnitude of the issues that may stand in your way. If and when you find yourself procrastinating and avoiding the task of getting your depression under control, you have no cause for self-criticism and abuse. Rather, you need to realize that you're experiencing a normal, human fear of change. In the following sections, we tell you about the two most common types of fear that inhibit change.

Fearing more losses

If you have significant depression, you inevitably have experienced profound losses of various types. Such losses include

- Belief in positive possibilities
- Relationships
- Security
- Self-esteem
- Status

TECHNICAL STUFF

Hunkered down with homeostasis

Even at a biological level, our bodies attempt to maintain a consistent, stable state — a process known as *homeostasis.* The body works very hard to sustain stable levels of temperature, hormones, fluids, carbon dioxide, blood sugars, and so on. When any of these conditions rise or fall beyond certain close parameters, the body goes into overdrive to reestablish the proper level. Many experts believe that homeostasis operates at all levels, from the cellular level to the psychological level, and even in social situations.

Your depressed mind fears additional loss; it inevitably overestimates the difficulty of making changes and underestimates your ability to make them. The fear of hope itself is a big obstacle, because you assume that lost hope feels more horrible than no hope at all. Perhaps you're like most folks who are mired in depression and believe that

- ✔ If you seek friendship, you'll experience more rejection.
- ✔ If you take a new job, you'll fail.
- ✔ If you take a risk, you'll be humiliated.
- ✔ If you work on your problems, your efforts will be useless.
- ✔ If you dare to hope, you'll fall into an abyss.

If these beliefs apply to you, it's no wonder that you avoid the challenge of change. The fear of additional losses is no trivial matter. It's so easy to conclude that not trying at all is better than trying and failing. Thus, your depressed mind tells you that making no attempt at least preserves a smidgen of self-esteem, whereas working hard at self-betterment and then failing means that you have sunk even further into an abyss of "in's" — incompetence, ineffectuality, incapability, incapacity, insufficiency, and inferiority.

Fearing inconsistency

The *fear of inconsistency* is another type of fear that frequently holds back attempts at recovery. Sounds a little odd, doesn't it? Psychologists have known for decades that people have strong motivations to remain consistent in their behaviors and beliefs. Consistency helps simplify the world. And consistency makes life feel more predictable.

And when you encounter information about yourself that runs counter to firmly held beliefs, you may find ways to reject the new information. This process tends to occur whether you're depressed or not.

The quest for consistency works to sustain depression. If you're depressed, you'll likely find yourself tossing out every piece of positive evidence about you or your world like yesterday's newspaper. You may fear success, especially if it comes with a less-than-Herculean effort, because such an outcome would contradict your long-held negative self-views of inadequacy.

Although you certainly don't like depression, it probably feels familiar and predictable. By comparison, seeking a life of joy likely sounds frightening, unfamiliar, and unpredictable. Staying in the depths of depression hurts, sometimes horribly so, but at least you feel as though you have a little more control.

We wouldn't be writing this book if we didn't completely believe that you have effective ways to remove yourself from the morass you find yourself in. In fact, each chapter is packed with suggestions, tools, and exercises for doing just that.

Finding change-blocking beliefs

Depression is usually accompanied by a variety of deep-seated beliefs that support and sustain the melancholy and add fuel to the fears of change. Even though you may have first become depressed many years after passing through childhood, these beliefs generally have roots back to those early years. When you're not depressed, the beliefs hang around in the background, where they usually don't cause huge problems. But when depression strikes, they take center stage and diabolically disrupt your attempts at recovery.

Change-blocking beliefs are the thoughts and negative expectations you have about yourself and the world that make change seem impossible. Exploring the childhood roots of your change-blocking beliefs can help you discover not only where they came from but also that these beliefs have more to do with a child's interpretation of events than with current day reality.

Occasionally, change-blocking beliefs have roots in adulthood. Usually, traumatic events or chronic, repeated occurrences cause these beliefs to come about later in life. Nevertheless, change-blocking beliefs grounded in adulthood can be dealt with in much the same way as the more common, change-blocking beliefs that originate in childhood.

In the following sections, we describe what we've found to be the most common change-blocking beliefs. We describe each one and give you some tools on dealing with them on a case-by-case basis. Then, in the "Analyzing your findings" section, we provide an exercise that enables you to challenge any or all these beliefs when they get in your way.

You may be able to think of other change-blocking beliefs than the ones we list here. For example, in Chapter 7, we discuss the core beliefs that often intensify depression and hinder attempts to recover. Any of these beliefs may also act as change-blocking beliefs. We suggest carefully reviewing each of the beliefs we list to see if they may be making you feel like avoiding, procrastinating, or viewing your situation as hopeless. After you've worked on this list, you may also find it useful to review and work on the beliefs in Chapter 7.

Dealing with dependency and inadequacy

When you believe in your feelings of dependency or inadequacy, you quickly throw the brakes on taking risks. If you feel *dependent,* you probably believe that your depression must be cured by someone other than yourself. And if you think of yourself as *inadequate,* you likely feel incapable of doing anything for yourself. These change-blocking beliefs make taking risks seem particularly scary.

Yet, all efforts to change involve risk — you risk the possibility of failure. Unfortunately, feelings of dependency and inadequacy are almost universal among people who have depression. We can't even think of a depressed client that we've worked with in the past few years who felt competent enough to independently tackle difficult, challenging tasks.

The dependency/inadequacy belief usually sends a series of related thoughts running through the mind, such as

- ✔ Whatever I try, I usually manage to screw up.
- ✔ I can't do this without a lot of help.
- ✔ I need help, but no one can help me enough.
- ✔ I don't want to take this risk; I know I'll fail and feel worse than ever.
- ✔ I'm not strong enough to do this.

The dependency/inadequacy belief, and the related thoughts, paralyzes its victims into inaction. And the belief fuels the fear of change because of the assumption that failure will inevitably result. Devin's story demonstrates how his dependency developed in elementary and middle school.

After **Devin's** father dies when Devin is only 4 years old, his mother becomes increasingly attached to him. As a result, she can barely stand to see him deal with pain or frustration. If he cries or whimpers, she rushes to provide comfort. If he wants candy or a cookie, she fulfills his wish because she doesn't want him to whine. Later, when he can't figure out the answers to his homework assignments, she provides them for him. She has the absolute best of intentions, but she inadvertently fosters the development of Devin's dependency/inadequacy belief.

Devin never has the opportunity to learn what his real capabilities are, because his mother inevitably steps in before he has a chance to work through his problems. Although the school tests Devin's I.Q. and finds it to be in the gifted range, his teachers describe him as an underachiever. As a result, Devin believes that he's inept. Devin's I.Q. stands in contradiction to his basic belief of inadequacy. He has more than enough brainpower, but his mind tells him otherwise.

Devin's history depicts one of a number of ways that this destructive belief comes into being. Dependency and/or inadequacy can also emerge in childhood when a child receives excessive, harsh criticism. In addition, when parents aggressively push their children toward independence too soon, they can paradoxically cause their kids to feel overly dependent. For example, if parents never provide assistance that is truly necessary, their children may give up too easily. A similar result may occur if parents neglect their children, frequently leaving them alone to fend for themselves at too early an age.

If you think that you may have some degree of a dependency or inadequacy belief, reflect on your own childhood. Is it possible that

- ✔ One or more important people harshly criticized you over the years?

- ✔ One or both of your parents stepped in to help you too quickly when you felt frustrated?

- ✔ You rarely got help that you truly needed when you asked for it?

- ✔ Your parents pushed you way too hard?

- ✔ Your parents neglected you and left you alone too often at an early age?

If you answer "yes" to any of the questions in the previous list, please realize that your dependency or inadequacy belief has a very legitimate basis. In other words, you came to this conclusion for good reasons. You need to remember that those reasons don't mean that you're actually dependent or inadequate! If you don't agree, we provide you with some strategies for dealing with this and other dysfunctional beliefs in the "Analyzing your findings" section later in this chapter (and in Chapter 7 as well).

Uncovering an undeserving outlook

The belief that you're undeserving can also derail your recovery train before it works up a good head of steam. Many people who believe that they're undeserving think that something is inherently wrong with themselves. Thus, they beat themselves up for the slightest flaw or mistake. They literally think that they don't deserve to feel good or have good things happen to them.

When people feel as though they're undeserving, they exert little effort to overcome their depression. They may feel as though depression is what they deserve and expect out of life, and that depression is an appropriate punishment for their miserable existence on this planet.

If you frequently have any of the following thoughts, you may believe that you're undeserving:

- ✔ I feel like other people deserve more out of life than I do.
- ✔ I don't expect much out of life.
- ✔ I think that having needs indicates weakness.
- ✔ I feel guilty when people do things for me.
- ✔ Because bad things only really happen to bad people, I must deserve my depression, not happiness.
- ✔ I don't deserve to get what I want.

If you believe that you're more undeserving than other people, you'll likely find your depression more difficult to tackle: You probably fear that any happiness you bring your way will literally lead to punishment, because the happiness is undeserved. You need to clear this belief out of your way before making serious attempts to drain depression from your life.

You can start working on getting rid of this undeserving outlook by searching for its roots. People don't feel undeserving for no reason at all. A series of childhood events builds the foundation for the undeserving belief. Did any of the following themes permeate your childhood?

- ✔ Were your parents emotionally unavailable to you?
- ✔ Did you frequently feel slighted (compared to one of your siblings)?
- ✔ Did one of your caretakers use *guilt tripping* (criticism and messages that made you feel ashamed) as a major form of punishment?
- ✔ Were you harshly abused or punished?
- ✔ Were your parents exceptionally unpredictable in the things they punished you for?

If these situations ring a bell with you, your undeserving belief is anchored in childhood. You formed this conclusion about yourself because, as a child, you tried to make sense out of the things that happened to you. It's natural to conclude that you're undeserving if your parents shamed you and/or failed to express love consistently. Desiree's story illustrates one way this undeserving belief can form.

Desiree's mother, Charlotte, is what psychologists call a *narcissist.* Charlotte thinks far more about her own needs than her child's. When Desiree exhibits the slightest crankiness at the age of 3, Charlotte whisks her off to spend the rest of the day in her bedroom. Charlotte's motivation is to eliminate an annoyance from her environment, not help Desiree learn self-control. Charlotte deals with Desiree's desires with similar harshness. If Desiree wants something that will inconvenience her mother, Charlotte informs Desiree that she's selfish, greedy, and ungrateful. Desiree decides early on that she's undeserving of good things.

Clearly Desiree deserved as much happiness and good in life as any other child. She didn't think that she deserved happiness — she still doesn't today, as an adult — only because of her upbringing.

Fighting the unfair fight

When people bog down and avoid working on their depression, they sometimes proclaim, "It's unfair; I shouldn't have to work at this! Why did this happen to me?" The belief that depression is unfair and that you shouldn't have to work on the problem is true to a certain degree.

We agree that coming down with depression isn't fair, and we sure wish that you didn't have to put in much work to do something about it. The truth is, we fully believe that

- ✔ No one truly wants to be depressed.
- ✔ No one deserves to have depression.
- ✔ No one is to blame for having depression.

Depression has many causes (see Chapter 2 for more on this topic) including genetics, diseases, childhood, tragedy, abuse, and trauma. You're not to blame for your own depression.

However, as unfortunate and unfair as it may be, you must work to overcome your depression. You won't find a fairy godmother to come into your life and wave depression away with a magic wand. Even if you choose to treat your depression with the path that often requires the least effort — medication — you still have to work closely with a trusted physician or psychiatrist in order to monitor your progress and any possible side effects.

Like other change-blocking beliefs, excessive concerns with unfairness usually have connections to childhood. More often than not, people who focus on unfairness were dealt with quite unfairly by their parents when they were children. Exploring the early causes helps you realize what change-blocking beliefs are about and lays the groundwork for changing them.

Rejecting the long-term victim role

Unfortunately, bad things sometimes happen to good people for no reason at all. Certain negative events have great potential for disrupting people's entire worlds and the ways they view themselves. This disruption usually occurs when

> ✔ Something really bad happens, such as serious illness or trauma.
>
> ✔ The negative event was undeserved or unfair.
>
> ✔ The person feels upset, angry, and/or anguished about the negative event.

When such undeserved events happen to people, their views about who and what they are change. They naturally begin believing that they're sick patients or victims. And beliefs about sickness and victimhood involve an entire set of related self-views and altered behaviors, which we now describe.

People typically shift both their feelings and behaviors — from independent to dependent, from well to sick, from capable to incapable, from in control to helpless, from serenity to rage. This type of change in beliefs, behaviors, and expectations (that come from perceiving yourself as well versus sick) is normal and natural when traumatic events occur.

In a sense, these new beliefs and behaviors about sickness and victimhood require the individual to take on a new role, like an actor in a play. The individual takes on the leading role of patient or victim, and society, friends, family, mental health providers, and physicians carry out auxiliary roles as helpers. These helpers typically have certain expectations for the patient or victim role as well as for their own roles. For example:

> ✔ Helpers feel motivated to help.
>
> ✔ Helpers don't view the patient as someone who deserves to be blamed.
>
> ✔ Helpers view themselves as mainly responsible for creating improvement and the patient as a passive recipient of their assistance.
>
> ✔ Certain helpers may provide compensation to the victim.
>
> ✔ Helpers believe that it's natural for the patient to feel upset or angry.
>
> ✔ Helpers usually provide sympathy, concern, and support.

The sick patient and victim roles are legitimate, reasonable, and deserved. In a sense, society created these roles so that people can receive predictable assistance when bad things undeservedly happen to them. We suspect that virtually everyone has occupied one or both of these roles at one time or another. So what's the problem? Nothing at all if you only take on one of these roles for a short period of time.

Unfortunately, over time, these roles easily become entrenched in the mind. As the belief in one's sickness or victimhood sets in, most people focus more and more on the unfairness and awfulness of what's happened to them. They feel angry and enraged. The worst part is that they frequently feel helpless to do anything about their predicament.

The best way to determine whether a belief in the sick patient or victim role has taken over your life is to ask yourself the following questions:

✔ Do I frequently think about how unfair life has been to me?

✔ Do I feel enraged by what has happened to me?

✔ Do I frequently complain to others about my circumstances?

✔ Do I feel helpless to do anything about my plight?

✔ Do I feel that doing something about my problems would somehow discount the importance of what's happened to me?

If any of the thoughts from the previous list apply to you, you may have slipped into a victim or sick patient role for more than a short stay. These roles provide no guidance for how to move on, and that's the problem: They keep you stuck.

Here are alternative roles that you may want to consider — the role of coper and the role of rehabilitation client. Copers and rehabilitation clients have also experienced bad (possibly horrible), undeserved, unfair events. The people who assume these roles are no more to blame than are victims and sick patients. But they find a way to dig down deep, let go of their anger and rage, and focus on what they can do to improve their circumstances. Rehabilitation sometimes takes months or years of hard work, but most people find that the results are worth the effort. Even chronic, debilitating diseases are often dealt with better by adopting the coper and rehabilitation roles.

If you find yourself trapped with prolonged, unrelenting sickness or victim-hood beliefs, seek therapy for additional assistance.

Please realize that we blame no one for taking on a victim or sick patient role. It's a normal, expected, and virtually universal reaction to terrible circumstances. And the more traumatic the events (such as rape, physical abuse, and serious mental illness), the more one is likely to stay in the role for a longer period of time.

However, even in cases of severe trauma, shifting into a coper mode and working arduously to find a better life is the ultimate but highly challenging goal you need to achieve. To accomplish this shift, you need to understand that you deserve peace. And most importantly, you need to know that rediscovering happiness in no way discounts or diminishes the awfulness of what happened to you.

Sometimes people wrestle with the idea that seeking happiness discounts past trauma. They may think that a renewed pleasure and zest for life would somehow mean that nothing truly horrific ever occurred. If this type of thinking sounds familiar, you may want to get back on the road to happiness with a technique we call "Putting It in a Vault." This technique is based on a strategy suggested by our colleague, Dr. Robert Leahy, who has written extensively on the topic of why people resist change.

If you've had one or more horrific traumas in your life, try imagining a large bank vault with thick steel doors in your mind. Put your mind's videotape of the trauma into the vault and lock it away. The tape will remain there, and you can play the video of the trauma to appreciate the meaning it has for your life anytime you feel a need to do so. However, when you finish viewing the tape, lock the trauma away and live your life safe in the knowledge that the trauma doesn't need to harm you any further while it's locked in the vault. In this way, you can learn to take charge of your trauma rather than allow the horror to continue controlling your life.

Analyzing your findings

Ridding yourself of change-blocking beliefs isn't the easiest thing in the world to do because, as we mention throughout this section, they usually originated many years ago in your childhood and adolescence. We suggest that reviewing your personal history to more fully appreciate how and why you acquired these beliefs is a good place to start. This knowledge can help you to stop blaming yourself for having the beliefs in the first place.

After you figure out which change-blocking beliefs you have, you can conduct an "Advantages and Disadvantages Analysis" of them. This analysis will provide you with important ammunition for challenging these beliefs when they get in your way. To do an Advantages and Disadvantages Analysis:

1. **Get a notebook out and construct a chart.**

   Draw a line down the middle of your paper. Write down the change-blocking belief that you want to tackle at the top of the page. Then label one column "Advantages" and the other "Disadvantages." See Table 3-1 for a sample analysis.

2. **Write every imaginable reason that your change-blocking belief feels advantageous to you.**

   Perhaps it feels like it helps you avoid risks and losses or that other people will like you more if you adhere to this belief.

3. **Write down all the reasons your change-blocking belief gives you grief.**

   Perhaps the belief keeps you from exploring new opportunities or prolongs your state of unhappiness.

4. **Review your two lists carefully.**

   Ask yourself whether the advantages or disadvantages seem more compelling. Typically, you're likely to find that the disadvantages greatly outweigh the advantages. If so, commit yourself to challenging your change-blocking belief by reading over the disadvantage column frequently. And see Chapter 7 for more ideas on how to challenge problematic beliefs.

Hayden's story shows how he uses this analysis technique to his benefit. **Hayden** puts off working on his depression for nine months. He hopes his bleak mood will simply go away all on its own, but his depression only deepens. His therapist suggests reading a particular self-help book. After three more months of procrastination, Hayden reads a chapter. He discovers that he has an entrenched belief that he is undeserving. This belief prevents him from tackling his depression because he literally feels that he doesn't deserve happiness. He currently believes that he's particularly undeserving of pleasure because his depression has caused him to be unproductive in his work as a freelance writer. Although he's a bit skeptical, Hayden conducts an Advantages and Disadvantages Analysis of his undeserving belief. Table 3-1 shows the results of Hayden's advantages and disadvantages analysis.

Table 3-1	Hayden's Advantages and Disadvantages Analysis
Belief: Undeserving Outlook	
Advantages	**Disadvantages**
I don't have to feel guilty if I avoid pleasure.	This belief stops me from trying to get to a better place.
People won't think I'm self-centered.	I actually feel guilty all the time, whether I have a good time or not.
I'll be satisfied with less.	I always feel unhappy.
I won't be disappointed by hoping for good things.	I keep myself stuck when I think I don't deserve better.
If I feel undeserving, maybe it will motivate me to be more productive.	Actually, I hate being unproductive, but I think it's my depression that makes me less productive. And if I don't think I deserve better; I'll never be more productive.
	Whenever I feel good, I end up trashing the feeling because I think I didn't earn the right to feel that way. This thinking makes me less motivated to do anything positive.

Hayden concludes that his advantages and disadvantages analysis looks stronger on the disadvantage side of the equation. This inference motivates him to battle his undeserving belief each time it tells him to shy away from doing anything good for himself.

If you use the advantages and disadvantages technique on one or more of your change-blocking beliefs and it doesn't seem to help, don't get too discouraged. We provide many more ways to bust these and other problematic beliefs in Chapter 7.

Shining a light on myths about therapy

Myths and misconceptions about therapy and self-help resources are another major reason why many people avoid seeking help for depression. We repeatedly hear some people discuss therapy and self-help in uncomplimentary terms. Of course, rarely do these people actually undertake a regimen of therapy. They avoid therapy like the plague because they truly view the process as misguided and useless. If they do begin therapy or self-help, they typically avoid full participation and then quit too early because of their misperceptions.

These people buy into the many myths and misconceptions about therapy. We now discuss each of these myths and why we believe that they're inaccurate:

Therapy is a long, complicated process. Therapy and self-help involve some work. However, numerous studies have demonstrated that most cases of major depression can be treated successfully with about 20 sessions of the types of therapy we discuss in this book. Other studies have shown that, for more than a few people, self-help alone can provide sufficient assistance for overcoming mild to moderate cases of depression. Studies have also shown that self-help can be a valuable addition to therapy.

But, if you're battling chronic, long-term depression, you may indeed discover that you require a relatively lengthy course of therapy. However, you'll likely experience a lift in mood within a few months of starting your therapy, and odds are good that you'll feel that the long-term payoff from continued work is more than worth the effort.

Therapy just provides excuses. People who ascribe to this myth often view themselves as inferior and believe that they deserve to suffer from depression. If this belief holds for you, please read the "Uncovering an undeserving outlook" section, earlier in this chapter.

Other folks who view therapy as an excuse generator believe that certain therapies (especially cognitive therapy; see Part II) simply push positive thinking. The truth is that these therapies don't ask you to simply see everything as positive. Rather, they require you to collect and examine evidence (much like scientists do). When you discover evidence that supports a negative aspect about yourself or your world, you work to change what you can and accept what you can't change.

Therapy and self-help merely trivialize depression. Throughout this book, we state that depression is a serious problem — sometimes deadly serious in that suicide poses a significant risk. All good therapists understand the seriousness of this condition.

On the other hand, we do realize that both self-help and therapy give you techniques that are fairly straightforward and not particularly complex. These strategies may indeed feel trivial. After all, you may have battled profound depression for years, and the idea that some simple techniques may help you overcome your depression can feel very discounting. But therapists try to take complicated ideas and information and break them into easily understood, digestible units. If you were to ask anyone to comprehend and execute all of this information at once, most folks would naturally feel overwhelmed by it all.

Sometimes you may feel that a therapist or self-help author is asking you to change too quickly or easily, which can make you feel diminished, as though your depression is simple and easily changed. If you're in therapy, discuss these feelings with your therapist. If you're attempting to treat yourself with self-help and you feel as though you're being asked to change too quickly, you may benefit from adding therapy to your efforts. And if you feel that we're trivializing your depression, feel free to contact us through our Web site (www.psychauthors.com) and let us know.

Therapy and self-help ignore the importance of emotions and feelings. The mental health field appreciates the agony and pain behind depression. That's why this field has devoted decades of professional exploration and research to finding ways to alleviate the pain of depression.

Emotions and feelings are of paramount importance to therapists. Nevertheless, sometimes therapists ask you to focus on your thoughts in addition to the emotions generated by those thoughts. As a result, it may feel like your emotions aren't fully appreciated. If you're in therapy, discuss this feeling with your therapist. If you have this reaction while reading a self-help book such as this one, you may want to supplement your efforts with a therapist who can listen to and appreciate your feelings more completely than an author can from afar.

Neither therapy nor self-help can give me what I need. Well, this thought has some truth to it. No therapist or book can possibly give you everything you need. Most therapists and authors realize that they have limitations. For example, you very well may feel disappointed by one or more parts of this book. And we want to hear from you if that's the case.

But try to approach both therapy and books with the realization that your needs will only find partial fulfillment. Your needs are more likely to be met through multiple sources — books, therapists, friends, relatives, and so on. And, unfortunately, we don't know of anyone who can truthfully report feeling 100 percent fulfilled all of the time.

Therapy doesn't work. Literally hundreds of studies have demonstrated the effectiveness of the therapies we describe in this book. As we discuss each of these therapies, we also briefly make note of the research behind them. However, not every type of psychotherapy has convincingly demonstrated such effectiveness. If you get therapy, make sure it's one of the ones we discuss in this book.

I can't change unless I feel totally understood, and no author or therapist can ever understand the complexity and depth of my problems. The idea that no author or therapist can ever completely understand every aspect of your depression is absolutely true. In fact, many mental health professionals haven't experienced a major depressive episode, so they can't truthfully say that they fully grasp the entire entanglement of your torturous emotional experience.

However, most therapists do their best to listen and connect with the devastating impact of depression. Hopefully what they write reflects a reasonable understanding of what they hear. And research shows that therapy works quite well even though most therapists can't claim a 100 percent understanding of the agony you may be experiencing.

People who go to therapy are weak. Although this thought effectively blocks more than a few people from seeking help, we fully believe that it is grounded in falsehood. In truth, seeking help is a courageous act. It requires letting down your guard and pondering your vulnerabilities. Think about it. Who is more courageous? Someone who feels compelled to present a false front and avoid exploring any personal vulnerability, or someone who owns up to problems and decides to face them head-on? We think the latter is more courageous.

People just go to therapy to whine and complain. The vast majority of people who seek help do reveal some "complaints" about their lives, but then they set about trying to do something about their problems. Therapy has about as much to do with whining and complaining as rapidly flapping your arms has to do with flying.

Saving Yourself from Self-Limitations

The earlier sections of this chapter review the considerable fears that change evokes, as well as the powerful beliefs and myths that support those fears. It probably doesn't surprise you that most people avoid anxious apprehensions whenever possible.

In the case of deciding to deal with depression, avoidance means turning to self-limitation in order to stay clear of your fear of working toward recovery. *Self-limitation* is anything you do that prevents you from working on your depression and therefore reaching your true potential. You may be engaging in self-limitation if

- You find reason after reason to avoid working on your depression.
- You view your situation as hopeless.
- You insist that there must be a perfect solution before trying to do anything at all.
- You demand to see a guarantee of improvement before you undertake the task of changing.
- You quit at the very first sign that things aren't working out.
- You repeatedly engage in harsh self-criticism when you put forth some effort, thereby robbing yourself of motivation.
- Whenever evidence indicates that things are a little better than you thought they'd be, you immediately discount and discard the data.
- You wait for the "perfect time" for making changes, which never seems to show up.
- You become confused, disoriented, or "out of it" whenever you try to deal with your problems.
- You repeatedly blame other people for your predicament rather than look at what you can do to solve your problems.

If any of the items in this list apply to you when you consider working on your depression, you're not likely to make any progress until you do something about your self-limitation.

Please be aware that everyone who has depression avoids dealing with the problem and engages in self-limitation at various times in life. Avoid pummeling yourself with harsh judgments, which only work to prolong the sabotaging process.

Instead, read the following sections to find out how to dig your way out of your depression. We discuss a number of ways to stop self-limitation and get your recovery train moving down the tracks. If one strategy doesn't do much for you, try the others.

Tracking saboteurs

Saboteurs prefer to work in the dark. Their chances of success escalate substantially when you can't detect their movements. Therefore, you need to monitor the sabotaging activity that your depressed mind engages in.

Light (awareness) is the arch foe of your mind's saboteurs; if you start monitoring how these saboteurs work, they won't be able execute their intentions as effectively. Monitoring your thinking increases your awareness of when your mind's saboteurs are at work and therefore enable you to stop them.

Find that notebook we suggest you keep around and start a "Self-Limiting Diary." Write the days of the week in a column to the left. Then title a column on the right "Self-Limiting Strategies." (See Table 3-2 for a sample diary.) Each day, write down anything you find yourself doing that keeps you stuck in depression and avoiding doing something about it. Consulting the list of self-limitation strategies in the previous section may help you get started. When you see what you're doing to limit yourself, you're likely to break out of the self-limiting pattern. Morgan's example shows how this technique works.

Morgan's melancholy manages to endure for more than a year before he decides to do something about his predicament. He seeks the services of a psychologist who practices cognitive therapy (see Part II for more information about cognitive therapy). The psychologist quickly sees that Morgan, because of a fear of change, inadvertently sabotages his own recovery efforts at every opportunity. Morgan shows up late to appointments, his mind wanders when he attempts to read self-help materials, he complains about how others treat him, and he insists that his therapist can't do anything to help him.

Morgan's psychologist helps him understand that his behavior only deepens the hole he finds himself in and prevents him from productively working toward improving his condition. It takes some time, but Morgan eventually gets the point. His psychologist then suggests that he keep a diary of his self-limiting strategies. Table 3-2 shows Morgan's results for the first five days.

Table 3-2	Morgan's Self-Limiting Diary
Day	*Self-Limiting Strategies*
Monday	I stayed in bed for hours and got to work late. I lost track of time later in the day and showed up to therapy 30 minutes late, which gave me only 20 minutes to deal with my issues. Then I spent ten of those minutes telling my psychologist how hopeless I am. *Not very helpful I guess.*
Tuesday	My boss said my report was terrific, and I told him it wasn't really that good and proceeded to point out several flaws in it. *What will that do for me?*
Wednesday	I got a speeding ticket. Then I told myself I was an idiot for letting that happen. My insurance might go up, and I'll probably start screwing up other things too. I dwelled on the stupid ticket all day long and had an unproductive day at work. *I guess that wasn't too useful.*

(continued)

Table 3-2 *(continued)*	
Day	**Self-Limiting Strategies**
Thursday	I met Sheila last week, and she seemed to like me. I really want to call her again, but I found myself not doing it. Maybe she was just being polite and doesn't like me at all. I started thinking I can't stand any more rejection and put off calling. *Where will that get me?*
Friday	I must have looked at that book my psychologist recommended ten times. But did I pick it up to read it? No, of course not. Then I beat myself up for being such a pathetic loser that I don't even do a simple thing like that to help myself. *I guess that doesn't help my cause either.*

Morgan reviews his diary and finds out how many ways he avoids productive work when it comes to improving his problems. He fears further loss and rejection, so he stays stuck in his depression, thereby insuring that he will fail to find a new relationship. When he hears something positive about his work, he refuses to believe his boss and actively argues with him. His self-criticism only serves to push his mood lower; it hardly helps motivate him to do something better. And his insistence on his own hopelessness only backs him into a corner.

Morgan's psychologist helps him understand that he self-limits for a good reason — the fear of change we review in the "Flushing out the fear of change" section earlier in this chapter. Tracking his self-limitation does seem to help him tackle his problems. As Morgan sees the myriad of ways he avoids efforts to recover and maintain his current sad state, he starts to recognize his self-limitation before the fact. Then he ever so gradually stops backing away from change and starts taking on his problems.

If you find yourself avoiding and self-limiting, try keeping a self-limiting diary. But don't use your diary as a trigger for self-criticism and abuse. Beating yourself up will only perpetuate self-limitation by making you feel worse about yourself.

Suspending judgment

If you bog down in a web of self-limiting thoughts when reading this book or participating in therapy, suspend judgment for a while. Experiment with the idea that just maybe therapy can work for you. While you're suspending judgment, work as hard as you can at following the techniques that we describe throughout this book or that your therapist suggests.

The deeper your depression, the more we recommend starting with Part III. That's because getting yourself moving is important, and Part III gives you a variety of ways to jump start into action. After you start moving, your energy will likely pick up and give you a boost for tackling the rest of the important techniques.

As you work on the various antidepression tools we provide you, you may find yourself practicing self-limiting from time to time. Fight it with all you can muster. Although simply repeating positive, self-affirming statements to yourself won't do much for curing depression, sometimes repeating certain ideas can serve as important reminders. Therefore, consider repeating one or more of the following statements to yourself on a regular basis:

- ✔ What do I truly have to lose by trying? I don't have to tell anyone what I've been doing, so no one will even know if my efforts don't work.

- ✔ The only real failure comes from never trying.

- ✔ Focus on progress, not perfection.

- ✔ When I dump on myself, it doesn't help. I will try to focus on what I do right more than what I do wrong.

- ✔ Don't judge, just do.

Going slow

You can also limit yourself in a rather surprising way — by working too hard and fast on your depression. Believe it or not, tackling your depression head-on at full speed can cause unexpected problems. Be sure to go slow. Going too fast sets you up for unrealistic expectations. Focus on small successes. If you happen to experience a big success, that's great. But savor it a bit and pull back from pushing ahead for just a little while.

You're more likely to overcome your depression by taking a gradual, steady approach rather than swinging away for home runs.

Pacing yourself has another advantage — it can help keep you from feeling overwhelmed by the tasks at hand. Some people look at a book such as this one and notice that it contains more than 300 pages along with numerous exercises. They then conclude that they could never get through it all. If you think that you may not be able to get through this book, consider the following ideas:

✔ You don't need to read every single chapter and do each and every exercise to derive significant benefits. If a particular exercise doesn't look that pertinent to you, don't do it! And certain chapters may not be important for you to read. For example, if you have a very good relationship, you may not want to read Chapter 14.

✔ Looking at the whole picture at once can lead to self-limitation because doing so can feel overwhelming. Focus on one small step at a time. For example, if we focused on writing this entire book as though it had to be completed in a single week, we'd stop writing this instant!

If you have a serious level of depression that includes thoughts of death and hopelessness, or you work on the strategies in this book for six weeks or longer without experiencing any success, please consult a professional for additional assistance.

Appreciating how progress proceeds

Many people who come to us for help with depression expect to improve, and they're correct to have that expectation. But all too often they also expect to see prompt progress that proceeds in a smooth, steady, upward fashion. The only problem with this second expectation is that we have yet to see it happen! Why?

To be honest, we're not entirely sure why, but we do know that humans almost inevitably progress gradually, with many peaks and valleys along the way. It's important not to expect your change efforts to move ever steadily upward. Change just doesn't progress in that manner. Your progress will likely resemble Figure 3-1.

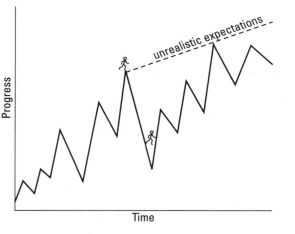

Figure 3-1:
The usual path of progress with depression.

As you can see in Figure 3-1, progress contains both peaks and valleys. Like the stick figures on the chart, you're going to occupy various positions as you work to overcome your depression:

- ✓ **Standing on a peak:** When you occupy this position, you're more likely to form unrealistically positive expectations about how you will progress in the future. You need to remind yourself that you will experience both ups and downs.

- ✓ **Walking in a valley:** At this point, you may be tempted to conclude that you have never been at such a low spot before. The truth is, you may have made progress, but at these downturns, it may be impossible to see the progress you made — especially after being on the higher peak earlier. Try to resist making judgments on your progress during the inevitable downswings.

When you're on an upswing, you can probably assess your progress fairly realistically, but you need to resist the temptation to predict a too rosy progression in the future. And when you've taken a dip, try not to judge how you've been doing overall, because it won't be possible at those times.

Finally, we want you to know that the inherent downswings in the process of change has its advantages. That's because each decline, though unpleasant, can provide you with useful information about the events that trigger your low moods. You can see what to do with such events in Chapters 5 and 6. The key lies in expecting these downturns and not bashing yourself for experiencing the inevitable ups and downs in overcoming depression.

Rewriting your reams of failure stories

If you're depressed, you've probably written hundreds of failure stories of doom and gloom. Oh, you may not have actually put the words on paper, but your mind undoubtedly has pictured rejection, shortfalls, wasted efforts, botched attempts, and humiliation more times than you care to recall. And those images more than likely include a rich detail of your anticipated bungling along with an itemized list of horrors that would have resulted from your failure.

Stories about potential failures can cause people to avoid efforts that are aimed at improving depression. In essence, the stories become another form of self-limitation. So, how about considering something different?

Get out your notebook and a pen. Or, if you prefer, sit down in front of your computer. Write a story about how you just may actually succeed at something! Include details about how you're going to approach the challenge, your plans, and the difficulties you anticipate.

Write down how you imagine you're going to overcome those difficulties. Be sure to include any thoughts about your fears, but also include strategies for working your way through the fear. If you have trouble coming up with ideas for getting around the obstacles, ask yourself what someone else might do. Make your story long enough to include the specifics; don't skimp.

Low self-esteem helps build barriers to change

A group of researchers at the University of Washington and the University of Waterloo in Canada conducted a series of studies on self-esteem and its effects on the motivation to break bad moods. In one of these studies, the researchers put a group of students (some of whom had low self-esteem and others had normal self-esteem) in a bad mood by making them listen to depressing, sad music. Then the researchers offered the students a choice of videos to watch, including a comedy. All the students believed that the comedy would do the best job helping them get into a better mood. But surprisingly, slightly less than half the students with low self-esteem chose to watch the comedy, whereas about three-fourths of the other participants chose the comedy. The students with low self-esteem appeared to believe that it's not particularly appropriate to change a bad mood. Furthermore, the students with low self-esteem also seemed to think that their bad moods were more acceptable than the other students did.

Low self-esteem usually accompanies depression. This fact supports the idea that people who are dealing with depression and low self-esteem typically fall into inaction. Therefore, you need to work on breaking your mind's barriers to change before you attempt other recovery techniques.

Chapter 4

Finding Help for Depression

*A*re you feeling blue? Okay, we're going to guess that, because you're reading this book, you or someone you love has been feeling depressed to one degree or another. Perhaps you merely feel a little down in the dumps, or maybe you're desperately despondent. The good news is that you can find help in a number of places, from the bookstore to the therapist's office. The bad news is that the shear number of choices can confuse the issue. In this chapter, we clear up the confusion by laying out your options for obtaining help and giving you the tools you need to make an informed decision.

We provide you with background information on three primary options for dealing with depression — self-help, psychotherapy, and medication — so that you can figure out what's right for you. We help you decipher the differences among the various mental health professionals and determine whether you have a good match with the professional you choose.

Stumbling onto a Solution

People often neglect to think through their decision to seek help or investigate their options carefully. Sometimes this approach works out just fine — even though the options for dealing with depression are numerous and strikingly different.

Consider **Betty,** for example. She takes a job as a head librarian in a new city. She feels excited about her new position. Nevertheless, she misses her friends and family far more than she expected. At the age of 52, she's considerably older than her coworkers, and she finds it difficult to relate to them. After talking to her adult daughter on the phone one evening, she's surprised to find tears welling up in her eyes. Over the next few weeks, her mood deteriorates, and she begins to cry frequently. She feels rising guilt and remorse for having moved away from the ones she loves.

Betty receives a new shipment of books and notices one about fighting depression. She begins to leaf through it. The book's message resonates with her. After reading a few chapters, she concludes that her mood reflects an adjustment disorder with depressed mood. Over the next six weeks, she picks the book up many times and tries out its many suggestions. Her mood gradually brightens, and she starts to enjoy her new job and the new city.

Betty stumbled upon the self-help option, and it worked for her. Other folks find their way into therapy or medication, and they meet with great success. (Believe it or not, people with depression usually deal with it successfully when they seek reasonable help.)

But many people don't just luck out and find the best option to deal with their depression. A more surefire approach is to really consider all your options for help and weigh the information carefully to make the best choice for you.

Exploring the Self-Help Option

Everyone who is dealing with depression can benefit from self-help. *Self-help* refers to efforts you make on your own, without professional assistance, to deal with your depression. Scores of studies have demonstrated the value of self-help for a variety of emotional, behavioral, and medical difficulties. For some individuals, self-help appears to be all they need. However, self-help may not be enough. But even if your own efforts fall short, self-help can provide a potent addition to therapy, medication, or a combination of both.

Deciding whether self-help is a singular solution

Should you consider self-help as an exclusive means of overcoming depression? Before making the decision to try self-help alone as your strategy, ask yourself the following questions:

> ✔ **Am I having any suicidal thoughts?** If the answer is yes, you need to obtain an evaluation from a mental health professional. That person will likely recommend psychotherapy, medication, or a combination of the two in addition to self-help.

> ✔ **Is my depression seriously interfering with my life in areas such as work, relationships, sleep, appetite, or recreation?** Once again, if the answer is yes, you may be suffering from a major depressive disorder (see Chapter 2 for more information), which means that you probably need more than just self-help.

If you answer "no" to both of these questions, self-help may be the right place to start. However, you need to consider another question before you begin: "Do I have the desire and motivation to work on the advice I receive from self-help sources?" We're not talking about hours of study every day. But, self-help does require more than a quick read of an article or book. And you, like plenty of folks, may do better when you have a coach or leader inspiring you. Only you can answer this question. If you can't confidently answer "yes" to this question, talk to a mental health professional about your options.

If you make the decision to stick with self-help — great. This book is a terrific place to start. Then, if you want to obtain extra self-help resources, you can choose additional books, videos, self-help groups, or whatever combination of resources you think will help. Work for a while at applying what you learn, and monitor your progress carefully. You can use the mood monitoring form (the "Mood Diary") that we outline in Chapter 2 to help keep track of your improvement.

If you don't see progress through self-help after a couple of months of effort, look into additional assistance. If at any point you feel discouraged, start having suicidal thoughts, or your depression worsens, get additional help. See the "Discovering who's who in psychotherapy" section, later in this chapter, for more information on mental health professionals.

Reviewing the resources

Choosing the right self-help approach depends in part on your personal preferences and style. The fact that you're already reading this book suggests that the written word may appeal to you. The following list covers the most common self-help options (we provide specific suggestions in the appendix):

> ✔ **Books:** This is the only book in the entire literary world that has value in helping people with depression. Just kidding, folks! Reading several different self-help books is a pretty good idea. Even though you may hear some suggestions more than once, repetition helps you remember, and all authors have slightly different ways of explaining concepts. The best books for dealing with depression give you information about treatments that are known to work (such as cognitive therapy, behavior therapy, interpersonal therapy, and medication).
>
> Books are an inexpensive way of getting help, which is an obvious advantage. But more importantly, books can also provide you with a

whole lot of information that would take a therapist many sessions to cover. And you can refer to the information as often as you need to. Finally, if you combine reading with therapy, it may just take you less time to get better.

Make sure that the authors of any self-help book that you purchase have credentials and experience helping others deal with depression. (We cover the credentials issue in the "Discovering who's who in psychotherapy" section, later in this chapter.)

✔ **Tapes and videos:** For folks who learn best by hearing or seeing, tapes and videos have merit. Look for the same author credentials and information on effective approaches that we note for books.

✔ **Self-help groups:** Self-help groups offer support and understanding. People with common problems gather in these groups to share information and experiences. The members help themselves and each other by expressing feelings and solving problems together. Unfortunately, we don't know of any major, organized groups like Alcoholics Anonymous or Take Off Pounds Sensibly with a nationwide network of self-help groups for people with depression. However, the National Alliance for the Mentally Ill (Internet: www.nami.org) is a self-help support and advocacy group for people with emotional problems and their families. They offer information concerning the availability of local support groups. In addition, your local chapter of United Way likely has a directory of community resources.

✔ **Web sites:** You can find a wide range of resources related to depression on the Internet. You can join a chat room or download articles. But take particular care if you venture away from the Web sites we give you in the appendix. First, the Internet has more than its share of unqualified, though well-meaning individuals serving up advice. Second, outright frauds also market their products and ideas on the Internet.

Numerous unscrupulous entrepreneurs hawk various types of books, tapes, herbs, videos, and other types of merchandise that promise prompt relief from depression with little or no effort. Buyers beware! No miracle cures exist for overcoming depression.

Pursuing the Psychotherapy Option

Psychotherapy involves work with a therapist using psychological techniques to alleviate emotional problems. And psychotherapy works well for treating depression. Incredibly, psychotherapy comes in literally hundreds of different forms and types; it's also practiced by a wide array of professionals. Yikes! How are you ever going to figure out how to get the help you need in this maze of options?

Never fear. In this section, we give you the information you need to find your way through the maze. First, we discuss the types of psychotherapy that are known to work for treating depression, and then we tell you how to sort out who's who among mental health professionals.

Uncovering the effective therapies

Feel free to read the vast literature that encompasses hundreds and hundreds of articles on the effectiveness of psychotherapy for treating depression. We're guessing that you probably don't want to read all that info, so we did the research for you. (Don't feel too bad for us; it's our job.)

The following therapies have been proven to be effective and produce excellent results within a reasonable timeframe:

- ✓ **Cognitive therapy:** In brief, cognitive therapy operates on the assumption that the ways in which people think about, perceive, and interpret events plays a pivotal role in how they feel. For the treatment of depression, no psychotherapy has received as much support as cognitive therapy. Flat out, it works. It works at least as well as medication does for treating depression, and it appears to provide a degree of protection against relapse — something that medication can't do. See Part II for a wide array of techniques and ideas based on cognitive-therapy principles.

- ✓ **Behavior therapy:** Studies have found that changing your behavior can also improve the way you feel and alleviate depression. Behavior therapy focuses on helping you to change behaviors (such as increasing your pleasurable activities and teaching you ways to solve problems). Most practitioners of behavior therapy also include cognitive techniques in their work. Many of these professionals call themselves cognitive-behavioral therapists. See Part III for a review of various behavior-therapy–based techniques.

- ✓ **Interpersonal therapy:** This type of therapy attempts to help people identify and modify problems in their relationships, both past and present. Considerable evidence supports the value of interpersonal therapy for decreasing depression. Like cognitive therapy, this approach has also been shown to alleviate depression about as well as medication. Sometimes this method of therapy delves into issues involving loss, grief, and major changes in a person's life, such as retirement or divorce. A fair portion of this approach also involves the relationship between the therapist and client (like learning to relate to the therapist in ways that may help you with other relationships), which a book can't provide. Check out Part IV for strategies such as learning to replace losses that are derived in part from interpersonal therapy.

Most people aren't aware that hundreds of different types of therapy exist. If you cast around, you may run into practitioners of psychoanalysis, hakomi therapy, eye movement desensitization reprocessing (popularly referred to as EMDR), client-centered therapy, transactional analysis, and Gestalt therapy, just to name a few. We fully believe that many of these therapies have value, and some may work for depression. However, the scientific literature on these other types of therapy as applied to depression is quite limited. We suggest that you start with therapies that have been fully established as effective.

Discovering who's who in psychotherapy

Most people don't realize that, in the majority of states, just about anyone can call themselves a therapist without getting into trouble with the authorities, because the title "therapist" isn't typically covered by licensing laws. Instead, states regulate specific professional titles and the right to practice psychotherapy or prescribe medications.

In the following list, we review the most common professional titles controlled by state professional licensing boards. We also describe the usual training required to obtain each type of professional license, although requirements vary slightly from state to state. You need to ask about a practitioner's specific training in particular types of psychotherapy, because not all professionals have been trained in the types of psychotherapy that have been found effective for depression (which we outline in the preceding section).

- **Clinical psychologists:** To become a licensed clinical psychologist, an individual has to earn a doctorate degree in psychology. In addition, she must complete a yearlong internship followed by one or two years of supervised postdoctoral training. Doctoral programs in psychology generally emphasize the science of human behavior and provide training in psychotherapies that have been validated by research. Nevertheless, you need to check on the psychologist's expertise in cognitive-behavioral or interpersonal therapy before you commit to working on your depression with her.

- **Counselors:** Licensed, independent counselors have a master's degree and two years of postgraduate supervision. In a few cases, counselors may only have bachelor's degrees in education, psychology, or theology. *Pastoral counselors* have theological training in addition to their training in counseling. Most counselors provide a range of psychotherapies. Inquire about their specific experience with the types of psychotherapy that have been found to be successful for depression.

- **Psychiatrists:** Psychiatrists earn a medical degree and participate in a four-year residency program that trains them in the treatment and diagnosis of emotional disorders, including depression. Their training typically emphasizes biological treatments. Therefore, many psychiatrists strictly deal with medication management and/or alternative biological therapies such as electroconvulsive shock therapy (see Chapters 15 and 16). However, some psychiatrists do receive extensive training in psychotherapy. If you're interested in obtaining psychotherapy, be sure to ask if the psychiatrist you're thinking about working with offers it.

✔ **Social workers:** Social workers sometimes go by various titles such as *licensed social worker* and *independent social worker.* The titles *qualified clinical social worker* and *diplomate in clinical social work* are given to folks who reach the most advanced levels of training. To become a qualified clinical social worker, the applicant must have earned at least a master's degree in social work, worked two years under supervision beyond the master's degree, and passed a comprehensive national examination. Social workers provide a range of psychotherapies, although some of them focus on arranging social services and helping people access resources. A social worker's title doesn't necessarily indicate the extent of his psychotherapy training. So just ask to find out whether the social worker you're planning to work with offers psychotherapy and has been trained in therapies found effective for the treatment of depression.

Finding the right therapist for you

Some people take less time choosing a therapist than they do picking out the best cantaloupe at the grocery store. That's too bad, because the right therapist can help you recover and reach new levels of adjustment and well-being. And in the worst case, the wrong therapist can take your time and money, actually causing increased emotional distress.

Important issues to consider when you look for a therapist include:

✔ **Finances:** Ask how much the therapist charges and whether your insurance covers that specific professional. Some insurance companies have lists of so-called preferred provider therapists that they cover. Some policies allow you to see almost any licensed therapist, while others restrict access to a very narrow panel of providers. Though unusual, a few companies only cover psychotherapies known to be effective, such as the ones in this book. Be sure to check your coverage rather than make an expensive mistake based on your assumptions. Some people choose not to use insurance because they want to see a particular professional or they have special concerns about privacy.

Investing money in therapy ultimately pays off in numerous, unexpected ways. For example, studies have shown that psychotherapy actually reduces medical doctor visits; it also appears to improve physical health in addition to mental health.

- **Reputation and recommendations:** Therapists can't provide you with the names of satisfied customers, because they're bound to respect confidentiality. However, you can inquire about therapists' reputations from other sources. Ask around. Talk to your friends and/or your family physician.

  Beware of advertisements in the newspaper, television, or phone book: They *are not* especially reliable sources of information about therapists' reputations.

- **Scheduling:** Some therapists have extremely full practices with very limited options for appointment times. You may need to find someone who sees people in the evenings or on weekends. Be sure to ask what hours the therapist keeps.

- **Training and licensure:** We discuss the general training requirements for various licensed mental health professionals in the "Discovering who's who in psychotherapy" section, earlier in this chapter. Consider this entry on our list as a reminder to ask about training and experience in the therapies that are known to work for depression, such as cognitive therapy, behavior therapy, and interpersonal therapy. (For a definition of these therapies, check out the "Uncovering the effective therapies" section, earlier in this chapter.)

Knowing if the shoe fits: Do you have a good match with your therapist?

Most of the time when people choose a therapist, they feel a good connection, and they get better. Therapists generally are bright, kind, and skillful. However, therapists and clients sometimes just don't make a good match.

You may find that your therapist is a poor match for you. Maybe the therapist looks just like your ex-spouse, and every time you go to therapy, you feel a flood of painful memories. Or maybe you don't feel connected to your therapist for some reason that you don't understand. The quality of the therapeutic relationship has been found to consistently predict good or bad therapy outcomes, so it's critical that you feel comfortable.

Here are some questions you may want to ask yourself to help determine your comfort level after you see your therapist a few times.

- Do I feel like I can tell my therapist just about anything?

- Does it seem like my therapist cares about me?

- Does my therapist understand me?

- Does my therapist seem interested in my problems?

✔ Does my therapist hear what I'm trying to say?

✔ Do I trust my therapist?

✔ Is my therapist nonjudgmental and noncritical with me?

✔ Do I feel safe discussing my problems with my therapist?

If you answer any of these questions with a strong "no," or you answer several of them without a clear "yes," discuss your concerns with your therapist. If you feel that you can't discuss these issues with your therapist, ask yourself why.

If you have good reasons for feeling so unsafe that you can't imagine speaking frankly, you probably need to search for another therapist. On the other hand, if your reticence comes from shyness or embarrassment, please realize that therapists are trained to hear your concerns, and you have an absolute right and need to express them.

How your therapist reacts to your concerns about the quality of your client-therapist relationship will tell you if the relationship can be repaired. Following is an example of how a good therapist might respond to a client's concerns:

Client: I need to talk to you about something.

Therapist: Sure, what is it?

Client: I've been feeling like I can't be honest with you because I'm afraid you'll be critical.

Therapist: I'm glad you brought that up. Can you help me understand when it's felt like I've been critical of you?

Client: Well, last week I told you about my plans to look for another job and you said I shouldn't do it.

Therapist: That must have sounded like criticism, as if I wasn't supporting you.

Client: Yes, it did. It felt like you thought I was stupid.

Therapist: That must have felt awful. Can you think of any other reason I might have made that suggestion?

Client: No. Was there one?

Therapist: Well, yes. I've simply found that when people make major life decisions while they're in the throes of a major depression like you, they often regret their action later. It's just so hard to look at things objectively at times like this. On the other hand, I certainly want to explore your unhappiness at your job. Come to think of it, I probably didn't ask you enough about that. Would you like to tell me more now?

That exchange seems to work out fairly nicely, doesn't it? The therapist listens carefully to the client's concerns, acknowledges having failed to adequately explore the issue, and demonstrates interest in doing so. If your therapist responds to you in this manner, we suggest that you remain in therapy a little longer to see if the relationship can become more productive.

But sometimes therapists have their own problems, and they don't respond very well to clients' concerns. Here's an example:

Client: I need to talk to you about something.

Therapist: Sure, what is it?

Client: I've been feeling like I can't be honest with you because I'm afraid you'll be critical.

Therapist: Well, I certainly don't think I've ever criticized you. What would make you think such a thing?

Client: Well, last week I told you about my plans to look for another job, and you said I shouldn't do it.

Therapist: That's because you're in no condition to be looking around for work. You're far too depressed to do something like that. You really thought I was criticizing you?

Client: Yes, I did. It felt like you thought I was stupid.

Therapist: That's ridiculous! You're obviously feeling overly defensive. We need to work on that.

Client: To be honest, I'm just not feeling heard by you.

Therapist: Well, you're wrong; I'm clearly listening to you.

In this case, the conversation does nothing to repair the strained relationship. The therapist reacts defensively and shows no support, empathy, or connection with the client. If your discussions with your therapist often sound like this one, you probably should consider going to another professional.

Talking to a Professional about Antidepressant Medication

The actual decision regarding whether or not to use medication for your depression is a complex one to make. In Chapter 15, we review both the upside and the downside of treating your depression with medication in detail. However, if you opt for antidepressant drugs, you still need to know who to get them from. A variety of different professionals prescribe medications for depression.

Professionals who prescribe most medications

As you may imagine, physicians prescribe most antidepressant medications. Two types of physicians prescribe these medications far more frequently than other physicians:

- ✔ **Primary care physicians:** These physicians are the ones most people go to for their routine care such as annual physicals and treatment for colds and flu. This group includes specialists, such as family practice physicians, internists, geriatric physicians, and sometimes even gynecologists. Talking to your family physician about symptoms of depressions can be a reasonable way to start your treatment.

  In fact, you may be surprised to know that primary care physicians write more than 60 percent of the prescriptions given for emotional disorders. Nevertheless, if your depression is quite severe or complicated by the presence of other problems, such as anxiety or substance abuse, you need to consult a psychiatrist.

  Before you ask for antidepressant medication from your primary care physician, be sure to find out whether your doctor is comfortable with these medications. Some general practitioners have considerable training in using medications to treat emotional disorders, while others know relatively little about this specific area.

- ✔ **Psychiatrists:** Keep in mind that psychiatrists receive more extensive training in the biological treatments of depression than any other prescribing group of professionals. (See the "Discovering who's who in psychotherapy" section, earlier in this chapter, for more info.) In addition, they regularly see patients with depression and other emotional disorders. Thus, they have considerable experience with the tricky side effects and drug interaction issues involved with antidepressant medication.

Occasional prescribers

A few professionals, in addition to physicians, are allowed to prescribe antidepressant medication and do so from time to time. However, this group of professionals typically has relatively less training in emotional problems like depression.

You're probably only going to want to seek a member of these groups out if your depression is fairly mild and has not been a chronic, long-term condition:

✔ **Nurse practitioners and physician assistants:** A majority of states allow these professionals to prescribe antidepressant medication in addition to other medications. Most of these practitioners have quite limited training in the treatment of emotional problems such as depression. If your depression isn't severe or complicated by the presence of other emotional problems (such as physical maladies, substance abuse, or suicidal thoughts), you may consider obtaining antidepressant medication from these mid-level providers.

✔ **Pharmacists:** In several states, pharmacists are lobbying for the right to prescribe certain types of medication. Usually this privilege involves collaboration with a primary care physician. Pharmacists also have quite limited training in the treatment of emotional problems, but you can consider obtaining your medication from a pharmacist if you have a mild, uncomplicated form of depression. (See Chapter 2 for more information about the different types of depression.)

Mental health professionals who generally don't prescribe medications

The vast majority of mental health professionals don't prescribe antidepressant medication. Although they may have received some training and education about the use and effects of these drugs, they don't prescribe. See the "Discovering who's who in psychotherapy" section earlier in this chapter for more information on the training of these professionals:

✔ **Counselors:** Though frequently well trained in psychotherapy, counselors don't currently prescribe medications in any state.

✔ **Psychologists:** Most psychologists don't prescribe medications of any kind. However, a small number of psychologists in the armed services and Guam who have considerable additional training in psychopharmacology prescribe medications for emotional disorders only. Legislation was recently passed in New Mexico (and is pending in many other states) to enable more psychologists to ultimately prescribe these medications (for emotional disorders only) following additional training. These practitioners recommend a complete physical examination to rule out any possible physical causes of your depression prior to prescribing an antidepressant.

✔ **Social workers:** Many social workers have received excellent training in psychotherapy, but at this time, they're not allowed to prescribe medications in any state.

Tired and stressed? You must be depressed!

While we were writing another one of our *For Dummies* books, *Overcoming Anxiety For Dummies* (Wiley Publishing, Inc.), Laura was also working as a clinical psychologist at a local hospital. In the midst of writing the book and fulfilling her duties at the hospital, she visited her primary care physician and complained of fatigue. The doctor asked about stress, which Laura had to acknowledge was fairly high. The doctor suggested that she was depressed. Laura said, "No, I'm quite sure I'm not depressed." She explained that she was still interested in things and didn't have any pessimistic thinking about the future. The doctor stated that mental health professionals were the worst at diagnosing themselves. Laura still protested, but the doctor insisted that she was in denial. Laura reluctantly went home with a prescription for an antidepressant medication.

The next day, the doctor's office called with the results of Laura's blood test. It showed that she was actually suffering from hypothyroidism, which fully explained her fatigue. Laura tossed the antidepressant prescription into the trash after discussing the findings with the doctor. Had the doctor known to inquire about other symptoms of depression, such as low self-worth, guilt, loss of interest in pleasurable activities, and so on, she would have realized that the cause was more likely physical in nature.

Laura's example describes one of the problems you can encounter when seeking treatment from your primary care physician. Generally, a brief ten-minute office visit proves insufficient for diagnosing emotional disorders; the short visit can actually lead to an erroneous initial impression. But don't get us wrong. Your primary care physician is usually a great place to start for most physical problems, and sometimes for emotional difficulties, as well. More and more primary care physicians are now receiving training in the recognition and treatment of depression.

If you decide to take medication and also receive psychotherapy from another provider, encourage your therapist to communicate with the health care professional who is prescribing your medications. Communication ensures that both professionals are working on the same page.

Part II
Untwisting Your Thinking: Thought Therapy

The 5th Wave   By Rich Tennant

"My hunch, Mr. Pesko, is that you're still making mountains out of mole hills."

In this part . . .

Thought therapy, which is also called *cognitive therapy,* is the most widely researched approach to the treatment of depression. This research has consistently shown that cognitive therapy alleviates depression as well as or better than any other strategy in this book. For most of you who are battling depression, cognitive therapy will be one of your main weapons.

In the chapters that follow, we give you a recipe for understanding the connections between depression and habitual ways of thinking. You can discover how depression distorts thinking. We also provide you with tools that you can use to smooth out the mental wrinkles. Digging deeper, you can discover your core beliefs that may be fueling your depressive thinking and ways to adjust the troublesome beliefs. Finally, depression often interferes with memory, so we show you what you can do to manage this problem.

Chapter 5

Discovering Depression-Driven Thinking

. . . .

In This Chapter

▶ Understanding the thoughts and feelings connection

▶ Tracking your thoughts and feelings

▶ Exploring the four major types of distorted thoughts

. . . .

*H*ave you ever been caught in a traffic jam? Horrible, right? Some people respond to traffic snarls by pounding on the steering wheel and muttering a few choice obscenities. Others turn up the radio and relax to soothing music. What's the difference? The angry people have angry thoughts: "It's awful to be caught in traffic. People in this town don't know how to drive, and I can't stand to be late." Those folks who are more laid back have thoughts like, "No sense in getting upset by things I can't control; I'll get there when I get there. And it's nice to have the chance to listen to this music."

The way you think about or interpret events greatly affects the way you feel about them. In this chapter, we discuss the relationship between events and the thoughts and feelings that follow those happenings. We also show you how to track your thoughts and feelings to see specifically how they operate in your life. Then we look at the four major types of distorted thinking that deepen and maintain depression. Finally, we give you some tools for smoothing out any troubling distortions in your thoughts.

Thinking about Cognitive Therapy

Thought therapy, also known as *cognitive therapy,* is by far the most widely researched approach to the treatment of depression. Numerous studies have confirmed time and again that thought therapy alleviates depression and reduces recurrences of depression.

Thought therapy is a type of psychotherapy. All psychotherapies involve work with a therapist using psychological techniques to alleviate emotional problems. Cognitive therapy primarily uses techniques designed to change thoughts in order to improve the way you feel.

A major idea underlying thought therapy is the interconnected nature of feelings (which we also refer to as emotions) and thoughts. Thoughts strongly influence feelings, and feelings alter thoughts. So thoughts and feelings both play a role in depression.

But the story doesn't end there. Physical factors can also play a role in depression. Factors such as fatigue, illness, and blood chemistry can produce dismal feelings, which, in turn, sow the seeds for dark, depressing thoughts.

For example, **Carter** tosses and turns through a third night. He's not sure what's causing his recent bout of insomnia, but every time he thinks he's about to fall asleep, another part of his body itches, or a position becomes uncomfortable. Carter's day begins with a long rush-hour drive; his usual calm acceptance dissipates into irritability. His fatigue compounds his growing worry. He starts to think, "What's wrong with me? I'm not going to be able to get through another day. I feel horrible. I can't focus. I'm going to lose my job. What's wrong with me?"

Carter's thoughts have spiraled out of control. Why? Too many days in a row of poor sleep shift his thoughts into negative gear. One good night of sleep just might allow Carter to return to normal. Or not. Sometimes, a physical event can start a cascade of bad thoughts and feelings that may just stay and visit for a while.

No one knows how to determine which of the three components (feelings, thoughts, or physical factors) kicks off depression for any particular person. But the good news is that you can interrupt the cycle of depression in various ways, using thought therapy, no matter what started the downward spiral. The goal of thought therapy is to help you be fully aware of your negative thinking when it occurs and then actively rethink those thoughts in more realistic terms. After you've done so, your depression is quite likely to lift.

Research shows that thought therapy is as effective as medications in treating depression. And, surprising as it may seem, learning new thinking habits through thought therapy, like medication, has actually been shown to have positive effects on brain chemistry — one of the physical components of depression. But therapy doesn't have to be an either/or proposition. Deciding which combination of medication, thought therapy, and behavior therapy (see Part III for information on behavior therapy) is right for you is complicated. We discuss the issue of combining medication with therapy in more detail in Chapter 15.

Tracking Thoughts, Feelings, and the Related Events in Your Life

A core component of cognitive therapy (see the preceding section on "Thinking about Cognitive Therapy") involves increasing your awareness of how thoughts, feelings, and events in your life interconnect. In this section, we show you how to uncover your feelings about events and examine the thoughts that accompany those feelings.

Some people truly have little awareness of their feelings. Others have trouble figuring out what's going on in their heads. So we help you understand what feelings are and how to identify them, and we explain how to figure out what you're thinking. You may think you know what your feelings and thoughts are, but it isn't always that obvious. After you have that info down, you can connect your thoughts and feelings and the events that lead to them, and record them on what we call a "Thought Tracker."

After you see how events, thoughts, and feelings intertwine, you can analyze your thoughts for possible distortions, which depression inevitably causes. We show how in the "Digging Up Distortions in Thinking" section later in this chapter.

Finding feelings

Believe it or not, experiencing a full-blown major depression but remaining unaware of sad feelings is possible. People sometimes try to suppress, deny, and/or avoid unpleasant feelings. They try to feel better by not feeling at all. And this strategy could even make a certain degree of sense — except that denying feelings doesn't work and only makes things worse.

Stuffing your feelings down inside is like filling a grocery bag with too many cans. You might just walk out and find that your bag rips apart, spilling its contents all over the place. The bottom line from research: Denial and repression are linked to poor emotional health, whereas expressing feelings improves both body and mind.

When people find *denial* and *repression* (either conscious or unconscious attempts to avoid thinking about uncomfortable emotions and thoughts) failing to blot out their unpleasant feelings, they sometimes turn to other strategies, such as immersing themselves in their work or abusing drugs and/or alcohol to drown out their sorrows. Unfortunately, avoidance of bad feelings by distracting yourself through excessive work or by ingesting substances only provides fleeting, temporary relief. In the end, they both actually cause you to dig yourself into a deeper hole.

A lot of people (with and without depression) have trouble finding their feelings. If you often don't know what you're feeling or people say that you're out of touch with your feelings, you can change things.

If you start tuning into your bodily sensations, we think you're likely to find feeling words to capture what's going on. It may take you a little time, but tapping into what your body is telling you will facilitate your efforts in getting to a better place. After you know the feelings you're experiencing, you'll be ready to connect these feelings to your thoughts, which prepares you for the important Thought Tracker step we describe in the "Building a Thought Tracker" section later in this chapter. You can start tuning into your bodily sensations by paying attention to the following:

- Muscle tension
- Your breathing (Is it fast, slow, deep, or shallow?)
- A sense of heaviness in your chest
- Dizziness
- Posture (Are you relaxed, rigid, or stiff?)
- Queasiness
- A constricted sense in your throat
- Discomforts of any type

Spend five minutes a day actively tuning into such bodily sensations. Everyone experiences such sensations, so just start tuning into your body and recognizing when you have them. Try to think of feeling words that capture your complete physical and mental state. Here's a partial list to start you out:

Afraid	Low
Apprehensive	Melancholy
Despondent	Morose
Disturbed	Nervous
Embarrassed	Obsessed
Frustrated	Sad
Guilty	Shaky
Heavy	Somber
Inadequate	Tense
Insecure	Worried

On the other hand, some people know all too well how horribly down and distressed they feel. But if someone asks them what they're thinking in response to events, they may say, "Absolutely nothing. I just feel terrible." If that reaction fits you, read the next section.

Ferreting out thoughts

Upon hearing about thought therapy, some people declare with total conviction, "But I don't have any negative thoughts in my head!" If you have that reaction, we believe you and know that you may not hear specific words and sentences running through your mind like many people do. However, we're referring to thoughts in a broader sense.

Consider thoughts as your *interpretations* or *perceptions* of the important events in your life. They're the way you see or look at happenings. In other words, thoughts are the *meanings* you consciously or unconsciously assign to what's going on around you.

TIP

You may not be aware of an actual dialog going on in your head when something happens to you, but humans have a way of assigning meaning to the occurrences in their lives. If you feel a sudden rush of feelings, try asking what event immediately preceded the feelings and then ponder your perception or interpretation of the event.

For example, if someone says to you, "I like your outfit," you may not be aware of any particular thoughts. But ask yourself how you interpreted that event. Did you hear the message as a positive statement about your clothes? Or did you hear the comment as sarcastic, meaning that your outfit is hopelessly out of style? Or, perhaps you heard the statement as a mere attempt at politeness. Those interpretations are your thoughts. And they'll all result in different feelings about the comment.

Pink elephants and negative thoughts

When you hear that negative thinking increases negative emotions, you might think of a quick solution — just stop thinking negatively. In other words, just shove any dark thoughts out of your mind the moment you detect them. You're cured! Well, not so fast. Drs. Richard Wenzlaff and Daniel Wegner recently reviewed research on the topic of this technique, which is known as *thought suppression.* Fifteen years of research demonstrated that suppressing unwanted thoughts doesn't work. Even worse, attempting to do so virtually assures that you'll end up experiencing the very thoughts you were trying to avoid in the first place, and to a greater extent than if you hadn't tried to suppress the thoughts at all. It's a bit like the old saying, "Don't think about pink elephants." Suddenly, you find yourself seeing pink elephants in your mind, whereas if no one had told you not to think about them, you probably wouldn't have done so!

You may think that thought therapy advocates thought suppression, because one of its goals is to help you think in less distorted, negative ways. But we urge you not to attempt ridding your mind of negative thinking merely by suppressing sad thoughts. Instead, figure out how to use the skills we provide you with for developing new thinking habits — it's worth the effort.

You may find these questions useful for helping you figure out your thoughts about events:

- ✔ What meaning does the event have for you in your life?
- ✔ What concerns do you have about the event?
- ✔ What implications does it have for your future?
- ✔ What do you think the event could mean about you?
- ✔ What passed through your mind as you noticed the event?

Building a Thought Tracker

Use the "Thought Tracker" when you experience troubling feelings. It can help you track and understand the connections between your thoughts, feelings, and the events that trigger them. In addition, the Thought Tracker can help you become more aware of the types of events that trouble you and prepare you to do battle with your problematic thoughts. Turn to a page in the notebook we've suggested you use and divide it into three columns. Fill each column out with the following information (check out Table 5-1 for a sample):

- ✔ **Feelings:** Use this first column to write down bad *feelings* (not thoughts) and rate them on a 1 (very mild) to 100 (extremely severe) scale. People often notice their feelings before anything else, even though thoughts usually precede the feelings, so focus first on what you're feeling. (Besides, bad feelings are what depression is all about.) Sometimes you'll notice yourself experiencing more than one feeling. Record all the bad feelings you notice.

- ✔ **Events:** Use the second column to write down the *event* that preceded or triggered the feeling. Such events are usually things that happen to a person, but sometimes, they involve a daydream or image that floats into the mind. If you notice the event before the feeling, feel free to fill out the event first. In either case, events do occur before the feelings, so if you first notice an unpleasant feeling, ask yourself what happened in the preceding moments to minutes. Only occasionally will the feeling emerge more than a half hour following the event; most times, the feeling comes on almost instantly.

When writing down the event, try to be as specific as possible: Include where you were, who was there, and what happened.

- ✔ **Thoughts:** Use the third column to record the thoughts or interpretations you have about the event — in other words, how you see the thing that happened. These thoughts generally occur automatically without careful, conscious reflection. Be sure to take time and reflect on all possible reactions or interpretations you have.

Sometimes you'll have slightly different thoughts that relate to different feelings that all stem from the same event. Look at the thoughts you have that relate to each feeling you list under the feelings column. For example, if you recently got promoted and your new boss asks you to rush a report to her desk, you may have feelings of both fear and despair. Fear-related thoughts may center on concerns of being reprimanded if you don't finish on time, and despair-related thoughts may focus on the belief that you're overwhelmingly inadequate for handling this new promotion.

Here's an example of how the Thought Tracker works. **Sharif** works at a software engineering firm. He tends to be quite a perfectionist, which adds further stress to his already highly demanding job. When one of the computer programs he's working on repeatedly crashes, Sharif crashes. He can't sleep; he can't eat; and thoughts of suicide enter his mind. Sharif confides his despair to a close friend. His friend strongly urges him to see a therapist. Sharif objects at first, but his friend insists.

His therapist suggests that Sharif fill out a Thought Tracker whenever he finds himself feeling down. Take a look at Table 5-1 to see what Sharif came up with.

Table 5-1	Sharif's Thought Tracker	
Feelings (0 to 100)	*Events*	*Thoughts (or Interpretations)*
Despair (80)	The computer program I'm working on crashed again.	My boss is going to figure out that I don't know what I'm doing and fire me.
Helplessness (95)		I'll never be able to figure this out.

You can see how Sharif's thoughts probably contribute to his bad feelings and overall depression. We suggest you fill out a Thought Tracker for a week or so. Try to capture at least one or two problematic events each day. After you've accomplished this task, you'll be ready to tackle the thoughts that lead to your depression.

Digging Up Distortions in Thinking

A primary premise of cognitive therapy rests on the well-established idea that certain thoughts you have in response to events (see the "Building a Thought Tracker" section earlier in this chapter) lead to depressed feelings.

Now we show you that those thoughts are almost always distorted. By *distorted,* we mean that these thoughts don't accurately reflect, predict, or describe events. In this section, we help you analyze your thoughts for these distortions. In doing so, you can start on the road toward seeing your world in more accurate terms.

By asking you to examine your thoughts for various types of distortions, we are *not* trying to get you to *rationalize* everything bad that happens to you. The goal of cognitive therapy is to teach you how to ponder, reflect, and weigh your distorted thoughts in order to later rework them in such a way that they match reality (see Chapter 6 for information on developing accurate, replacement thoughts). When reality sucks, we don't want you to deny that fact. Rather, we want you to cope when events turn negative.

You may find it helpful to know that people with depression don't own exclusive rights to distorted thinking. Every single human on this planet has, at times, significantly distorted thoughts. Depression merely makes these distortions more frequent and intense. Even those people who aren't especially depressed could likely benefit from taking a look at our strategies for ironing out such distortions. And if you are depressed, discovering new ways of thinking may lead to a far more joyous existence.

If you find yourself objecting to the material in this chapter because the information sounds overly simplistic or that it seemingly discounts the importance of your feelings, please read (or reread) Chapter 3, which discusses common barriers to change as well as myths about therapy. The depressed mind very well may resist hearing some of the information that follows. If you're depressed, take your best shot at reading this material, and take your time before you form conclusions.

We group the various types of thought distortions into four major categories. In the following sections, we discuss each of these types of distortions and show you how they can shape your perceptions of reality as easily as you can mold cookie dough into images of people, trees, or monsters.

Scrambling signals

Reality-scrambling distortions involve twisting reality in ways that make events appear as bleak as you feel. The human mind has a rich variety of ways for distorting incoming information. And the depressed mind escalates these distortions to the point that reality morphs into a tangled mess of mangled misinformation. In the section that follows, we discuss each of the most common types of reality-scrambling distortions. We then use a Thought

Tracker (see the "Building a Thought Tracker" section earlier in this chapter) to show you examples of how these distortions gang up on you and work together to deepen depression. Understanding how these distortions operate can start the process of more accurate thinking.

Meeting the reality scramblers

Everyone scrambles reality from time to time. Depressed minds just use reality scramblers more often, and they more fully buy into them. In the following list, we review common reality scramblers — the tactics that the mind has for scrambling signals from your world. We call this bag of tricks "The Mind's Seven Sinister Reality Scramblers." Read carefully to see if your mind ever resorts to using these reality scramblers.

- **Enlarging and shrinking:** Your mind uses this scrambler to magnify or catastrophize the importance or "awfulness" of unpleasant events. In a similar fashion, the mind minimizes the value and importance of anything positive about yourself, your world, or your future.

- **Filtering:** The depressed mind typically searches for dismal, dark data while screening out more positive information. The not too surprising result? The world (or yourself) looks dreary and bleak.

- **Seeing in black-and-white, all-or-none terms:** This reality scrambler views events and your character in absolute terms, with no shades of gray. Thus, a single bad grade or performance would indicate complete and utter inadequacy. The problem with such polarized thinking is that it sets you up for inevitable failure, disappointment, and self-abuse. All-or-none thinking imposes standards that no real human could reach.

- **Dismissing evidence:** This scrambler looks at evidence that just might contradict the mind's negative thoughts and dismisses that evidence as inadmissible and/or completely irrelevant. For example, suppose you have the thought that you're a failure. Then your boss gives you a promotion for your performance. Your mind may quickly conclude that the promotion was meaningless and that your failure runs much deeper than mere job performance. This trick is sort of like being accused of a crime, and the judge throws out every single piece of evidence that proves your innocence as irrelevant. We suppose you can guess the verdict. In this case, your own mind is throwing out evidence and determining the verdict.

- **Discarding positives:** Somewhat similar to "dismissing evidence," impugning positives is a gimmick the mind uses to trivialize successes, good outcomes, and positive personal attributes. So if you win the audition for your city's symphony orchestra, you conclude that the organization is a low paying, ill-supported group that anyone with minimal musical talent could join.

> ✔ **Overgeneralizing:** This ploy involves looking at a single, unpleasant occurrence and deciding that this event represents a general, unrelenting trend. Thus, if you drop your fork on the floor, your mind concludes that you're a clumsy klutz who's *always* dropping things.
>
> Words like *always* and *never* are tip-offs to this reality scrambler.
>
> ✔ **Mind reading:** Mind reading occurs whenever you assume that you know what others are thinking without checking it out. Thus, someone may not ask out a new acquaintance because, "I just know she wouldn't go out with someone like me."

Adding reality scramblers to your Thought Tracker

A good way to understand whether your thoughts about events that happen to you are distorted or not is to add a fourth column to your Thought Tracker (see the "Building a Thought Tracker" section, earlier in the chapter). Label that column "Reality Scramblers" (see Table 5-2 for an example). Examine your thoughts about events carefully and ask yourself which reality scramblers apply. You may be surprised to see how often your thoughts are scrambled.

Brandon's story illustrates how reality scramblers distort his thoughts and intensify his negative feelings. **Brandon** works as a supervisor for the city bus system. He arrives home from work one day to find a note from his wife saying that she's decided to file for divorce and has taken the kids with her. The note says that she's had enough of his long work hours, and she plans to find happiness some other way than with him. Brandon's grief (see Chapters 2 and 13 for more information about grief) fails to dissipate, and he slowly sinks into a deep depression over the following year. At this point, his department head strongly urges him to see a psychologist for help, out of concern for his obvious distress.

Brandon's psychologist quickly diagnoses a major depressive disorder (see Chapter 2 for more information about this problem) and decides that cognitive therapy will likely help. First, as part of this therapy, the psychologist discusses the types of reality scramblers (see the previous "Meeting the reality scramblers" section) that the depressed mind usually employs. Brandon isn't sure that he distorts anything in his life, but he agrees to look into the possibility.

Next, the psychologist prescribes an exercise called a Thought Tracker, in which Brandon fills out various items so that he can see how he's looking at events. Brandon then adds a fourth column to see whether he's scrambling his reality. Table 5-2 shows what Brandon discovered, somewhat to his surprise, when he filled out his Thought Tracker for a few days.

Table 5-2		Brandon's Thought Tracker	
Feelings (0 to 100)	**Events**	**Thoughts (or Interpretations)**	**Reality Scramblers**
Fear (75)	The city bus drivers said they will go on strike. The drivers' representative said if it weren't for me, they would have done this long ago.	I will lose my job when the strike lasts more than a week or two, and then I'll lose my home. I can't imagine anyone else hiring me.	Enlarging Overgeneralizing Mind reading Discarding positives
Despair (80)		I have so little education, I'll never find another job. I'll bet the drivers' rep is lying; he probably thinks the strike is my fault for not keeping the drivers happier.	Filtering
Sad (70)	Amanda said I looked worn out.	I've had a thing for her, and now she says I look like hell.	Enlarging Black and white
Embarrassed (85)		I've made a fool of myself. She probably thinks I'm the last man on earth she'd go out with. No one's ever going to see me as attractive.	Mind reading Overgeneralizing
Upset (78)	I bounced a check.	I'm messing everything up lately. My credit rating is going to plummet if I do things like this! I'll never get that car loan I need.	Overgeneralizing Enlarging All or none
Apprehensive (35)	I got a very positive job evaluation.	The department head is just trying to butter me up. He wants me to work more hours, and I just can't do it. Next time, I'll probably get a terrible evaluation if I don't do everything he wants.	Dismissing evidence Discarding positives Mind reading

Do you see in Table 5-2 how consistently Brandon's depressed mind scrambles his thoughts or interpretations of the things that happen to him? Time and again, his mind enlarges the meaning of negative events and puts them into all or none terms. Even positive events are either filtered out or dismissed. Is it any wonder that he ends up feeling fear, despair, sadness, and apprehension?

Notice that Brandon's reaction to the first event contains five types of reality scramblers. For example, when he says he "will" lose his job and his home, and that no one will ever hire him, he's engaging in automatic, reflexive thinking without any reflection on true probabilities whatsoever. He's *enlarging* on the event by the unquestioned assumptions that the strike will continue to the point that he'll lose both his job and home. He's *overgeneralizing* when he concludes that should he lose his current job, he'll never find another. How does the fact that a person loses one job mean that no other job will be found? He's *mind reading* as well as *discarding positives* when he concludes that the representative is lying to him. In addition, he's *filtering* out the positive message from the representative and focusing on imagined negative catastrophes.

Perhaps you're wondering if, just possibly, Brandon's thoughts are *not* actually distorted with reality scramblers. For example, maybe he really will lose his job, and maybe the drivers' representative does believe that Brandon deserves blame for not keeping the drivers happy. Possible? Yes, of course. However, you can tell that reality scramblers are at work by the fact that Brandon doesn't use qualifiers, such as "possibly," "maybe," or "perhaps," and that he fails to factor in other considerations, such as the likelihood of his assumptions in relation to other possible outcomes.

Consider using a fresh page in your notebook and dividing it into four columns and as many rows as you need. Start tracking your feelings and see whether you can connect them to the events in your life and the interpretations you make of those events. Then subject those thoughts to scrutiny. Find out whether your mind scrambles the meanings of the various occurrences that pop up each day.

If you find it easy to spot these reality scramblers, you're one step ahead of the game. You'll probably soon start seeing doubt creep into the unquestioned truth of your depressed mind's reflexive interpretations of events. In other words, it's not a big leap to go from seeing that those interpretations might contain distortions to realizing that a less twisted view of happenings might be more valid, as well as make you feel better to boot. That's the purpose of looking for distortions in thoughts — doing so starts to shake the hold that your depressed mind has on your thinking. (We show you many other ways to actively untwist distortions in your thoughts in Chapter 6.)

Table 5-3 contains three more sample events and sample thoughts (or interpretations) and feelings about those events. It also has a space for you to think about possible reality scramblers embedded within those thoughts. See if you can figure out which scramblers apply. After you've filled in the reality scrambler column, check out the correct answers that follow.

Table 5-3	Practice Finding Reality Scramblers		
Feelings (0 to 100)	*Events*	*Thoughts (or Interpretations)*	*Reality Scramblers*
Anger (55)	You arrive home an hour late from work and your husband says, "Gosh honey, I was worried about you. What happened?"	He's actually being paranoid that I was out having an affair. He's always jumping on me about things.	
Sadness (70)		I think maybe he wants me to have an affair, so that he can get out of this marriage. After all, with my depression, I haven't been such a great wife lately.	
Anxiety (50)	You're a coauthor of *Depression For Dummies,* and your project editor e-mails you that he really likes the first submission and reminds you the next portion is due in two weeks. But you're running behind.	I'll never get this in on time. And when I don't get my part finished, my coauthor (and wife) will be really angry. And the editor is bound to lower the boom. We might even lose the contract. It won't matter that they liked the first part if the second portion comes in a few days late.	
Despair (65)	You ask someone out for a date. She tells you, "Sorry, I'm busy that night. Perhaps some other time?"	Obviously, she thinks I'm a zero; she's just being polite when she says "perhaps some other time." I'm never going to find someone to go out with. What's wrong with me?	

Here are the answers to this quiz:

> ✔ **Event 1, Arriving Late:** enlarging, overgeneralizing, mind reading, filtering

> ✔ **Event 2, Running Behind on Work Due:** enlarging, filtering, discarding positives, overgeneralizing, mind reading

> ✔ **Event 3, Turned Down for a Date:** enlarging, mind reading, filtering, overgeneralizing, black and white

Making misjudgments

The depressed mind more often than not acquires a nasty habit of making harsh, critical judgments about almost anything you do, thus deepening depression with each faultfinding episode. We can't remember the last time we worked with a seriously depressed client who didn't resort to harsh self-judgments. Thus, the fact that guilt is an important symptom of major depression is no coincidence. Even people who have little or no depression often judge themselves more negatively than they need to, but those with depression sometimes walk around as though they have a scarlet "G" for *guilty* tattooed on their foreheads.

The "making misjudgments" type of thought distortion comes in three forms:

> ✔ Shoulds

> ✔ Unfair comparisons

> ✔ Self-labels

Like the reality scramblers earlier in this chapter, all three of these distortions occur instantly, reflexively, and without careful consideration of reality. Keep reading for detailed info on each form and how they lead to bad feelings. When you see how often you resort to using "shoulds," "unfair comparisons," and "self-labels," you're likely to use them less often and feel better as a result.

Shoulding on yourself

Psychologist Dr. Albert Ellis deserves the credit for the phrase, "shoulding on yourself." We're amazed at the extent to which people use the word to pummel themselves for the slightest misdeed. You've probably heard people say the following:

> ✔ I *should* have known better.

> ✔ I *should* be more careful.

> ✔ I *shouldn't* even have thoughts like that!

> ✔ I *shouldn't* have eaten that cake!

If you think that people don't use this word a great deal, start listening to what people say. Tune in and notice whenever you hear the word *should*. Some folks use it so often you'd think someone had offered them a dollar for every time they used the word. The depressed mind not only uses the word *should* frequently, but it also takes it quite seriously.

But what's so bad about *should*? Nothing much, if you only mean it in the sense of conveying an expectation of what's to come, such as, "The package should arrive today." But when used to judge yourself or your behavior, the word can add a mound of unnecessary judgment and harshness to your self-evaluations.

Ah, but some folks think that using "shoulds" as a way to motivate themselves to do better is a good idea. The only problem with that approach is that motivation based on guilt doesn't work very well. For example, imagine two types of teachers — R.F. (for rewarding, yet firm) Chalky and G.I. (for guilt inducing) Fails. R.F. Chalky treats his kids kindly and with warmth, but responds with firm guidance when they steer off course. G.I. Fails judges her students harshly, tells them they shouldn't be so lazy when they aren't working hard enough, and humiliates them with dunce caps when they perform poorly.

Which teacher would you prefer? Which one would make you feel more motivated to do good work? Psychologists know, in general, that kind reinforcement, offset with firm limits as needed, works better than guilt induced by *should* statements. But which approach do you take for yourself? All too many people judge themselves with contemptuous, critical evaluations for even the slightest misdeed.

Start tracking your "shoulds" today. See if you can substitute terms such as "I'd rather," "I want to," "it would be better if," and "I'd like to." See the following examples for ideas:

> **Should statement:** I *should* have done a better job on that project.
>
> **Alternative statement:** I *would like to have done a* better job on that project.
>
> **Should statement:** I *shouldn't* have eaten that doughnut.
>
> **Alternative statement:** I *wish* I hadn't eaten that doughnut; I'll try to make up for it in other ways later.

Another approach to "shoulds" is to ask yourself where you've seen it written that you *should* do this or that. Is the rule you've made for yourself with your should statements chiseled in granite somewhere? If not, you may want to rewrite the rule. Finally, ask yourself if "shoulding on yourself" helps you or just makes you feel bad. Keep in mind, as we note earlier in this section, that guilt and shame do little to motivate positive behavior, especially when used to excess.

By the way, if you're an astute reader, you're bound to catch us using the word *should* from time to time in this book. Although we usually try to avoid "shoulds," the word is so engrained in everyone's psyche that we, too, slip once in a while. Of course we know we *shouldn't*, but we suppose we're human just like everyone else.

Calling up crass, critical comparisons

If you really want to make yourself depressed, or deepen your depression, comparing yourself in unfair ways to others will do the trick about as easily as anything we can think of. Many people make these comparisons with frightening frequency and without forethought. And their feelings of personal worth slowly disintegrate with each putdown of the self that occurs every time they contrast themselves negatively with someone else. Do any of these comparisons sound familiar to you?

- You have a friend who has far more successes than you do. Therefore, you conclude that you've failed.

- You're a student, and you receive an A- grade on an exam, but you denigrate your performance because a few others did even better.

- You don't get as many dates as a few of your friends, so you conclude that you're undesirable.

- You're a teenager who isn't as popular as some kids, so you assume that you're a total reject.

- You're a pretty successful writer of self-help books, but a friend of yours writes a *New York Times* best-selling book, so you conclude that your writing sucks.

- You're overweight, and you have friends who are as skinny as rails, so you conclude that you're a fat pig with no self-control.

- Your neighbor buys a new 60-inch plasma TV, which you can't afford, so you think of yourself as inadequate, as well as deprived.

This list contains some really great ways to pound yourself into the ground! But you may wonder how such comparisons distort reality. After all, in each case, one or more people stand higher on the totem pole than you do for a given success or self-quality. But the distortion doesn't lie in seeing others who do better than you do. That fact is true and alright as far as it goes. The problem comes about in the self-destructive conclusion that if you don't equal or surpass others, you amount to nothing. The issue is similar to all or-none, black-and-white thinking we discuss earlier in this chapter in the "Meeting the reality scramblers" section.

Further distortion occurs in the fact that these comparisons focus on a single factor that the other person has, which you don't have. The comparison zeroes in on one isolated issue and ignores the bigger picture. For example:

> ✔ The highly successful friend also happens to overwork himself to the point that he feels miserable.
>
> ✔ Your skinny friend happens to spend money like water and is saving nothing for retirement.
>
> ✔ The neighbor with the new, expensive television happens to have $45,000 in credit card debt.

If you focus on a single end result, you can always find someone you know who either has or could better you. For example, we have no doubt that neither of us has a sole quality, trait, success, or achievement that someone else couldn't best us on. Whether we concern ourselves with our intelligence, personality, writing, appearance, income, or accomplishments, certainly we'd have no trouble finding others in the world who rate higher. If we compared ourselves on each isolated quality, we could quickly dig ourselves into a black hole by summing up these comparisons as personal failures.

When you find yourself making comparisons to others, try to:

> ✔ Realize that focusing on single issues where others do better is a waste of time and only saps your feelings of worthwhileness. Instead, learn to appreciate both your strengths and weaknesses as a totality.
>
> ✔ Don't just compare yourself to the top. Look at the whole picture. How do you stack up against the middle, or even the bottom?
>
> ✔ Allow yourself to accept average, normal, and even less-than-average qualities into your self-perceptions. All humans have a few or more qualities that lie in that range, and we assume that you're human.

If you struggle with the preceding suggestions, we suggest that you read about the destructive influence of certain core beliefs in Chapter 7. The *perfectionist belief,* which we discuss in that chapter, may lie behind your difficulty.

Tagging yourself with loathsome labels

The final distorted method for making misjudgments involves finding a particularly obnoxious label to apply to yourself, such as *disgusting, pathetic, idiot, pig, bungler, clod, misfit, freak, oaf, nerd,* and so on. And don't make the mistake of thinking these labels have no consequence. The old adage your mother may have told you, "Sticks and stones may break my bones, but words can never hurt me," sounds great. But it isn't true. People use words to hurt themselves all the time.

What do you say to yourself when you stumble, trip, or drop something? Do you call yourself a total klutz or a clumsy oaf? Labels like *klutz* and *clumsy oaf* erode your sense of self-worth. And low self-worth is a symptom of depression (see Chapter 2 for more information about symptoms of depression). In the following example, Aaron uses lots of negative self-labels and feels rather rotten as a result.

Aaron works as a DJ at a popular radio station. People know him all over town because, as the station's marquee DJ, billboards exhibit his face everywhere. But Aaron doesn't feel particularly notable, special, or accomplished. He's a lifelong perfectionist who berates himself for every mistake. A single mispronunciation, and he calls himself a jerk. If he inadvertently says something that a few listeners take offense to, he thinks he's an idiot.

Labels like *freak, monster, a nobody,* and *fool* regularly ramble through his mind. His self-worth erodes to the point that he believes his audience is only temporarily fooled; someday soon, they'll all turn away from him. Thus, he turns down a high-paying job in a larger city because he knows that the more sophisticated listeners in that city will see right through him and understand what an imposter he really is.

If you're a bit like Aaron, start tracking your self-labels. See how often you apply them to yourself in response to mistakes, failures, and quirks. We call this tool the "Label Replacement Strategy." Grab a notebook. Write down the event in one column and the label you attach to yourself in the next column. Then in the third column try reworking your labels with alternative phrases. By doing so, you can start to view yourself more realistically and stop the pain brought on by negative self-labels. See Table 5-4 for examples of replacing your labels.

Table 5-4	Label Replacement Strategy	
Event	*Label*	*Label Replacement Thought*
You gained a few pounds.	I'm a *pig!*	Okay, I gained a few pounds. I'll try to work on that.
You wrecked the car.	I'm a *pathetic loser.*	Well, I didn't like wrecking the car, and it was my fault. Guess I'll have to try and be more careful. Statistics say this happens to most people at one time or another in their lives.
You didn't get the hoped for promotion.	I'm a complete *failure.*	Although I didn't get the promotion, I've had plenty of successes. I have to learn to take the good with the bad.
You get turned down for a date.	I'm a *nerdy, freak.*	One person turned me down. How does this make me a freak? If I'm going to succeed at dating, turndowns will happen.

Self-labels may run through your mind so often that you can't possibly catch them all. If so, don't worry. Just write down the ones that particularly grab your attention and see if you can replace them with other kinds of thoughts. If you find this exercise difficult, you may want to read Chapter 6 and return to it afterward.

Assigning blame to the wrong source

Another type of thought distortion involves blaming the wrong source(s) for your problems. This distortion can take one of two forms:

- ✔ Most often, people with depression *personalize* problems and blame themselves entirely for their current plight.
- ✔ Alternatively, some people place blame for all their problems on others, thereby disowning any responsibility for making changes in their lives.

Neither of the these strategies is productive. As an alternative, try combing through all the possible causes of your particular problem at hand and allocating responsibility in a reasonable, fair manner. Generally speaking, you can only work on the portion of your problem that you own — the part that you actually are responsible for.

A number of years ago, **Rachael** complained to her psychologist that her son was having major problems with his behavior at school. Rachael's conclusion? She was a *bad mother,* period. In addition to using a global self-label, Rachael was personalizing the entire problem as totally resulting from her poor parenting.

So, her psychologist asked Rachael to list all the possible causes for her son's misbehavior. With some thought, she realized that Logan's father had a lot to do with how he's behaving, that the school was failing to set limits for him, and that he was hanging around with a rough bunch of kids at school.

Then her psychologist asked her to consider what overall proportion of the problem she may have caused and due to what specific things she'd done in raising Logan. Finally, he asked her to think about what she could do with her part of the issue. We call this the "Responsibility Reallocation and Action Strategy."

With the "Responsibility Reallocation and Action Strategy," you avoid immersing yourself in guilt and self-blame. Rather, the approach allows you to take responsibility for an appropriate portion of the problem and do what you can with it. If it involves something that's over and done with, no action is possible. But you can try to let go of the guilt because feeling guilty will lead nowhere and holds no advantages for you.

This strategy asks you to turn to a new sheet of paper in your notebook and draw columns for listing all the causes of your problem, the percentage of the problem that's truly your responsibility, your role in the cause of your problem, and any specific actions you can take to alleviate your problem. When you complete this chart, you're likely to understand that you're not totally responsible for your problem and hopefully forgive yourself more easily. And you'll develop ideas for what you can do about your problem.

Table 5-5 shows what Rachael came up with when she did this task.

Table 5-5	Rachael's Responsibility Reallocation and Action Strategy		
Problem: Logan's Behavior			
Causes	*Percentage I Own*	*My Specific Role*	*Specific Actions I Can Take*
Peers, school, father, myself (mother), biology and genetics, neighborhood, television, culture at large, the self-esteem/feel good movement, random events, Logan himself (he is 15 years old after all)	Realistically, I think I own about 20% of Logan's problem. His father is way too critical, which I think contributes quite a lot in addition to every-thing else. But I have to own that much.	I overcompensated for his father's parenting by being way too lenient. As a result, I let Logan get away with too much.	1. I can go to family therapy and work out our parenting differences. 2. I can read, *Why Can't I Be the Parent I Want to Be?* by Drs. Laura Smith and Charles Elliott 3. I can start setting firmer limits with Logan.

Using emotions, the misleading cues

Most people with depression have countless negative thoughts about events. Then the mind uses emotions as cues or evidence for supporting the truth of those thoughts. The reasoning goes something like this:

✔ I've done something wrong: I *feel* guilty, so I must have done something wrong.

✔ Something is wrong with me: I *feel* ashamed, so there must be something defective about me.

✔ I'm hopeless: Because I *feel* so horribly hopeless, I must truly be hopeless.

✔ I can't clean the garage because I don't *feel* like cleaning the garage.

✔ I can't work on my depression because I don't *feel* like working on my depression.

The problem is that feelings all too often occur in response to distorted views of events. So the very feeling that you're using as a way of proving your thought probably came about in connection with a negative or distorted thought in the first place.

Feelings are *not* facts.

Frankly, if all those suffering from depression constantly catered to the directives of their feelings, few would ever improve with therapy. If you're depressed, you most likely don't feel like devoting energy toward doing anything about your condition because you have little energy to start with. And if you listen uncritically to feelings of hopelessness (see Chapter 3), you'll likely similarly conclude that you have no reason to improve your lot.

Don't get us wrong; feelings and emotions are important. Positive feelings give you information about what you like and don't like. Negative emotions alert you to danger and assist you in knowing that something isn't right in your life. Feelings make us human. We value and respect feelings. Much of the intent of this book is to help you find ways of feeling better.

However, we suggest that you resist using feelings as though they're facts. Dr. David Burns, a psychiatrist, calls the temptation to view feelings as facts, "emotional reasoning." He also notes that a common example of such flawed reasoning is to determine your personal worth based on feelings. Thus, if you *feel* awful, you conclude that you must *be* awful. But what if you feel really wonderful? Does that actually mean that you *are* wonderful, or merely that you're feeling pretty darn good?

Start tracking your use of emotional reasoning. Tune in when your mind tells you to avoid an undertaking merely because you don't *feel* like it. Ask yourself if you've felt that way in the past but successfully plowed through the feeling anyway. Did you end up feeling better when you pushed on, or when you gave in to the feeling?

Also, take a look at Chapter 6 for considerable information on how to talk back to distorted thoughts and the feelings they cause. As you see how many ways these distortions lead to unpleasant feelings, you're likely to understand that feelings surely don't equate with facts.

Don't conclude that we're saying negative feelings are wrong, and positive feelings are correct. If that idea were so, people should consume fattening foods, certain drugs, and alcohol in copious quantities simply because they feel good! We simply mean that feelings can obscure your vision of reality and yourself if you let them.

Chapter 6

Breaking Up the Dark Clouds of Depressive Thinking

- -

In This Chapter

▶ Tracking events, thoughts, and feelings

▶ Taking thoughts to court

▶ Weighing the evidence

▶ Designing evidence-based thoughts

▶ Rummaging through a thought repair toolkit

- -

*A*fter six months of delightful retirement, **George's** golf handicap has decreased by three strokes. He swings his nine iron and grins as the ball flies down the fairway. He resists renting a cart; walking the course is part of his exercise routine. Today, he notices an uncomfortable tightness in his chest; he feels nauseous and begins to sweat. He's suddenly dizzy, and pain radiates from his chest down his right arm. He collapses on the grass.

Five weeks later, after successful bypass surgery, George sits at home depressed and hopeless. He believes that life will never be the same. He can't imagine ever being able to play golf again. His retirement will surely be one of illness, misery, and dreary boredom.

His doctor prescribes rehabilitation at the hospital's gym and predicts that George will be out playing golf in a few months. George cancels his rehabilitation appointments. He can't muster the energy to get dressed in the morning, let alone go to a gym. His dreams destroyed, George contemplates suicide.

George experienced a triggering event (his heart attack) that set off a slew of gloomy thoughts about his future health and retirement. Those thoughts led him directly into a depression. However, the good news is that his thoughts can be changed in ways that will make him feel better. He merely has to practice a series of skills we discuss in this chapter.

You need skills to defeat your depression. You can start with the "Thought Tracker" we describe in Chapter 5. In this chapter, we build upon the Thought Tracker by telling you how to subject your thoughts and perceptions to scrutiny using objective evidence. You can then use this evidence to construct new "evidence-based" thoughts. Furthermore, we give you a large toolkit for repairing distorted thoughts, which will lead the way to feeling better.

Thought Court Is Now in Session

As we mention in the chapter introduction, the investigation of depressive thinking begins in Chapter 5 where we show you how to track down thoughts, emotions, and events that relate to depression with a Thought Tracker. A Thought Tracker lets you record the events that trigger your emotions and explore the interpretations, or *thoughts,* you have about those events. This tool helps you see various examples of how feelings naturally result from your thoughts. In that chapter, thoughts also stand accused of seriously distorting reality.

Now, we take the basic Thought Tracker a significant step further and demonstrate how to take your depressive thoughts to what we call "Thought Court." The goal of Thought Court is to put your thoughts on trial and, if you find them guilty, to develop accurate, believable replacement thoughts (not overly positive spins on the events). Although Thought Court is a mildly playful term we use to describe the rethinking process, keep in mind that the strategy is both serious and powerful.

Thought Court forms the core work of cognitive therapy. Therefore, we suggest that you keep using these strategies frequently, regularly, and persistently. The good news is that you don't have to spend huge amounts of time. Generally speaking, devoting 10 to 20 minutes, 4 or 5 times per week, will provide a noticeable boost to your moods within 8 to 12 weeks. And after your moods start to lift, we suggest that you continue the work for at least another 8 weeks or so to be sure that your new ways of thinking have plenty of practice.

Here's a brief summary of the Thought Court process for you to review. We give you the complete rundown in the sections that follow.

1. **Thought Tracker:** This part of Thought Court consists of recording all your thoughts, interpretations, or perceptions of the event that triggered your ultimate cascade of difficult feelings. You also rate the severity of the resulting feelings. (See Chapter 5 for more details about filling out Thought Trackers.)

2. **Take the thought to court:** This step involves gathering evidence that both prosecutes and defends the truthfulness of your thought. We ask you to carefully examine your thoughts and weigh the evidence to determine whether you should hold onto your thoughts or judge them guilty of making you unnecessarily depressed and toss them in jail.

3. **Find replacements for jailed thoughts:** This step occurs if you find your thought guilty. You develop a reflective replacement thought that seems believable, not unrealistically positive. These thoughts often include a small portion of the original negative thought, but they incorporate credible positive information as well.

You need to develop replacement thoughts because having no perspective on or interpretation of the events in your life is impossible.

4. **Rate the results:** Take your reflective replacement thoughts for a test drive. It's important to know if your replacement thoughts feel better than your old, depressive thoughts. Therefore, this step asks you to rate how you feel with the new thought versus the old one.

Persistence is key to successfully prosecuting negative, depressive thoughts. Practice regularly and keep at it until your feelings of depression have quelled for quite a while. Realize that improvements take time. But if things get worse instead of better, consider seeking professional help.

Don't make the mistake of trying to use these techniques simply "in your head." Work in the head makes a great supplement to the work you do on paper, but it *can't* stand alone. Writing all the elements down in a notebook helps you utilize the objective part of your mind, which you need for this task. Furthermore, writing facilitates memory.

Review doesn't hurt either, and we recommend going over your thought records from time to time for additional help. In one sense, any good principle of education is a good principle for thought therapy, including summaries and a little repetition.

With the Thought Court process, we're not suggesting that negative thoughts and feelings have no validity whatsoever and that you should banish such thoughts and feelings from your life. Before we go any further in our discussion, we want to clear up these possible misconceptions. Consider the following points:

> ✔ **Negative thoughts often (though not always) have a grain of truth.** We want you to appreciate any such truth. Denial isn't a useful undertaking. When things are truly bad and difficult, you're better off finding ways to cope than rationalizing and fooling yourself.

✔ **Sadness isn't the same as depression.** Losses and adversities of various types will make you unhappy, and we wouldn't dream of suggesting that you shouldn't feel sad when such occurrences come to pass. The death of a loved one, loss of a job, severe illness, financial reversals, and physical disabilities all present serious challenges, emotional upheaval, and profound sadness or despair.

Typically, reactions to losses don't cause a deterioration in your basic sense of self-worth, and they do ease over time — sometimes, it takes a very long time, but the feelings do get better eventually. See Chapter 2 for more information about the difference between grief and depression.

Tracking the thought and making the arrest

You must find the accused party before going to trial. Recall a time when you felt strong negative feelings such as sadness, despair, guilt, or shame. What's to blame for those feelings? A Thought Tracker can tell you by uncovering the links between events, thoughts, and feelings. A Thought Tracker will show you that most of the time, your unpleasant emotions come from the thoughts or interpretations you make in response to events that have happened to you.

To understand the relationship between thoughts, feelings, and events, you need to record your thoughts along with the events that came before them and the feelings that followed. Rating the intensity of those feelings in order to know just how much trouble your thoughts are stirring up is also a good idea. See Chapter 5 for more information about Thought Trackers and the connections between events, feelings, and thoughts.

Here's a brief reminder. First, turn to a page in your notebook and divide it into three columns. Then, record the following information for each column:

✔ **Feelings:** Write down any and all feelings you notice. (If you have trouble coming up with the right words, see Chapter 5 for ideas.) Then *rate* the feeling on a scale from 0 (absence of feeling) to 100 (the highest intensity imaginable).

✔ **Event:** Include as many specifics as possible, such as *when* the event occurred, *where* it happened, *who* was there, and *what* exactly transpired.

✔ **Thoughts (or interpretations):** Thoughts include the meaning the event holds for you, your concerns about the event, its implications for your future, what it means about you, and anything passing through your mind at the time. If you write down several thoughts, we recommend that you then underline the thought that causes you the greatest amount of distress.

Ramon's story illustrates how to track down the thought suspects and prepare a case. We follow Ramon throughout this chapter to show you how the entire process works.

Ramon reluctantly reaches out for help after feeling seriously depressed for a month. He isn't sure how his depression started, but he feels its impact on his sleep, energy, interests, and concentration. He's starting to show up late for his college classes and decides to drop two of them in order to keep his head above water. At the strong urging of one of his friends, Ramon calls the student mental health center.

The counselor at the center recommends *thought therapy,* also referred to as *cognitive therapy,* because it has the longest and best established track record for treating depression. Furthermore, the approach helps prevent relapse. The counselor asks Ramon to start noticing the times when he feels especially sad, depressed, and/or upset. Then he tells him to record these feelings on a Thought Tracker that he gives to Ramon. After Ramon fills the form out completely, the therapist suggests that Ramon underline the most troubling, inflammatory thought — the one that stirs up the most difficult emotions. Table 6-1 shows one of Ramon's records.

Table 6-1	Ramon's Thought Tracker	
Feelings (0 to 100)	*Events*	*Thoughts (or Interpretations)*
Shame (90)		
Guilt (80)		
Despair (85)	I failed the English midterm last week. I scored in the 38th percentile for the class as a whole. Two classmates next to me saw my grade when the instructor plopped it down on my desk in full view of the entire world.	I should never have taken this class in the first place. <u>This F means that I'm stupid and that I'll never graduate from college.</u> I really studied for that exam, and the best I can do is an F. Now I look like a fool to everyone in the class.

Ramon diligently records the specifics of his unpleasant event and carefully rates his feelings. He contemplates what thoughts instantly passed through his mind after receiving his exam. At first, all he comes up with for thoughts are that he shouldn't have taken the class to begin with. However, when he considers the implications for his future and what he thinks the grade means about him, he finds more information to write down under his thoughts column. Finally, he reviews his various thoughts and concludes that one of them troubles him the most by inflaming his feelings of shame, guilt, and despair. That inflaming thought is that an F on an exam means that he's stupid and will never graduate.

Taking the thought to court

After you identify a particularly troubling thought, take that thought to court. In this court you play the role of defense attorney for the thought as well as the prosecutor. Your job is to prepare a case for both sides. The depressed mind usually has no difficulty coming up with evidence for the defense of the negative thought (that is, evidence in support of the thought). You're likely to have more trouble coming up with evidence for the prosecution (evidence that refutes the negative thought).

We have a list of evidence-gathering questions to help you prepare the case for prosecuting the troubling thought:

✔ Do I have any experiences or evidence from my life that would contradict my thoughts in any way?

✔ Have I had thoughts like these in the past that didn't pan out as true?

✔ Is this event as awful as I'm letting myself believe that it is?

✔ Is this negative thought illogical or distorted in any way? (See Chapter 5 for a list of common thought distortions.)

✔ Am I ignoring any evidence that would dispute this thought?

✔ Is my thought based on facts or reflexive, critical judgments?

Using a "Thoughts on Trial" form (see Table 6-2 for a sample), record the evidence both for and against your problematic thought on a page in your notebook. Divide the page into two columns: "Defense" (evidence in support of your thought) and "Prosecution" (evidence against your thought).

Now we return to Ramon to demonstrate how this process plays out. Ramon's counselor suggests that he take his inflammatory thought (that an F on a test means he's stupid) to court. To do so, he asks Ramon to play two roles — first, as the defense attorney and then as the prosecutor.

Next, the counselor gives Ramon a Thoughts on Trial form to fill out as carefully as he can. Table 6-2 shows what Ramon turns into his counselor after pondering both sides of the case.

Table 6-2	Ramon's Thoughts on Trial Form
Accused Thought: This F means that I'm stupid and that I'll never graduate from college.	
Defense: Evidence in Support of Thought	**Prosecution: Evidence Refuting Thought**
An F is clearly considered a failing grade in college.	Well, I suppose one F doesn't have to mean that I'll fail.
If I accumulate too many F's, I will no doubt fail.	I'm sure that a few smart people have failed an exam or two.
Generally speaking, only stupid people fail.	
This class was only freshman English. If I fail early classes, I'm sure to fail later ones.	
My mother said that I obviously either didn't try or wasn't cut out for college, so that means I'm stupid.	

As you can see, the defense attorney side of Ramon's thought has the upper hand with his initial efforts. He's obviously struggling to develop a plausible case for the prosecution in order to overthrow the negative thought. Here's a dialogue between Ramon and his counselor that shows how a few of the right questions can help.

> **Therapist:** So Ramon, you failed this English midterm and concluded that you're stupid and will never graduate, is that right?
>
> **Ramon:** Well, yes. What other, how do you say it, ah, conclusion could there be?
>
> **Therapist:** Think hard on this question. Can you think of any evidence that would suggest you're actually pretty smart? Anything at all.
>
> **Ramon:** I suppose so. I did get all A's in my high school. But it must have been a really bad school.
>
> **Therapist:** Okay, I'll get back to the quality of your high school in a moment. But do you have any other evidence that says you might be smart?

Ramon: I guess I did get an A in calculus, an A- in Latin American history, and an A in biology. But I know those subjects really well. They not count for much.

Therapist: So explain that to me. If you know a subject really well, it doesn't count? Is it possible that you're using the thought distortion known as *discarding positives?* How do you know a subject really well unless you've studied and mastered it? And can you really do that if you're stupid?

Ramon: Okay, you have a point there. Maybe I am discounting important information. But I still failed English.

Therapist: Oh yes, you did. And that reminds me, where did you go to high school?

Ramon: In Buenos Aires, why?

Therapist: How long have you spoken English?

Ramon: I took my first class two years ago, why?

Therapist: Is it possible that English would be a little more difficult for you than for most students, since you've only started learning the language in the past two years?

Ramon: I suppose, but I've always excelled at everything I do.

Therapist: And when you excel, does that mean you're doing so because you're just lucky or because you're smart?

Ramon: I suppose, sometimes, I'm smart.

Therapist: By the way, didn't you tell me that more than 40 percent of the class failed the exam? And didn't most of the students speak English as their primary language? If that's the case, is it possible that you're being a little harsh with yourself, to say the least?

Ramon: Okay, I get your point. Maybe I am, as you say it, ignoring positive information and focusing on negatives. Perhaps a little more work in English, possibly even a tutor, would help.

Armed with this nudge from his therapist, Ramon develops a list of additional evidence for the prosecution side of the case against his negative thought that an F means he's stupid and will never graduate from college. His list of evidence for prosecuting his negative thought now includes the following:

- ✔ I did get very good grades in three other classes that most of the students found difficult.

- ✔ I have usually succeeded in most of what I do.

- ✔ Because I usually succeed, I probably fall apart when I don't.

- ✔ How can I expect to excel in English when I just started learning it two years ago? I just need some extra work and help with the subject.

✔ My mother criticizes me all the time; just because she thinks I'm not cut out for college doesn't mean anything. Besides, I think she may just be trying to get me to return home. I will eventually, but not now.

✔ I suspect very smart people fail sometimes when they take classes that they know very little about and find challenging. I need to look at the big picture.

At first, most people find it difficult to come up with good evidence for refuting their thoughts. If that happens to you, try these tactics:

✔ **Take your time.** You can go back to the form over a period of several days if you need to. The goal isn't to feel better immediately, but to discover the skill of subjecting your thoughts to careful, objective analysis. Figuring out skills takes time.

✔ **Carefully review the evidence-gathering questions we list earlier in this section before the Thoughts on Trial form.** Ponder each question and push yourself to find evidence that can contradict your negative thought.

✔ **Consider seeking help from a professional to get you started.** Professional assistance can help you discover that the vast majority of your negative moods are fueled by thoughts that rest on a foundation of sand.

After Ramon completely fills in his Thoughts on Trial form, with his new evidence, he's ready to make a verdict. He declares his thought, "This F means that I'm stupid and that I'll never graduate from college," guilty of fraud and deception. He now sees that the thought causes him enormous shame and pain, but with little basis for doing so.

Finding replacements for jailed thoughts

After you judge the thoughts leading to your depressed feelings guilty, you need to develop an alternative perception, a *reflective replacement thought*. These thoughts are *reflective* because they require effortful consideration. And the reflective replacement won't help if it, too, is based on falsehood.

Pollyanna perspectives, overly positive spins, and simplistic dismissals of negative thoughts look very different from reasonable, reflective replacement thoughts. A *Pollyanna perspective* is a view that's overly optimistic without basis. An *overly positive spin* is a clumsy attempt to make a bad event or situation seem like a good thing (politicians are pretty good at positive spins). And *simplistic dismissals* are ineffective attempts to minimize the meaning of unpleasant events.

Returning to Ramon, and his discarded negative thoughts about his F grade, check out these examples of three ineffective types of replacement thoughts, followed by the later reflective approach:

- **Pollyanna perspective:** So I got an F on this test; I'm sure I'll get an A next time.

- **Overly positive spin:** One F on my transcript will show job recruiters that I'm human; it's really a good thing.

- **Simplistic dismissal:** So what? An F is meaningless. I know I'm smart.

- **Reflective replacement thought:** An F doesn't mean that I'm stupid; I have too much evidence to suggest otherwise. It does mean that I should take a serious look at this class and see if I need remedial work, a tutor, or whatever, in order to master this subject. I'm intelligent enough to get through this if I get the needed help.

After you've taken your thoughts to court and gone through the painstaking work of finding them guilty, don't replace them with equally bogus alternatives. Rather, craft a new perspective based on reason, logic, and solid evidence. In other words, develop a perspective that's a reflective interpretation of what's occurred in your life.

Such reflective interpretations include any partial truth contained in your negative thoughts. For example, Ramon realized that an F did mean something important, just not stupidity. And these interpretations are best if they include realistic positive information. In Ramon's case, that means recognition of his intelligence.

Rating the results of your replacement thoughts

If you find your thoughts guilty of fraudulent negativity and replace them with new evidence based on reflective replacement thoughts, you've made a great start. But the exercise is only useful if it does you some good!

We suggest that after you take your thoughts to court and replace them with alternative thoughts, you rate the outcome. How? Simple. List the feelings you originally rated as stemming from your negative thoughts. Then re-rate those feelings to see if they change.

Ramon wrote down each of his feelings and found that

- **Shame** went from **90** to **55**.

- **Guilt** went from **80** to **40**.

- **Despair** went from **85** to **65**.

These ratings indicate that Ramon's work on replacing his thought shifted his feelings significantly. However, the difficult feelings didn't go away entirely. And the fact is you can expect that some residual unpleasant feelings typically will remain. You'll have to practice this exercise a lot before you find them diminishing to the point that they feel almost inconsequential.

But what if the feelings remain the same or, even worse, increase? This outcome occurs occasionally, so try not to panic. Consider the following possibilities instead:

- ✔ **You've identified the wrong event.** To check out this possibility, ask yourself what else had been going on around the time you experienced the troubling feeling. Possibly, the event was actually a daydream, image, or thought that had just floated through your mind, and you failed to notice it. If you're able to capture another triggering event that seems more likely to have started the downhill slide, start over and run through the Thought Court process again.

- ✔ **You've arrested the wrong thoughts.** It could be that you've put a thought on trial that isn't as upsetting to you as some other thought about the event. For example, if you feel ashamed and inadequate after dropping a pass while playing touch football with your friends, perhaps you thought it was because you were a bit clumsy. So you take that thought about clumsiness to Thought Court and don't feel better after disputing it and developing a replacement thought.

   But maybe the event involves additional, more troubling thoughts. In addition to thinking that you were clumsy, perhaps you were bothered by seeing how upset your teammates were and thinking that you horribly disappointed them by letting them down. If so, you need to take the more troubling thought through the Thought Court process. If you don't benefit from Thought Court, be sure to ask yourself if you may have additional, more troubling thoughts to arrest and put on trial.

- ✔ **You may have additional thoughts that you need to deal with.** We told you to take your very most disturbing thought to Thought Court. However, you may want to take remaining thoughts through the same process. Do so with any such thoughts if they seem to arouse a lot of unpleasant emotion.

- ✔ **You came up with an unbelievable reflective replacement thought.** Ask yourself if your replacement thought is too much like the *Pollyanna perspective*, the *overly positive spin*, or the *simplistic dismissal* we discuss in the "Finding replacements for jailed thoughts" section earlier in this chapter. Develop a reflective replacement thought that seems truly believable.

- ✔ **You have a sense that you don't actually want to change your feeling about the situation.** If this concern seems correct to you, you may want to read Chapter 3, which deals with breaking barriers to change. You may very well find certain beliefs blocking your way toward feeling better. If so, you'll most likely find it helpful to work on those beliefs first.

If you work on the entire Thought Court process, as well as the potential change-blocking beliefs in Chapter 3, and you still struggle with feeling better after a number of weeks, please seek professional help. You should seek help sooner if you feel hopeless and helpless and don't pull out of those feelings fairly quickly. This book can still provide a useful accompaniment to therapy, but you shouldn't try to use it alone in such cases.

Trying another example

We introduce this chapter with a story about **George** and his bypass surgery, and we didn't want to end his story on such a down note. Plus, recalling George's progress provides another example for you on how to complete the Thought Court process.

George's cardiologist recently attended a continuing education conference that featured discussions about how often depression follows heart attacks and even increases the likelihood of additional heart problems. After additional research on cognitive therapy, the cardiologist suggested to George that he see a counselor. George agrees, and after his first session with his counselor, George decides to take his thoughts to court. Here's how George makes the most out of his Thought Court process.

First, George fills out a Thought Tracker form, as seen in Table 6-3.

Table 6-3	George's Thought Tracker	
Feelings (0 to 100)	*Events*	*Thoughts (or Interpretations)*
Despair (85)	Heart attack, bypass surgery, hospitalization, and the prospect of lengthy rehabilitation.	I'm old. I'll never recover from this heart attack. Rehabilitation sounds grueling. I can barely get out of bed. And I could never be happy without being able to play golf again.
Hopelessness (85)		

George's thoughts that arouse the most despair and hopeless include the idea that he'll never recover and that he could never be happy without playing golf again. He analyzes these thoughts with a Thoughts on Trial form, as seen in Table 6-4. To do so, he ponders the evidence-gathering questions (see the section "Taking the thought to court" earlier in this chapter for the list of questions).

Table 6-4	George's Thoughts on Trial Form
Accused Thought: I'm old. I'll never recover from this heart attack. And I could never be happy without being able to play golf again.	
Defense: Evidence in Support of Thought	**Prosecution: Evidence Refuting Thought**
I've seen good friends whither and die after a heart attack.	I guess I've also seen people get a lot better after bypass surgery and live a number of good, active years.
Rehabilitation does take months, and that assumes it would work.	I have thought things looked bleak in the past, and things got better. I thought I'd never recover from the loss of my wife. It was very hard and I still miss her, but I managed to feel happy again.
I don't have the energy for rehabilitation; maybe I'll go when I feel better.	I suppose maybe I'm ignoring my doctor's prognosis; he said I should recover.
If I don't get better, I'll never play golf again.	I think maybe I'm trying to make conclusions because of how I *feel* rather than the facts.
	They say that energy only comes after you start moving and that the body deteriorates when you lay around. Maybe that's true.
	Although it's true that I'll never play golf again if I don't get better, I'll never get better if I don't get moving.
	Even if I don't play golf again, I do know some friends who seem pretty content, even though they have physical limitations.

Based on George's Thoughts on Trial form, he formulates a reflective replacement thought: "The odds are pretty good that, with work, I can recover from this bypass surgery. It won't be easy, but it's better than the alternative. And if I don't recover to the extent that I hope, I can still find some interesting things to do."

Finally, George rates the results from his new reflective replacement thoughts by re-rating his feelings:

> ✔ Despair was at **85**; now it's at **30**.
>
> ✔ Hopelessness was at **85,** now it's at **10**.

George continues working with the Thought Court process for several months. He ultimately recovers from his surgery and plays golf again. His handicap never gets as low as it once was, but he feels good about the outcome.

Opening a Thought-Repair Toolkit

Going to court and weighing the evidence that supports and refutes your problematic thinking isn't the only method for dealing with problematic thoughts. We've designed a toolkit for detecting and ironing out any distortions and twists in these thoughts. You may want to review each one of these tools and try them out on your own thoughts.

Refer to Table 6-1, the Thought Tracker shown earlier in this chapter, and fill it out for yourself in your notebook. Underline the thought that arouses the most difficult emotions. Then run the thought through one or more of our thought repair tools in the following sections. As with Thought Court earlier in this chapter, the goal is to develop accurate, believable replacement thoughts rather than overly positive spins on events.

Giving your problem to a friend

What? Are we suggesting that you find a way to dump your problems over onto a friend? Not exactly. This thought-repair tool involves imagining that a good friend of yours ran into the identical event that you did and experienced the same exact thoughts and feelings. Giving your problem to a friend allows you to view the thoughts from a different, more objective perspective.

Thus, you literally imagine that friend sitting in a chair next to you, telling you about those negative thoughts. What would you say? Keep in mind that we're not asking you to simply make your friend feel better by lying or distorting the facts. Rather, we think that you should tell your imagined friend what you actually think makes sense. Paige's story illustrates how you can put this tool to good use.

Paige's childhood consisted of a barrage of criticism from her father; that is, when he noticed her at all. Now, as an adult, she serves as an assistant director of a large social service agency. Unfortunately, she has little confidence and finds fault with anything she does. In addition, she magnifies her mistakes and sees them as larger than life. However, her boss, impressed with her report on project development, insists that she make a presentation to the executive board of the agency.

Filled with fear, Paige complies with the request. She does a credible job, and several board members make positive comments. However, she forgets to pass out handouts until her talk is over, and one of the members suggests that her presentation would have made more sense with the handouts in advance. Paige feels horrible, so she fills out a Thought Tracker (see Table 6-1) and realizes that her feelings of shame and self-loathing relate to her unquestioned thoughts, which have concluded that her performance was an utter failure, and her job might be in jeopardy.

Although skeptical, Paige agrees to try the tool of giving her problem to a friend. She imagines her friend Kayla sitting in an empty chair next to her. Kayla relays the information about the speech and declares that she failed abysmally and might even lose her job. After all, the person with the critical remark was her agency's chairperson of the board of directors!

Oddly, when Paige hears those thoughts from the imagined Kayla sitting in the chair, she finds different, more reflective thoughts flowing through her mind. She tells Kayla, "What? Didn't you hear the boss say that he was so impressed with your report that he wanted you to make the presentation in the first place? And why are you discounting the positive comments made by several of the influential board members? Of course, it's true that remembering the handouts in advance would've been nice. Most likely, your anxiety got in the way. But other than that, you did a great job!"

You're probably thinking that this strategy is too easy to believe. How can something this simple possibly work? The tool helps because it allows you to back away from your problem a bit and ponder the issue from another perspective. After you've done that, you may find it easier to be a little more objective. In any event, many people benefit from this strategy.

Putting time on your side

It's amazing how much anguish people can generate over the things that happen in day-to-day living. When disagreeable events stick themselves in your face, gaining perspective is difficult.

Putting time on your side is a strategy that asks you to view your problem at a distant, future point in time. You consider how important your problem and your thoughts about your problem will seem weeks, months, or even years in the future. It's amazing how many of the things people find upsetting look insignificant in the future. Jacob's story shows how he makes use of this tool.

Jacob has a rather serious problem with anger. He's abrasive, curt, and hostile — more so than he even realizes. He has few friends, and his blood pressure has soared in the past year. He's depressed, and his psychologist tells him that anger contributes to his lack of friends and depression. His psychologist suggests that Jacob start using a strategy she calls putting time on your side.

She says, "It's pretty simple, actually. Jacob, what I'd like you to do is notice what's going on whenever you feel angry. Then take a moment to step back and ask yourself a question. How upsetting will this situation feel and how important will it be a year from now? Rate that importance on a scale from 0 to 100, where 0 represents no consequence at all and 100 is equivalent to terrorists capturing you and telling you that they plan to slowly torture you to death over the next two weeks, and the torture has just begun."

It takes Jacob awhile to start catching his angry moments and stepping back enough to answer the question. However, as he does so, he discovers that very few of the anger-arousing moments in his life manage to rise above a level of 10 on that 100 point scale a year later. Slowly but surely, he finds his anger going down.

Putting time on your side works especially well with anger-arousing events. However, it can also put a better perspective on other happenings that arouse different feelings, such as sadness or upset. See how it works for you.

Putting thoughts to the test

Many of the thoughts that disturb you can be put to the test. In other words, you can run various experiments to see if they really hold water. We have three such experiments for you to perform.

Playing out negative predictions

The depressed mind makes lots of predictions about the future. And these predictions typically look ominous and foreboding. In part, those predictions look bleak due to various distortions discussed in Chapter 5, such as filtering out positive information and magnifying negatives. Thus, positive possibilities are excluded, and negative outcomes aren't only assumed but are also enlarged.

If you're depressed and listen to your mind's forecasts, you'll probably avoid activities and events that hold the remotest chance of unpleasant outcomes. Try to push yourself to experiment with these predictions, though. In other words:

- Go to that party and see if you actually have a bad time like you're assuming.
- Make yourself volunteer to give that speech and see if you survive.
- Call your friend and see if she actually wants to have lunch with you even though you think she won't.

If you plan to use this strategy, your best bet is to test out at least ten of your negative thoughts and predictions. Some of them may very well prove true. But most of the time, nearly all of them prove false. Even when they do turn out to be true, the actual experience usually doesn't feel as awful as the prediction says it will. See Chapter 11 for more information about challenging negative predictions.

Performing a survey

You can also test out thinking by actively collecting data and information. In other words, you can carry out a survey of family, friends, or colleagues. For example, perhaps you believe that most people see money and status as the measure of a person's worth, and you just had to take a job at lower pay. You could ask a group of friends (or strangers for that matter) what they think makes someone important and worthwhile in their eyes. Is it earning power, prestige, or other qualities, such as honesty, friendliness, and so on? You may be surprised at what they tell you.

Or if you have a concern specific to a particular individual, you can approach that person and check it out. Tyler uses this tool to overcome a pervasive worry that his wife is losing interest in him.

Tyler notices that his wife has shown less interest in sex lately. He assumes that she no longer finds him desirable. So he withdraws from her out of fear of rejection. The more he withdraws, the more she seems to lose interest. He becomes irritable, and the relationship deteriorates further. His psychologist suggests that he ask her what's going on. He doesn't want to, but with prodding, he realizes that he has little to lose.

So he asks his wife what's going on. Tyler approaches his wife and says, "Honey, I've missed you lately. It seems we both work too much. How can we find more time for us?" He's surprised to find that she misses him and has been holding the same negative assumption (that he has lost interest in her). She explains that work was really intense for a few months, and her sex drive had waned for a while. When her interest returned, he seemed to have gone away. This discussion led to an improved relationship.

If you use this tool, be sure that you don't set your experiment up to fail. In other words, had Tyler approached his wife in an accusatory manner, the outcome likely wouldn't have been so positive. How do you think she would have responded if he'd said, "How come you don't ever want to have sex anymore? Don't you care about me or our marriage?" When you check something out, be sure to consider how your wording will sound.

And if you unfortunately encounter negative data when you check things out, at least you know what you're dealing with. Even if Tyler's wife said she was having an affair, he would now know what's going on and could decide what to do. We find again and again that avoidance rarely spares pain in the long run.

Honing your acting skills

A final method for putting your thoughts to the test involves acting "as if" you don't believe them. In other words, if you think that you'll be rejected every time you approach someone, play a new persona for a week or two. Imagine that you're someone who won't get rejected. Act as if you're that person and see what happens when you approach people. Don't take our word for it, try it out. Doing this exercise will increase your chances of social success because you will be putting yourself in a *position* to succeed. If things don't go well, you won't be crushed — you'll just try again with the next person. Go ahead. See for yourself.

Revisiting your all-or-none thinking

As we mention in Chapter 5, the depressed mind thinks in all-or-none, black-and-white terms all too frequently. Perhaps you've fallen prey to this kind of thinking from time to time. If so, you may think that you must achieve perfection, or else you're abysmally and totally inadequate. Similarly, you may think that you must

- Achieve everything possible, or else you're a complete failure.
- Live a totally moral existence, or else you're an egregious, guilty sinner, deserving of hell and damnation.
- Always think of others, or else you're completely selfish.

We aren't suggesting that you can't have high standards for yourself. It's just that the all or none thinking that usually accompanies perfectionism sets you up for misery. No one is perfect. See Chapter 7 for more information about the perfectionism belief.

You're likely to derive benefits from redefining and recalculating your all-or-none thinking. When you find yourself immersed in all-or-none, black-and-white thinking (and almost everyone does now and then) try the following:

1. Carefully define what you're talking about.

Clearly define and elaborate on what you mean by any labels you apply to yourself, such as "failure," "loser," and so on. Without having a clear idea of what these labels mean to you, you can't perform the second step.

2. Recalculate your new definition on a percentage or continuum basis.

Here's how you do the recalculation: Whenever you hear absolute terms in your mind, such as "always," "never," "failure," "loser," "horrible," and so on, try thinking in terms of a continuum, or a rating scale. In other words, recalculate and estimate a *percentage* of the time your negative thought is true.

Thus, if you think that you're a failure, estimate what percentage of the time you've succeeded and what percentage you've failed and what failure really means to you, rather than a global label. If you think that you're a horrible person, recalculate and ask yourself what percentage of your actions are truly "horrible," as you defined the term in the first step, what percentage are "good," and what percentage are "neutral."

Few things in life exist in all-or-none terms. Redefining and recalculating can help you see the shades of gray that your depressed mind may have blocked from your sight. When you define your terms and put your self-evaluations on a continuum, you're likely to find that your recalculated assessment feels a lot better — and, more importantly, better reflects reality.

Erin complains to her counselor that she's an inept mother because her kids are acting up in school. The therapist asks her to explain what an inept mother is; what does such a mother do that other mothers don't? Erin replies that an inept mother is one who doesn't know anything about parenting, is mean to her kids, and neglects them. The therapist asks Erin if that definition fits her, and Erin says, "Well, not really. I guess I mean that I just don't always know how to handle them."

"Okay, then instead of asking how often you're an inept mother, because that doesn't fit, let me ask you how often you don't have any idea of how to handle your kids versus how often you do know what to do?" her therapist inquires.

After considerable thought, Erin concludes that she probably knows what to do with her kids about half the time. This more realistic redefinition and recalculation of her problem leads to a fruitful discussion of how Erin might discover more about parenting and increase the percentage of time she feels competent in knowing how to handle her kids. She figures that, with work, she can increase the percentage to 60 percent of the time, and further work can keep the percentage going up.

Facing the worst

Facing the worst is one thought-repair tool that's especially important. Cognitive therapy doesn't work as well when you stick your head in the sand like an ostrich. Rather, you have to think about the worst possible implications and potential outcomes of your thoughts.

Putting your worst face forward

It's surprising how often people manage to see that they could cope with their worst imagined fears, if had to. Of course, no one would want to, but you're likely to discover that it's more possible than you think.

You can identify your worst imagined fears by asking yourself what you're most afraid of. Then, if what you fear actually happened, what would it be like for you? After you identify these scenarios, answer some fear-coping questions. These questions can help you deal with your feared worst-case scenarios. These questions include the following:

- ✔ How likely is it that your worst feared fantasy will come true? (Consider assigning a probability from 0 to 100 percent likely.)
- ✔ If the worst fear actually happens, what possible ways could you cope with it?
- ✔ If the worst occurs, can you think of options or alternative plans of action?

If you get stuck when reflecting on these fear-coping questions, you may find it helpful to review other thought-repair tools, as well as the Thought Court process discussed earlier in this chapter. And if anxiety and fear complicate your depression, consider reading another book we wrote, *Overcoming Anxiety For Dummies* (Wiley Publishing, Inc.).

Putting the worst to work

Jack's story illustrates how this process of facing the worst goes. Jack celebrates his 45th birthday with a sense of gloom and doom. He's worked at a high tech chip manufacturing company for the past 15 years. During those years, he's invested 90 percent of his retirement fund into his company's stock. For a while, that decision looked pretty darn good to Jack as his fund soared to heights he'd never imagined, well over $2 million.

Then the tech bubble popped, and the value of Jack's company's shares plunged so fast that he couldn't do anything to save his retirement fund from devastation. Jack naturally lamented the loss, and he fears that retirement may lie far into his future. His therapist suggests that Jack track his thoughts on a Thought Tracker, which he does (see Table 6-1). The event is the demise of his retirement fund; his feelings are despair rated as 80 and self-loathing rated as 85. Jack records his thoughts in response to the event as:

- ✔ I may not be able to retire before I'm 80 years old.
- ✔ I was stupid to invest so much money in my company.

Replacing your therapist with a computer?

Mental health professionals have played around with the idea of using computers to assist in delivering psychotherapy for almost 40 years. Some of these early ideas involved trying to simulate an actual therapist's responses with the computer. As you may imagine, these early attempts were fairly clumsy because the computer frequently misunderstood what the client meant.

In the 1990's, Dr. Barbara Rothbaum and colleagues explored ideas for using computers to assist in the treatment of various types of phobias through virtual reality. This approach has considerable promise but currently is hampered by the necessity of rather elaborate equipment.

Drs. Jesse Wright, Andrew Wright, and Aaron T. Beck have recently developed a multimedia computer program on DVD ROM called Good Days Ahead: The Multimedia Program for Depression (available at www.mindstreet. com). This program doesn't attempt to replace your therapist, but it does do a very nice job of teaching cognitive-therapy principles and strategies. It also has various assignments and checklists for enhancing understanding of this therapy. Early evidence has shown that it's well received and may even cut down on the total amount of contact needed with a therapist. On the other hand, it'll probably be a very long time, if ever, before any computer program completely replaces a therapist.

Of course, Jack and his therapist could've worked on these initial thoughts to see if they contain distortions and to gather evidence for refuting them. And in fact, they did so by using many of the techniques illustrated in this chapter. However, Jack experienced only a minor lifting in his troubling emotions of despair and self-loathing. Therefore, his therapist asked Jack the following:

Therapist: Even though we see evidence to the contrary, let's assume that you were stupid to invest so heavily in the company and that you won't be able to retire until you're at least 80 years old. What's the worst possible meaning that these thoughts hold for you if they did happen to be true?

Jack: It would mean I'd be ridiculed.

Therapist: Okay, and let's say you receive ridicule. What about ridicule feels so awful? What would happen next if that were so?

Jack: Everyone would see me as an idiot and a fool.

Therapist: So if you truly were an idiot and a fool, what makes that feel so horrible to you? What's the worst imaginable thing that would happen if that were so?

Jack: Everyone I care about would leave me and no longer love me; I couldn't stand that.

At this point, his therapist has reached some of Jack's truly core fears — abandonment and loneliness. So Jack's thoughts hold even greater meaning for him. They mean that not only is he stupid and can't retire for a long time, but that everyone he cares about will leave him and that he couldn't stand living on his own without them. Jack's therapist poses the following questions to him in order to help him gain a better perspective. Jack's answers follow the questions.

- ✔ **How likely is my worst feared fantasy to actually come true?** Actually, as I review the evidence, it seems quite unlikely that my family would conclude that I'm an idiot and leave me. Even if they thought I did something stupid, I have lots of evidence of their absolute loyalty. So I give this scenario about a 5 percent chance of happening.

- ✔ **If the worst fear actually happens, what possible ways could you cope with it?** Ugh, this would be very difficult. But I guess I would find a way to deal with the loss. People do. Perhaps I'd join a support group. I could stay in therapy longer. And I could immerse myself in some useful distractions, such as reading and exercise.

- ✔ **If the worst occurs, can you think of options or alternative plans of action?** I'd try to stay in touch with my kids, even if they despised me. I could always find a group of supportive friends. Even if my current friends think that I'm a fool, it doesn't mean other people will think similarly because they won't know about what I did with my retirement money. And I could master new job skills or find work in another tech company. Some of them are still hiring, and I'm not that old. I have time to rebuild my finances. Finally, over time, I could possibly find another wife. I'm not that bad looking after all.

Thought therapy works best when you don't deny, rationalize, or avoid the worst thoughts in your mind. Rather, this therapy delivers maximum results when you deal with dreadful possibilities directly.

Chapter 7

Discovering the Cracked Lenses Behind Depression

· ·

· ·

Riley, a consummate optimist gets a good job at a computer software company right after college graduation. He cheerfully assumes that he'll find a solution to every problem and that nothing and no one will ever stand in his way. He feels confident and superior. He boasts to coworkers about his successes. He buys an expensive luxury car on credit, convinced that his salary will grow. You could say that he sees himself and the world through rose-colored glasses.

Ashton, also hired by the same software company, is the exact opposite of Riley. Ashton always expects the worst. He conjures up pitfalls and problems that most of the software developers can't even imagine. Ashton sees himself as less accomplished than the way his colleagues view him. He worries constantly about losing his job. Ashton seems to peer through gray, smoky lenses when viewing life. Not surprisingly, he usually has a bleak and bleary outlook.

In this chapter, we show you that Riley and Ashton aren't particularly unusual folks. In fact, everyone views the world through various pairs of glasses that we call *life-lenses*. As you look at your world through these lenses, they filter what you see. The right lenses can clarify the scene, but others distort what you see. These lenses can be clear, gray, cloudy, rose-colored, cracked, dirty, or distorted.

Life-lenses alter your very perceptions of events, yourself, and people in the world. You'll likely be surprised by how powerful these lenses can be. And you may even be dumbfounded to discover that both Ashton *and* Riley eventually succumb to depression.

Ashton, whom we describe as feeling inadequate, fails to advance in his career because he lacks confidence. He eventually becomes depressed, which probably isn't surprising given his bleak outlook on life. But Riley looks at himself and his world as though nothing could ever go wrong for him. Nothing's wrong with a little optimism, but Riley also feels superior to all those around him. Eventually, Riley gets fired for his haughty insolence and he, too, quickly slides into depression. Opposite life-lenses lead to the same outcome for both of these software developers.

In this chapter, we show you how these life-lenses can work in a way that predispose people toward depression and other problems, such as anger and anxiety. We help you see which of these lenses may be influencing you, even though you probably don't know it. You likely have a number of different life-lenses that you use to view different types of events. After you discover which lenses you're looking through, we give you tools for breaking the problematic lenses and regrinding new ones.

Looking Closely at the Mechanics of Life-Lenses

In Chapters 5 and 6 we discuss how thoughts or interpretations of events directly lead to depressed feelings. For example, if you visit your mother and she tells you that "by and large" she feels proud of you for some accomplishment, you may instantly interpret that happening in either positive or negative terms.

You may consider the "by and large" phrase as trivial and take her statement as a sincere compliment. On the other hand, you may hear the words "by and large" as hypercritical. If so, you're likely to have the thought that you've failed and disappointed her, and your mood will plummet.

What lies behind those instant thoughts? You guessed it: life-lenses. In fact, these lenses can be so powerful that they cause two different people to view the very same circumstance in totally contrasting ways.

For example, **Haley** and **Olivia** attend the same university and obtain virtually identical grade point averages. They receive acceptance letters to the same prestigious graduate school. In the letters, they're both awarded partial scholarships. Haley feels ecstatic and calls everyone she knows to tell them the good news. Olivia feels sharp disappointment and shame that she failed to obtain the larger scholarship she'd hoped for and feels that the school failed to appreciate her talents.

Haley feels astonished by Olivia's negative reaction. And Olivia can't believe that Haley could be so happy about obtaining a meager scholarship when she obviously deserves more. What's going on with these two students?

The answer lies in the life-lenses that each of them looks through. Haley happens to have a pretty clear, undistorted pair of glasses for viewing her achievements. Olivia, on the other hand, looks through the life-lens we call "entitlement." The entitlement lens makes her believe that she deserves the best of everything and that anything less is totally unacceptable. Thus, Olivia's reaction, although perhaps a bit obnoxious, now at least makes sense, doesn't it?

Most folks don't realize that they look at their world through life-lenses, but even if they do, they're usually unaware of which ones their minds use. We've discovered in our work with depressed clients that 12 life-lenses stand out as particularly problematic.

The list of possible life-lenses is potentially endless. But don't worry, this list covers most of the problematic issues that mental health professionals deal with. By the way, Riley's so-called rose colored glasses that we discuss in the introduction to this chapter, actually consist of two lenses from the following list — superior and invulnerable. In other words, Riley felt superior to other people and invincible.

We give a brief description of each life-lens in the following list, and in the "Searching for Your Mind's Life-Lenses" section later in the chapter, we give you the opportunity to discover which ones your mind may employ. Some lenses aren't particularly problematic because they allow you to view events without significant distortion. We tell you how to create those lenses, if you don't already have them, in the "Writing New Prescriptions for Clear Lenses" section, which you can also find later in this chapter.

- **Abandonment fearful:** Worry that people you care about will eventually leave you

- **Entitled:** A pervasive perspective that you always deserve the best and feel outraged when your needs go unmet

- **Guilty and blameworthy:** A pervasive sense that you must always do the right thing or else

- **Guiltless:** Shameless disregard for ethics and morality

- **Inadequate:** A sense that you lack important skills, abilities, or other qualities

- **Inferior:** Viewing yourself as insignificant and less important than others

- **Intimacy avoidant:** A sense that you don't like getting close to people

- **Invulnerable:** No sense that you need to take even reasonable precautions because everything will be fine

✔ **Perfectionistic:** A compulsion to believe that you can and should do everything perfectly — see Chapter 5 for more information about the destructive influence of "shoulds"

✔ **Superior:** A view that you stand far above others

✔ **Unworthy:** A sense that you don't deserve good things or have good things happen to you

✔ **Vulnerable:** A belief that the world is a dangerous place and horrible things are about to happen

Writing prescriptions for life-lenses

So who writes the prescriptions for life-lenses, and when and where do people go to pick them up? In other words, where do they come from?

Knowing the answer to this question helps you understand that no one deserves blame for having a variety of problematic, distorted life-lenses. After all, who'd visit the EZ To Go Eyeglass Shoppe and request a pair of cracked, distorted glasses? Similarly, no one wants distorted life-lenses. Nevertheless, people end up with them for good reasons.

Generally speaking, the life-lenses that you see yourself and the world through today were created in childhood. From infancy onward, children actively work to make sense out of an array of activities and actions on the part of parents, friends, teachers, relatives, and others. From children's perspectives, these lenses reflect a reasonable understanding of the events bombarding them. And during childhood, they make pretty good sense.

Thus, people who look through a guilt and self-blame life-lens likely had parents who criticized them frequently and harshly. Rather naturally, they came to the conclusion that they're quite blameworthy. Similarly, people with the entitled life-lens were likely spoiled and received excessive praise and flattery.

The problem lies in the fact that the world inevitably changes as people mature and enter adulthood. For example, a boy who hears innumerable messages about how inadequate, inferior, and unworthy he is isn't likely to continue hearing those messages as an adult. However, he will continue to look at the world through the same old prescriptions. Because of those long-held distorted views, as an adult, he may interpret comments from others as criticism, even if that's not the intent.

Although events later in life may shape or reshape a person's life-lenses, childhood usually is when the most difficult, distorted lenses originate.

Seeing the world through life-lenses

Now, to show you precisely how these lenses operate, here's an example of how viewing the *exact same event* through different life-lenses leads to totally contrasting thoughts and feelings (see Chapter 6 for more information about the interconnections between events, thoughts, and feelings).

Pretend that you gave a presentation to a group of colleagues. You felt slightly nervous at the beginning of the talk, but you quickly relaxed and gained confidence that you got your point across. After the talk, a coworker comments, "Gee, you were a little nervous up there."

Depending on your particular life-lens, your reaction to the comment may lead to very different thoughts and feelings. Table 7-1 illustrates how these lenses work.

In Table 7-1, you may notice that the final lens, "adequate," wasn't on the list of problematic lenses listed earlier. If so, you observed correctly. That's because some life-lenses are less distorted and provide a relatively clearer view of yourself and the world. We discuss such clear life-lenses in the section on "Writing a New Prescription for Clear Lenses" later in this chapter.

Table 7-1	Life-Lenses Lead to Contrasting Thoughts and Feelings	
Event: You give a speech, and a friend says that you looked a little nervous.		
Life-Lens: Definition	**Thoughts (or Interpretations)**	**Resulting Feelings**
Inadequate: I'm not particularly intelligent or skillful.	I'll never be a good speaker. I shouldn't even try. Everyone thinks I'm a fool and an idiot. How stupid could I be?	Shame Despair
Abandonment fearful: I worry a lot about whether people like and approve of me. Eventually, everyone leaves.	My friend isn't going to want to associate with me anymore. No one else will, either.	Worry Anxiety Isolation
Superior: I stand above others and, therefore, look down on them.	My so-called friend is trying to undermine me! Who is he to say something like that? As if he could do any better. I never did think that much of him.	Anger Rage

(continued)

Table 7-1 *(continued)*

Event: You give a speech, and a friend says that you looked a little nervous.

Life-Lens: Definition	Thoughts (or Interpretations)	Resulting Feelings
Guilty and Blameworthy: I'm very hard on myself whenever I don't do exactly the right thing.	It's my own damn fault. I let the audience down. I should've practiced more!	Guilt
Adequate: I know and accept that I have both strengths and weaknesses. I like to do well, but I can learn from mistakes, too.	My friend is right; I did feel nervous, and I'm sure it showed. I don't particularly like looking nervous, but I can certainly get better with practice.	Mild, Momentary Distress

Optimism |

Same event, different life-lenses. When viewing life through various lenses, people can't help but see starkly contrasting pictures. This process explains why people have such conflicting thoughts and feelings when facing the same occurrences.

The difference between a life-lens and thoughts about events (see Chapter 6 for more information about such thoughts) is that each lens causes your specific thoughts in reaction to many events. You apply the same lens to a variety of situations, whereas your thoughts are generally more specific to a particular event. Thus, if you have the guilty and blameworthy lens, you're likely to end up having many types of specific guilty thoughts when you mess up in the slightest way.

For example, **Lenny's** life-lens, inferior, causes him to have a myriad of thoughts that hold him back in different types of situations. At parties, he has thoughts about how insignificantly others view him, so he tries to meld into the woodwork. At work, he fails to put in for a promotion because he has thoughts that others in his same rank will be viewed as better than he. And at the neighborhood homeowner association meetings, he fails to contribute his ideas because he assumes that no one will take him seriously. Though his thoughts in each situation are somewhat different, they all relate to his one life-lens.

Searching for Your Mind's Life-Lenses

So, you're probably curious now about what kind of life-lens you look through. Well, in this section, we show you how to find that out. This discovery can reveal the root cause of much of your emotional distress — depression as well as other troubling feelings, such as anger, anxiety, and worry.

Awareness is the first step on the path toward change. Changing a problematic life-lens is difficult unless you know which one (or ones) you're dealing with. You need to find out the specific lenses that may be causing trouble in your life. Just like people suffer from nearsightedness and farsightedness, life-lenses come in opposite pairs. Lenses, like most concepts (long and short, heavy and light, wet and dry, and so on), can be viewed as contrasting opposites as seen in Table 7-2.

The "Problematic Life-Lenses" questionnaire in Table 7-2 contains a description of what we've found to be some of the most important distorted life-lenses. Before going through this questionnaire, please take a look at the following instructions:

- ✔ **Answer as honestly as possible.** Sometimes, people readily see how they think they "should" answer, rather than answer with an honest self-appraisal. Self-deception isn't useful.

- ✔ **Base your answer on how often you feel and react in situations that relate to each lens.** For example, if you frequently *feel* inadequate, but know in your head that you're really adequate, answer on the basis of how you feel when your adequacy comes into question, such as when you're asked to make a speech.

- ✔ **Take your time.** Reflect on various events and situations that have happened to you and that are relevant to each lens. For example, in answering questions about abandonment fearful versus intimacy avoidant, ponder the relationships you've had and how you feel and react to those close to you. You shouldn't rush this task.

- ✔ **Don't worry about inconsistencies.** Yes, the life-lenses come in opposite pairs. And you very well may frequently find yourself using both opposing pairs from time to time. Thus, if you're a perfectionist, you may also quite often feel inadequate when you make a mistake. Or if you normally feel unworthy and undeserving, you may find yourself feeling quite angry and entitled on occasion when your needs unexpectedly go unmet. People often flip between opposite lenses, so don't worry if you think that you look a little inconsistent.

- ✔ **Answer on the basis of how often each lens describes you.** If you see parts of the description that apply and others that don't, underline the parts that fit and rate yourself on those parts in terms of how often they apply to you.

- ✔ **Use a scale of 0 to 4 for your frequency rating.** Use **0** if the lens almost never describes you, **1** if it occasionally describes you, **2** if it sometimes describes you, **3** if it usually describes you, and **4** if it almost always describes you.

Table 7-2	Problematic Life-Lenses Questionnaire
Lens	**Opposite Lens**
____ **Inferior.** I feel less significant and important than other people. I see others as better than me. I feel like I don't fit in because something about me is defective.	____ **Superior.** I feel like I stand far above other people. Truly, few people are my equal.
____ **Unworthy.** I just don't feel like I deserve to have good things happen to me. I feel uncomfortable whenever someone does something nice for me.	____ **Entitled.** I deserve the best of everything. I should have almost anything I want. If my needs unexpectedly go unmet, I feel angry.
____ **Abandonment fearful.** I need lots of reassurance to feel loved. I feel lost without someone in my life, and I worry about losing those I care about. I feel jealous and cling to my loved ones due to my fear.	____ **Intimacy Avoidant.** I don't like to get close to anyone. I'd just as soon stay away from any emotional involvement. I don't need anybody in my life.
____ **Inadequate.** I feel like I'm not as talented or skillful as most other people. I just don't measure up. I don't like taking on things I've never done before if they look difficult.	____ **Perfectionistic.** I feel like I must do everything perfectly. And if I want something done right, I'd better be the one to do it.
____ **Guilty and Blameworthy.** I feel guilty and blameworthy. I worry about whether I've done the wrong thing. I can't stand hurting anyone else.	____ **Guiltless.** I don't let stupid things like morality and conscience stand in my way if I want to do something.
____ **Vulnerable.** Bad things happen all the time. I worry a lot about the future. I'm scared. The world feels very dangerous.	____ **Invulnerable.** I am invincible. Nothing can hurt me. I have great luck. The world treats me well. I never worry about taking precautions.

Any life-lens that you rated as 2 or higher, in terms of how frequently it describes you, probably gives you problems from time to time. Realize that these lenses set you up for bad feelings and depression. Even if you've overcome your depression by working on your troubling thoughts discussed in Chapters 5 and 6, you're likely to find it useful to do further work on these lenses. That's because if you change your life-lenses, you can change the likelihood of depression reoccurring in the future.

Don't despair if you rated many of these life-lenses highly. We've found that with work and diligence, most people can handle tackling multiple lenses in the same way they deal with just one or two.

Breaking Problematic Life-Lenses

Assuming you're aware that you look through distorted life-lenses, now what? We recommend that you take one such lens at a time and pulverize it into dust. Unfortunately, that's not such an easy task. Appreciate the fact that life-lenses are manufactured out of durable, emotionally intense material, hardened through the years. Therefore, you need to proceed slowly and take your time.

If the task of pulverizing your life-lenses ends up being too hard for you to do, we've found that many people can at least put their old, distorted glasses away in a drawer for a while. You may still find yourself using the old glasses from time to time, but less often and less frequently than before you started to work on them. In other words, with work, your old lenses will no longer remain the only way for you to look at yourself and your world.

You can expect the task to require considerably more time if you've been depressed for a long while, or if you've experienced multiple depressions through your life. However, with patience and diligence, you can succeed. If you start to waver, flip back to Chapter 3, which deals with breaking barriers to change.

Avoid going overboard with your approach to change. For example, if you have the life-lens of inadequate, you won't solve the problem by thinking that you need to be perfect. Perfectionism lies at the opposite extreme and will give you as much trouble as the inadequate lens. Similarly, if you've been extremely fearful of abandonment, avoid the temptation to believe that you need no one in your life (the intimacy avoidant lens). Later in the section on "Writing a New Prescription for Clear Lenses," we show you how to grind clear lenses that lie between such opposite extremes.

Finding self-forgiveness

Finding self-forgiveness is a crucial step that ultimately leads to breaking up your distorted life-lenses. All too often, people pummel themselves for having their distorted life-lenses. This self-abuse merely uses up crucial energy that they need for making difficult changes. It's sort of like running a race and pounding yourself on the head with a hammer because you haven't yet reached the finish line.

Instead, we suggest that you search for ways to forgive yourself, thereby freeing up that energy for better purposes. One approach has been quite helpful to many of those we've worked with over the years. We call it the "Childhood Review."

The Childhood Review strategy asks that you review the emotionally important events in your life, especially as they may have contributed to the origins of your life-lens. For example, if you have the life-lens of abandonment
fearful, look back on your life for possible causes, such as:

- Parents divorcing when you were four years-old
- An emotionally rejecting father
- Being left alone for long periods of time at an early age

After you identify likely causes, ask yourself whether those life-disrupting
events perhaps are more to blame than you for the development of your life-
lens. If so, try easing up on yourself. Appreciate that everyone is, in a sense,
at the best place that he or she can possibly be, given each person's unique
life history, genetics, biology, culture, and so on.

Focus on what you can do about future changes rather than beating yourself
up over a past that you can't change.

Understanding the difference between then and now

As we say more than once in this chapter, life-lenses are largely shaped by
emotionally intense events in childhood. As an adult, when you look at
current happenings in your life, the lens makes you see occurrences almost
as though they were the childhood events happening all over again. You may
find it useful to compare and contrast the events that trigger your problematic life-lens with the origins of that lens. When you do, try to appreciate that
your reaction likely has more to do with events from long ago than with
what's happening now.

Audrey repeatedly runs into trouble with her guilt and self-blame life-lens.
When she commits the slightest sin or social faux pas, she feels swamped
with guilt and self-loathing. She takes the Problematic Life-Lenses questionnaire (see Table 7-2) and fully realizes her struggle with this particular lens.

Her therapist suggests that she fill out a "Then and Now" form to help her
appreciate that her reaction relates more to the past than the present. He
suggests that she write down her life-lens in the left column, then, in the
middle column, record one or more images from childhood that may have
contributed to the development of the lens, and, finally, write about the event
that currently triggers the guilty feelings in the right column. Table 7-3 shows
what she does with this form.

Table 7-3	Audrey's Then and Now Form	
Problematic Life-Lens	*Childhood Image(s)*	*Current Triggers*
Guilt and Blameworthy. I worry about whether I've done the wrong thing. I can't stand hurting anyone else.	Mother used guilt-tripping constantly on us kids. She always said we were ungrateful, lazy, and worthless. She told us we were ruining her life.	When I didn't get the payroll in on time, I felt so guilty that I felt sick to my stomach. My boss told me it wasn't a big deal, but I couldn't forgive myself.
	The priest in our church bombarded us with messages that we'd all end up in hell if we committed sins. I was terrified and believed him for years.	I found a $20 bill in the parking lot. I kept it instead of turning it into the mall security department. And I felt like I'd committed a mortal sin. Like I broke a commandment.
	My father kept me away from boys until I was 18 years-old and said that all they wanted was sex, which is absolutely disgusting. He made me think that I was perverted for having any sexual feelings.	When I had a momentary fantasy about our neighbor, I felt guilty for weeks. And yet I know that I'd never cheat on my husband.

As Audrey reviews her Then and Now form, she realizes that the events in her present-day world pale in significance compared to her vivid images from childhood. Yet, the current-day events evoke almost identically miserable emotions. She starts reminding herself that her reactions today feel so intense only because of her earlier history. She starts saying things to herself, such as, "I feel exactly like I did when I was 13 years old, and my father yelled at me for looking at a boy. A momentary fantasy is pretty insignificant compared to my father's outrageous conduct."

Try using the Then and Now technique with your problematic life-lenses. You'll need to repeat the exercise numerous times, but as you do, you'll likely find your life-lens softening its impact on your emotions.

Conducting a cost/benefit analysis

In some respects, people would be willing to toss aside their problematic life-lenses more quickly than they do, except for the fact that they believe the lenses protect or benefit them in some way. At first blush, you may think that idea sounds rather unlikely. For example, why would someone think that feeling unworthy could possibly be beneficial?

Actually, the reason these lenses feel so beneficial is that people believe in them so profoundly that they fear incurring losses and/or looking like fools if they discard the lens. We give you a couple of examples of how such concerns play out for several different life-lenses:

- ✓ **Unworthy.** If a woman with this lens decides to discard it and believe that she's truly worthy of good things, she's likely to fear that others will see her as outrageously greedy and self-centered because, in truth, others know that she doesn't deserve those things.

- ✓ **Inadequate.** If a man with this lens decides that he actually has no horrible deficiencies, he may start taking some risks, such as volunteering to lead a project at work. But he doesn't do so because he's absolutely convinced that his inadequacy lens is true, and thus, he'll fail miserably if he tries to discard the notion.

- ✓ **Entitled.** Someone with this lens fears that if she gives up feeling entitled to everything she wants and needs, she'll find that she gets nothing of what she wants.

- ✓ **Superior.** A person who feels that he stands far above others fears that letting go of this lens will cause him to be seen as the opposite — inferior to others.

We suggest that you conduct a careful cost/benefit analysis of each problematic life-lens that plagues your life. Start by filling out the benefits side and list every possible value the lens may provide you. Table 7-4 contains an example as it relates to Tomas.

Tomas has a vulnerable life-lens. Due to an abusive childhood, he now worries constantly about every imaginable danger — financial losses, terrorism, auto accidents, health, and more. He goes to great lengths to protect both himself and his family. He saves every possible dime, he controls the family diet like a dictator, he exercises religiously, and he imposes strict curfews on his children. Tomas lists the following benefits for his vulnerable life-lens in Table 7-4.

Table 7-4	Tomas' Benefit Analysis of the Vulnerable Lens
Benefits	*Costs*
I take many precautions to stay safe.	
I'm less likely to be hurt.	

Benefits	Costs
I can plan for dangers and what to do when they hit.	
I do a good job of protecting my family.	
We all just might live longer.	

Table 7-4 contains a pretty impressive list of benefits, doesn't it? Tomas had little difficulty coming up with this list of benefits for his lens. Why would he possibly want to discard his vulnerable life-lens? To find out, Tomas worked to develop a list of costs for his vulnerable life-lens. With effort, he managed to discover a number of important costs. You can see his complete cost/benefit analysis in Table 7-5.

Table 7-5	Tomas' Cost/Benefit Analysis of the Vulnerable Lens
Benefits	**Costs**
I take many precautions to stay safe.	My wife says I'm like a prison guard and that she can't stand it.
I'm less likely to be hurt.	My daughter got so angry with her curfew that she ran away from home for three days.
I can plan for dangers and what to do when they hit.	We never do anything for fun because I feel a need to save every penny I make.
I do a good job of protecting my family.	I got in a car accident in spite of all my extra care.
We all just might live longer.	Sometimes, I wonder whether living longer matters if everyone is so miserable.
	Never eating anything but health food didn't prevent me from getting prostate cancer.
	I think that my obsession with safety is making me and the entire family miserable.

After Tomas finishes his cost/benefit analysis, he feels more motivated to break his problematic life-lens. No matter which lenses cause you problems, a cost/benefit analysis of each lens can help you do the same. You'll likely want to use all the lens-breaking strategies we discuss in this section, but a cost/benefit analysis can help you see the value in making the effort.

In addition to the techniques for breaking your problematic life-lenses in this section, we find that trying on new, clear prescription glasses through which to look at yourself and the world is also important. As you do so, you're likely to find that the new glasses not only help you see better but also lead you to feeling better. Eventually, as you become more comfortable with the new prescription, you'll have even more reasons to throw the old lenses away.

Writing New Prescriptions for Clear Lenses

If you've reached the point where you at least "know in your head" that your old, distorted lenses aren't doing you much good, the time's come to look for new ones. When you look for new life-lenses, giving them a new name, one that's more flexible and balanced, isn't a bad idea. For example, instead of *inferior* or *superior,* you could design a lens you call "equal to others." Or instead of *invulnerable* or *vulnerable,* you may come up with a lens you call "reasonably cautious." You get the idea.

The bad news is that the process of designing new lenses is neither quick nor easy. The good news is that you can get there with sufficient patience and diligence.

You need to proceed with alertness and care because acting against the distorted views you've been seeing through your life-lenses feels almost like driving in another country where they use the opposite side of the road from what you're used to. The engrained, habitual side of your mind says to drive on the right side, and the clear-headed, adaptive side says to do the opposite in the new country. Preventing the old habit from automatically seizing control takes vigilance.

We have four separate strategies that are likely to help you remember which side of the road to stay on. Remember to drive slowly and watch the road signs. You may find that one of these strategies works for you, or you may find it helpful to use all four.

Looking through contrasting lenses

Even people who feel overwhelmed with the effects of distorted life-lenses can usually access another clearer lens that sits neglected in their minds.

Most folks do know that they have this reasonable, logical, and somewhat less distorted way of thinking. Nonetheless, they may not have looked through that side of their minds in a while.

The "Looking through Contrasting Lenses" strategy is an effective way of getting in touch with the clear-thinking, level-headed side of your mind. And by the way, everyone's mind has a clear-thinking side. This type of thinking naturally develops in adulthood, but it too often goes into hiding when depression sets in. Sometimes, looking for the clear lens feels like searching for a contact lens that flew out of your hands onto the carpet. Though you think that it may have disappeared, rest assured that you can find clarity if you look around a bit.

1. **Arrange two similar chairs to face each other. Label one of these chairs the distorted lens that your mind uses all too often, and the other chair as the clear lens that looks at events more logically and objectively.**

2. **Sit in the distorted lens side first and literally talk out loud to the imagined other side of you sitting in the other chair, but which sees through a clear lens.**

   Tell that logical, clear side all the reasons you *should* feel as bad as you do. Argue forcefully!

3. **When you run out of steam, switch chairs and sit in the clear, objective lens chair. From the clear side, tell the negative, distorted chair all the reasons that the arguments you just heard are bogus.**

   Use evidence, data, and logic. Point out any distortions you heard from the negative chair.

4. **Keep switching chairs until you've run the argument into the ground.**

   And notice how you *feel* in each chair. Ask yourself which chair feels stronger and which side seems most reflective of reality.

Okay, perhaps this tool sounds downright silly as well as perhaps a little confusing. However, psychologists have used various versions of this technique for decades for one reason: It works. And if the strategy sounds a little confusing, perhaps Alyssa's story can help to clear things up for you.

Alyssa has felt depressed for about four months. About two months ago, she started reading a number of self-help books. In the last three weeks, she's noticed a significant lifting in her mood.

Then she crashes. Her boyfriend says that he must take a four-day trip out of town for work. She doesn't doubt what he says, but nevertheless, her mood plunges like a bungee jumper diving off a platform. She thinks to herself that she's foolish to believe that her depression will get better, and, perhaps, she's actually hopeless. She realizes that her abandonment fearful life-lens has led to her intense feelings of hopelessness. Here's how the Looking through Contrasting Lenses exercise plays out for Alyssa in tackling that lens:

Abandonment Fearful Life-Lens chair (Talking to the Logical, Clear Life-Lens chair): "Why did you even bother to hope? You're a loser, and you know it. Blake makes a lot of out-of-town trips. One of these days he's going to find someone else, and that'll prove that you're a loser who'll never have a successful relationship. Besides, the fact that your depression has returned also shows that Blake will eventually leave you. After all, who would want to stay with someone who's always depressed?"

Logical, Clear Life-Lens chair: "Did you think that your depression would just go away at once and be gone forever? It doesn't work that way — you read that in a number of books. Blake has stuck with you through thick and thin for more than a year now. He says that he wants to spend his life with you. He's concerned about your depression, and he says that he'll do anything it takes to help. Why not believe him?"

Abandonment Fearful chair: "Well, you've had other boyfriends who left you after they said nice things, too. Why should Blake be any different? Remember how hurt you were when Seth left?"

Logical, Clear chair: "For one thing, you know that a couple of those guys who left were pathetic nobodies; you didn't really want them anymore than they wanted you. And yes, I was hurt when Seth left. But first of all, most of my friends have had a great guy leave at some point or another. It doesn't mean that they all will. Natasha had five guys leave her, but then she got married four years ago, and things look great for her. Besides, you know that you practically pushed Seth out the door because of your fears. Don't do that again for God's sake!"

Abandonment Fearful chair: "But I couldn't stand it if Blake left me! I'd die."

Logical, Clear chair: "Well guess what? You felt hurt, but you didn't die when Seth left. What do you have to lose by hanging in there, trusting, and not pushing Blake away?"

Abandonment Fearful chair: "I guess you have a point, but I'm afraid."

Logical, Clear chair: "Of course, you're afraid, but you can handle it. Hang in there with me and try something different for a change."

Repeated practice of the Looking through Contrasting Lenses technique can help convince you that the new, clear lens is more accurate and also feels better to look through than the old, distorted life-lens. Repeat the exercise every time you waver in your efforts to use the new way of looking at yourself and the world.

Modeling new lenses

This strategy for finding clear life-lenses is like shopping for clothes. One of the most common ways people decide what they like in clothes is by looking at friends, acquaintances, and models for ideas. If you see an outfit that looks good on someone else, you may decide to choose something similar. Then what do you do? You probably try it on and see how it looks and feels.

Thus, if you have a life-lens that hasn't given you the results you want, look around at other people you know. Most likely, you won't have trouble finding someone else who has a clear lens in that area. We call this the "Modeling Technique." Modeling a new life-lens is pretty straightforward:

1. **Find someone you know who seems to look through a clearer lens than you do.**

2. **Give that new, clear lens a name and decide what it means to you.**

3. **Try on the new lens just as you'd try on a new outfit.**

Howard's story illustrates how to use this approach. **Howard** hardly looks like someone who'd fall into depression. He completed his residency in orthopedic surgery eight years ago and now stands atop his profession in terms of both income and prestige. However, in the past six months, he's been waking up at 3 a.m., unable to go back to sleep. His energy droops, his appetite wanes, and he loses interest in sex.

His wife convinces him to get help for his depression. He doesn't believe that he's depressed, but he agrees to see a psychologist. After four sessions, the psychologist manages to convince Howard that he's seriously depressed. And much of his depression seems to originate from a perfectionistic life-lens that causes Howard to work excessive hours and beat himself relentlessly for the most trivial of mistakes.

Howard tells his psychologist, "I can't possibly stop being a perfectionist; I'm a surgeon for crying out loud! If I don't obsess over every detail, patients could die!"

"Yes," Howard's psychologist agrees, "and don't you know of any colleagues who work hard, do an excellent job, but nevertheless aren't so completely driven by perfectionism?"

When pushed, Howard manages to think of his friend Rene. Rene is a successful surgeon, too, but she doesn't work the hours that Howard does. And Rene doesn't seem to clobber herself over trivial miscues. Howard agrees to try modeling Rene's life-lens.

Having accomplished Step 1 of the Modeling Technique, Howard moves on to the next step of naming the new lens. He can't bring himself to consider a lens labeled merely "adequate," yet he knows that the perfectionism lens is killing him. He settles his sights on a lens that he decides to call "productive and proficient." He defines this new lens as meaning that he wants to be highly competent and work hard, but not nearly as driven and obsessed. Howard tries on his new life-lens for a week. Thus, he essentially tries out acting "as if" he is his friend, Rene. After a week, he decides that he likes this new lens more than his old one.

With the Modeling Technique, you find someone else you know to mimic or model a new lens for you. You try on the lens and give yourself the option of going back to the old one if that feels better.

Taking direct actions

Now comes a scary approach — acting in ways that directly go against the views you see through your distorted life-lenses. Although it may feel a little scary, "Taking Direct Actions" against your lenses isn't especially complicated. All you do is

- ✔ Ask what your old, distorted life-lens has been causing you to do that's either self-destructive, not useful, or fails to give you what you want.

- ✔ Make a list of a few different things to do — actions that are likely to lead to long-term benefits.

- ✔ Start doing them, one at a time.

Starting with small steps never hurts. You've had your old life-lenses a long time; you don't need to rush the process.

Abby's abandonment fearful life-lens causes her to cling so tightly to every new relationship that the guy always feels smothered and eventually leaves. Her distorted lens, in fact, like most life-lenses, ultimately causes the very outcome she fears most. She feels lost without someone in her life, and her cost/benefit analysis (see the "Conducting a cost/benefit analysis" section earlier in this chapter) tells her that her abandonment fearful life-lens is inflicting far more harm than good. So she makes a list of a few self-destructive items that her life-lens has typically directed her to do:

- ✔ If I'm in a new relationship, I call the guy frantically several times every-day asking for reassurance.

- ✔ I do almost anything to keep from being alone, including something really stupid — going to bars and letting myself get picked up.

> ✔ I dress in really sexy outfits and come on strong to hook guys because I so hate being alone.
>
> ✔ I neglect my friends.

Abby decides that she wants to do something different than her past patterns. After mulling over her list for a bit, she thinks of some things she can do to change:

> ✔ I will call a girl friend once a week and spend time with her rather than obsess about guys.
>
> ✔ I will spend at least three evenings a week at home and line up a variety of activities to help me deal with the time by myself.
>
> ✔ I'll quit trying to find guys in bars and stop wearing sexy come-on clothes.
>
> ✔ If someone does come into my life, I'll force myself to call him no more often than he calls me. I'll enlist a couple of my friends for help on this one.

Abby works hard at implementing her new actions. Sometimes, she succeeds, and sometimes, she flops. But by frequently reviewing her list, she manages to maintain her focus on where she's headed. Slowly but surely, she grinds a new life-lens that she decides to call "intimacy comfortable." For her, intimacy comfortable means learning to feel okay by herself as well as when she's involved in a relationship.

As you can see, taking direct actions simultaneously breaks up your old lenses and grinds new ones for you to see life through. It's not the easiest task to launch, but you're likely to find this approach quite rewarding in the long run.

Writing letters to the optometrist

If, as a child, you tried on a new pair of glasses and they caused everything to look out of focus, you'd probably tell the optometrist that you couldn't see right with the new lenses. But imagine that the optometrist told you, "That's how this prescription is supposed to make things look! Give the glasses time, and they'll eventually feel just right." Perhaps, as a child, you'd feel like you had no option but to continue wearing them. And you'd probably make some kind of adjustment to the glasses even if they were wrong for you.

But eventually, at some point in your life, you'd figure out that you'd been hornswoggled by that optometrist. And you'd probably feel rather angry about having been forced to wear the wrong glasses for years. Writing a letter to the eye doctor wouldn't change anything, but it could let off some pent up emotional steam and set the record straight.

That's what the "Writing a Letter to the Source" strategy is about. We recommend that you write a heartfelt letter to the person or persons most responsible for the development of your distorted life-lens. Include details about what the person did and how you felt. After you've vented your emotions, also tell the person what you plan to do to create a new, clear life-lens — your plan for positive change.

In the vast majority of cases, you won't actually want to mail such a letter to the source. If you do decide to do so, give your decision time. And check out the decision with a trusted friend, clergy, or professional. Make sure that you've thoroughly thought through the advantages and disadvantages of sending the letter.

If the source that you're directing your letter toward is one or both of your parents, you may feel reluctant to express this anger. Perhaps you feel guilty and think you shouldn't express such feelings toward a parent, even if you don't plan to send the letter. You may be tempted to defend your parents' actions. We recommend that you write about your anger and distress nonetheless. You also may benefit from finding forgiveness for the source of your life-lenses. But forgiveness comes after releasing the boiling emotional caldron first.

Adam looks at the world through an inadequacy life-lens. As a child, his father had no patience for teaching Adam anything; instead, he ridiculed Adam anytime he made the smallest mistake. For his entire adult life, Adam has shied away from learning any new skill out of fear of looking clumsy and stupid. He even calls a repair service rather than attempt to read the simple instructions for restarting his furnace. When his wife says that they need to get out more and suggests dance lessons, he wants to dig a hole and jump in. However, Adam decides to try writing a letter to the source. Figure 7-1 shows the letter he writes to his father.

At first, Adam feels guilty when he starts to write the letter to the source of his life-lens. But he realizes that he has no intention of actually sending it and that he has a perfect right to feel the way he does. Note that he includes not only his feelings of anger, shame, and humiliation, but also his plan for grinding a new life-lens. If you've struggled long enough with a destructive life-lens, try the Writing a Letter to the Source exercise.

If you want even more ideas for how to regrind problematic life-lenses, we recommend *Reinventing Your Life,* by Jeffrey Young, PhD, and Janet Klosko, PhD, (Plume) and *Why Can't I Get What I Want?*, by Charles Elliott, PhD, and Maureen Lassen, PhD (Davies-Black).

Dear Dad,

I remember how so many times you'd get red in the face and walk off in frustrated disgust whenever you tried to teach me something. It didn't matter what it was, your temper had about a six-second fuse. What did I do to deserve that abuse? Do you know how ashamed and humiliated I felt when you expected me to master things on the first attempt, whether it was riding a bicycle or hammering a nail?

I remember I wore clip-on ties for years rather than ask you to teach me how to tie a tie. I felt like a stupid geek wearing them, but that was a lot better than watching you explode again. And then there's the fact that you were always gone on the weekends. Most of the time you didn't even manage to get off work to go on vacations with the rest of us. What was that about? I concluded that you didn't want to be around me.

But why were you so close to my older brother, Kyle? I imagined that he was so much smarter and skillful than I. I can't even express how hurt and angry I feel about all those times.

It's funny, too. Much later in life I learned that my talent is that I am actually very smart. I guess I can't make a piece of furniture like you can, but I can do an awful lot of things you can't. I'd like to see you try writing those magazine articles I write every week. I'm being promoted to Senior Editor next week, by the way. Not that you'd care or ever show any recognition of something I do.

Well, I must say that it feels good to get some of these issues off my chest for once. I realize that you must have your own problems, and that some deficiency of your own kept you from ever connecting with me. I think perhaps you lost as much as I did — maybe more.

At any rate, I'm sick of feeling like a total klutz. So let me tell you what I plan to do now. I'm going to go to the Home Warehouse and take their basic home maintenance class. Yep. And if I don't get it at first, I'm going to take it again. And again — until I master some things and feel better about myself. And, incredibly, I'm going to take dance lessons with my wife. I know that I'll feel just like I did when I was six years old and you screamed at me for dropping a hammer, but I'm going to keep at the lessons no matter what. I'm not going to live the rest of my life feeling like a complete geek and a klutz.

Perhaps someday you'll dig down deep and show interest in me and my life. And possibly not. Either way, I plan to move on and overcome what you instilled in me.

Love,
Adam

Figure 7-1:
Writing a Letter to the Source exercise: Adam.

Schemas: The astonishing power of life-lenses

Psychologists have a term for what we call life-lenses — *schemas*. Schemas indeed work like lenses you see the world through. They're the mind's way of organizing and making sense out of a bewildering bombardment of information. Upon birth, a human infant can't tell the difference between a face and a light bulb. However, in due course, the infant quickly learns to distinguish faces from other objects. And then the infant begins to distinguish one face from another. Later, the schema for faces develops to the point that the infant can interpret a circle with a few dots for eyes and lines for a mouth as a face.

The mind uses schemas to organize everything. For example, if cats are raised in a tubular cage with nothing but vertical lines on the walls, they later become physically unable to perceive horizontal lines because they have no schema for such lines. In a similar fashion, members of the Suku tribe in Africa reliably perceive vertical lines as longer than horizontal lines, unlike most Americans who have a slight tendency to see horizontal lines as longer. Why? The Suku tribe live and hunt in grassland areas where they can always see the horizon. For them, perceiving animals and enemies that rise vertically above the horizon is especially important for survival. Thus, their brains learn to magnify perceptions of vertical objects.

Chapter 8

Mending Your Memory

● ●

In This Chapter

▶ Understanding how your memory works

▶ Looking at the effects depression has on your memory

▶ Knowing when to worry about forgetfulness

▶ Checking out strategies for improving your memory

● ●

*D*epression is bad enough. You feel terrible. Your sleep may be disturbed, your appetite may be lousy, and nothing seems like fun anymore. What could be worse? Well, you can add to the mix a significant decline in your ability to remember names, dates, errands, and shopping lists.

But why would we single out memory as a special concern? Mostly because mucked up memory messes up your everyday life. In addition, when you notice memory problems, putting yourself down for having the problem is all too easy. You don't need more sources for negative thinking than depression has already given you.

Depression and memory impairment go hand in hand. Here's the good news — when your depression lifts, your memory will likely improve. But in the meantime, you have many options for aiding and improving your memory, which may in turn improve your mood.

In order to understand how depression damages memory, we first tell you how memory works and then describe the different kinds of memory. Next, we reveal the ways depression depletes and disrupts memory. Some forgetfulness is perfectly normal; we tell you how to know if your problem needs more attention. Finally, we give you sound strategies for dealing with memory problems and boosting your memory skills.

Making Sense of Memory

Think back to when you were a child. What is the earliest memory you can conjure up from childhood? Do you recall where the event took place, who was there, and what you looked like? Good. Now try to remember what you ate for lunch two weeks ago. What? You can remember something that happened years ago, but you can't remember something that happened two weeks ago?

This little exercise demonstrates that memory processes are complex. You don't remember everything that happens to you. We're pretty sure you were awake and paying attention to what you ate two weeks ago. But you probably can't remember the food unless it was unusual, special, or important to you in some way.

Scientists basically agree on how memories are formed. All memory begins with some perception of information or an event by one or more of the senses. Many factors determine the perception that forms a memory and whether or not you're going to recall it. Briefly, here are the most important processes involved in memory:

✔ **Immediate memory:** Think of immediate memory as a photograph or recording of each moment that quickly disintegrates. Right now, you're reading these words, but your senses are also aware of the temperature of the room you're in, the sounds of cars going by, the level of light, and the comfort of your seat. You can turn your attention willfully to any of those sensations, but most of them are never really brought into your awareness.

  Your lunch two weeks ago was in your immediate memory for a while. Unless something unusual occurred, such as choking on a chicken bone, the memory of your lunch will probably never move from your immediate memory to long-term memory (which we describe later). Rather, it will be lost forever.

✔ **Working memory:** When you pay attention to information, your working memory (a temporary holding zone) allows you to use, manipulate, elaborate, or send the information on to long-term storage. Working memory is like a blackboard in your brain that constantly changes. Without working memory, you'd be unable to solve many types of problems that involve thinking about more than one concept at a time. Here's an example: Say all the letters of the alphabet (which you pull from your long-term memory) that rhyme with the word *me*. In order to say these letters, you have to use your working memory to picture all the letters, scan through them, and figure out if they rhyme.

✔ **Long-term memory:** Most of the information that flows through immediate memory and working memory is quickly forgotten. But when the brain converts a memory into long-term storage, the memory may last a while (maybe even a lifetime). When asked to recall the alphabet, you (hopefully) have no problem remembering the letters. But unless you're a schoolteacher, you probably haven't had to write or recite the letters in order since you were a kid. You can thank your long-term memory for keeping this little nugget of seldom-used info on file. Long-term memory can store huge amounts of information; it's what most people think of when they use the word *memory*.

✔ **Retrieval:** You have billions of memories stored in various places in your brain. But sometimes you can't easily find those memories. When you can't remember someone's name and then a couple of hours later it just seems to pop into your brain, you've experienced a retrieval problem. Retrieval (or *recall*) is the process of pulling stored information into conscious awareness.

When all is well, the brain processes, stores, and recalls memories with efficiency and ease. However, memory has many enemies, including neurological injuries or diseases, attentional problems, drugs, alcohol, and emotional disorders. Depression is also a memory antagonist. It disrupts and may even damage the elegant memory system.

Depressing Disruptions

Depression fills your brain with sadness. Your ability to think clearly can be clouded by feelings of hopelessness, helplessness, guilt, and low self-esteem. But depression also affects your ability to think clearly by having a negative influence on all aspects of your memory. In the following list, we describe the ways that depression affects each facet of memory. (For more on each aspect, see the "Making Sense of Memory" section, earlier in this chapter.)

✔ **Immediate memory:** Depression decreases your ability to pay attention to what's going on around you; you may not even notice important information. Things that you normally pay attention to may slip right by.

An overwhelming depression keeps **Aidan** moving slowly through his morning routine. He notices the time and realizes that he'll almost certainly be late for work. Aidan searches frantically for his keys. He tosses papers aside, digs in his brief case, and scurries from room to room. "Damn, damn, damn," he says, as his irritation grows. Suddenly, his hand discovers the keys, in his pocket, where he put them just minutes earlier. "Damn, damn, damn." Everyone probably has something like this happen from time to time, but Aidan is running into this problem almost every day. Aidan's immediate memory is impaired.

✔ **Working memory:** Depression disrupts your ability to concentrate and hold on to information. Your ability to solve problems plummets.

Throughout her company, folks know **Isabella** as an energetic, kind, and intelligent manager. Lately, she has been experiencing a lack of energy, a poor appetite, and a huge decrease in her usual enthusiasm for her job. Today, she must chair a meeting with six other managers to work on solving a company problem. She begins the meeting by asking the managers to report on their perceptions of the situation. She anticipates finding a solution easily after all the aspects of the problem are exposed. As the meeting progresses, Isabella finds it difficult to listen and hold on to the various ideas in order to compare and contrast them. Her mind floods with negative thoughts. At the end of the presentations, she realizes that she doesn't have a clue about how to approach this problem. Her working memory isn't working very well.

✔ **Long-term memory:** Depression makes learning new material much harder. Tasks such as studying for an exam can become extremely difficult. Not only is concentrating more difficult, but also the information just doesn't seem to stick.

The cold, slush, and dreary days of winter are especially depressing to **Ethan.** His mood matches the dimming light of the season. But this winter seems worse than past years. Ethan loses his job at an Internet company, which deepens his depression. The job market looks terrible, so he decides to get his real estate license. He gathers all the study materials, but when he reads a paragraph, he finds that he can't even remember what he read. He never experienced this kind of problem before. He reads through the book twice, and keeps notes. He takes a practice test and fails miserably. His struggle adds to his depression. Ethan is having trouble getting information to stick in his long-term memory.

✔ **Retrieval:** Depression makes recalling information like dates or mental shopping lists more difficult. It renders previously learned names, faces, and facts inaccessible. When you're depressed, you're more likely to remember sad and depressing memories, because depression floods your brain with negative memories. You may actually have trouble remembering the periods in your life when you were happy.

"I'll never find a guy," **Emma** complains to her friend Hayley. "Every time I think someone's nice, he turns out to be married, a jerk, or not interested in me. And even the guys who seem interested are only interested in one thing. Sex. I've never had a good relationship. They all turn out horrible. I may as well give up."

Hayley is a bit astounded. She remembers plenty of guys who were interested in Emma, and she recalls several long-term, stable relationships that Emma actually broke off. Emma has more dates than anyone in her circle of friends. In fact, Hayley has always been jealous of Emma's ability to attract guys. What gives? Emma is suffering from depression. She really can't remember the good times.

Picturing the depressed brain

Researchers are certain that depressed people have real problems with memory. Exciting new brain-imaging techniques are now helping scientists see what depression looks like in the brain. With this knowledge, they're beginning to understand the complicated relationship between mood and memory.

One explanation for poor memory during depression may be found in increased levels of *corticosterone,* a hormone that's released when people experience severe stress. Corticosterone levels increase during depression. Research at the University of California found that high levels of this hormone impaired

rats' ability to retrieve information that was previously learned or stored in long-term memory. Another possible explanation for poor memory may be the decreased levels of the brain chemical serotonin found in depressed people. *Serotonin* helps regulate attention as well as the ability to be interested in pleasurable activities.

Research at the Washington University School of Medicine has shown that people who have suffered from depression may have a smaller *hippocampus,* a key region in the brain that is important in learning and memory. According to some speculation, the stress hormone *cortisol* may have toxic effects on the hippocampus.

Worrying About Forgetting

When you experience memory problems as a result of depression, worrying about these problems may deepen your depression, which will no doubt increase your forgetfulness. If you're depressed, don't be too surprised if you forget where you parked, can't remember a word or someone's name, or misplace everyday items. Getting upset about minor problems with your memory can easily make you even more depressed.

Try to lighten up on yourself and realize that your memory glitches are most likely merely symptoms of depression. These memory problems will likely resolve when your depression lifts. And to take a more active approach in bulking up your memory muscles, use the tips and techniques we provide in the "Boosting Broken Memory" section, later in this chapter.

An underlying disease or disorder sometimes causes poor memory. A little forgetfulness is a normal part of aging, too much stress, or depression. But extremely poor memory may be a sign of a more serious problem.

If you notice any of these symptoms, make an appointment for a complete physical:

✔ You become confused when performing activities you're very familiar with, such as doing laundry or cooking.

> ✔ You get lost when going to places you routinely visit, such as the post office or grocery store.
>
> ✔ You get disoriented, unsure about where you are or what you're doing, for more than a brief moment or two.
>
> ✔ Your memory problems begin to significantly interfere with your everyday work or relationships.

Your doctor may find that a treatable, physical cause is at the heart of these problems. Or she may confirm that your memory problem is due to depression, too much stress, or anxiety.

Boosting Broken Memory

So, you have some problems with your memory. If you're depressed, you probably don't have lots of enthusiasm for rigorous exercises that can help improve your memory. So we provide *quick, simple* tips and tricks to help you get by until your depression lifts and your memory improves.

In addition to using the following techniques, practice forgiving yourself for memory lapses. Self-criticism only worsens your memory problems as well as your depression.

If you're ready for some advanced memory training, several good books are available to assist you. For example, you can check out *Improving Your Memory For Dummies,* by John Arden, PhD (Wiley Publishing, Inc.), or *The Memory Bible,* by Gary Small, MD (Hyperion).

Writing stuff down

Admit that you have a problem with your memory, and then compensate for it. Keep a day planner next to you at all times, and make sure that you use it. Write down everything you need to remember. You need to write down not only your appointments but also shopping lists, names of people you recently met, and things you want to accomplish. Check your day planner frequently.

If you choose to use a personal digital assistant, just make sure that you input all the important appointments and daily reminders. Sophisticated technology can be very useful for people with memory problems. For example, some electronic devices ring scheduled alarms to remind their owners to check their calendars, take their medications, or perform other daily chores. On the other hand, you may find the old-fashioned pen and paper easier to use.

Developing routines

Here's the scene: You finally managed to force yourself to do some shopping, and now you're tired. You push your shopping cart out the door and, suddenly, you can't remember where you parked. This situation can happen to anyone, but when you're depressed and distracted, it becomes more likely, it feels horrible, and it gives you one more reason to feel bad about yourself.

Here's one way to avoid this type of situation: Every time you go to a store, park at the end of a row on either the right or left side of the entrance. If you have a favorite mall or grocery store, pick out a space that is rarely used. Park in that spot even when another space is open right next to the door. Parking in the same spot will not only take care of the problem, but it will also help by making you walk a little more (see Chapter 10 for information about the benefits of exercise for depression).

Developing habits and routines for other annoying tasks can also help. For example, find a decorative hook or basket for your keys, and make sure that you put them there every day. Don't forget to write these tasks down in your daily planner.

Smelling (and touching and seeing) the roses

Most people experience the world through sight, sound, touch, smell, and taste. Memory experts have discovered that when you use more than one sense, your ability to remember something improves. For example, when you listen to several instructions, you're more likely to remember them if you also see them in writing.

When you need to remember something, try to experience it with as many senses as possible. For example, if you want to remember an address such as 10 Greene Street, you can picture ten people mowing grass alongside a residential street. Use both the image of the green grass and the smell of the grass to plant the address in your memory.

You can also use a familiar tune to help you remember information. You change the lyrics of a song to include the information you want remember.

Have you ever noticed how kids learn the alphabet? But don't forget, the best way to remember something is to write it down. Both writing and singing involve more than one sense.

At times, you may find that experiencing something through all the senses doesn't, well, make sense. When you want to remember the names and faces of people you meet, reaching out and tracing the shape of their faces (or other personal places) probably isn't a good idea. And please don't lick anyone you just met. Okay?

Remembering names

Many people complain that they aren't able to remember names. Have you ever forgotten someone's name only seconds after being introduced? If so, try this: Next time you're introduced to someone, use the name at least three times in the conversation. "Hi, Riley, nice to meet you, Riley. So, do you live here in town, Riley?"

Try to look directly at the person and take a mental photograph. As you make eye contact, use the name again in conversation. When you turn away, visualize the name, face, and anything interesting you learned about the person. Repeat the name to yourself several more times, and then go write the name down in your day planner.

Chunking

Chunking involves grouping or organizing large amounts of information into small units. Doing so facilitates memory. Here's an example of how chunking helps.

First, read the following numbers and then close your eyes and try to remember them.

632895745

This exercise may be hard for you to do. One effective technique for remembering strings of unrelated numbers is to put them together in shorter units or chunks. Now read the following numbers and then close your eyes and repeat them.

554-759-823

Did you do a little better this time? Your brain can hold on to small amounts of information better than it can hold on to large amounts.

Yakking it up

University of Michigan psychologist Oscar Ybarra examined the relationship between memory and cognitive ability and social engagement. He studied more than 3,000 Americans between the ages of 24 and 96. He also studied 2,000 people from the Middle East. He found that, across cultures, the more people talk to others, the better their memory and cognitive functioning.

Does this mean that if you start talking to people more, your memory will improve and your IQ will sky rocket? Well, it's not that easy. We can't conclude from this study that social engagement either causes improved memory or prevents your memory from declining. It could be that people with good memory tend to get together with friends or family more often, and that people with memory problems or depression tend to stay away from other people. So don't feel like you have to become a social butterfly. On the other hand, the more support you get from others, the better you feel. And getting together with other people can be an excellent distraction.

Getting rid of distractions

Do you ever talk on the phone at the same time you answer e-mail? Do you listen to news shows and read the newspaper simultaneously? The modern world encourages, and sometimes demands, multitasking. However, when you're depressed, your ability to pay attention is compromised. And multitasking takes considerable attention.

Understand that, during a time of depression, your concentration may not be as good as usual. If you need to remember something or figure out something new, do so in a quiet setting. Concentrate on one thing at a time.

Following through

Do you have several uncompleted projects hanging over your head? The stress of knowing that you have unfinished business may increase your negative mood. When you're having problems with your memory, tracking progress on several different fronts becomes especially difficult.

When you start something, make sure that you finish it. Don't begin another project until you complete what you start. Alternatively, you can finish a portion of your project and then organize the balance for tackling later. For example, with something as time-consuming as doing your taxes, you may want to tackle it in logical pieces, rather than all at once. And finally, make sure that you plan ahead so that you can devote sufficient time to your project.

Eat your spinach

The foods you eat and drink can affect your memory. Eating lots of fruits and vegetables may help you remember more, as well as retain the memories you already have. In 2000, research presented at the Society for Neuroscience showed that rats who were fed a diet of spinach performed better on tests involving memory and learning than did rats who ate regular rat chow.

Although the results are preliminary, this study supports the theory that *antioxidants* (substances that destroy harmful oxidants which rust away your body), which are found in fruits and vegetables, may neutralize the free radical molecules (the byproducts of oxidation) that likely contribute to the cell damage and memory loss associated with aging.

Revving up recall

The most annoying memory problem may be forgetting a word or name in the middle of a conversation. You know that you'll remember it tomorrow or in a couple of minutes, but you can't get it out. You feel like kicking yourself. The more you try to remember it, the madder you get.

Stop, take a deep breath, and relax. It happens to us all. Stop trying to remember the word, and think about something else. Then, a little later, take some time to think about associations you may have with that name or word. Most likely, you'll remember it. Don't forget, depression disrupts memory.

Part III
Taking Action Against Depression: Behavior Therapy

The 5th Wave   By Rich Tennant

Mike's doctor said exercise can help alleviate depression. So I thought I'd surprise him with a Stairmaster exercise machine.

In this part . . .

Depression stops people in their tracks. Inactivity and a sense of inertia often go hand in hand with depression. This part explores behaviors that you can take in order to get moving again. Just taking a few initial steps can pose what seems like an insurmountable barrier. So we start this part off by showing you how to break through the obstacles to activity thrown up by your mind. Then we take Exercise Avenue, a great route for improving mood. Next, we encourage you to reconnect with pleasurable activities — whether you feel like doing so or not. Finally, we provide a step-by-step method for solving some of life's most vexing problems.

Chapter 9

Getting Out of Bed

● ●

In This Chapter

▶ Understanding motivation

▶ Monitoring your activity

▶ Curing "can't do-itis"

▶ Giving credit where credit's due

● ●

The clock chimes 1, 2, 3 . . . 10 a.m. Tears stream down **Paul's** face; he's still in bed. A new rush of shame floods over him. Another wasted weekend. He feels like a lazy failure. He lacks the motivation for even simple day-to-day tasks. The crushing sadness paralyzes him. He's a prisoner of depression, unable to escape. The pain deepens, with each day being worse than the one before. "When will it end? How can I end it?" he sobs.

Depression robs its victims of confidence, energy, motivation, and desire. If you're seriously depressed, you likely feel that you truly lack the ability to perform even the basic tasks of daily living.

In this chapter, we give you the tools for constructing a plan of action that works to get you moving again. First, we tell you how depression reduces motivation. Then we provide exercises and tools for overcoming inertia. At this moment, you may think that reading a few pages can't possibly help you deal with the overwhelming inertia you feel. But bear with us; what do you truly have to lose by reading what comes next?

If you've been virtually immobile for days and have thoughts of profound hopelessness or death, you need to consult a professional. And if making an appointment feels too difficult, ask a friend or family member to help you, or call a crisis line, such as 911 or 1-800-SUICIDE.

Taking Action

Doing the dishes, taking out the garbage, paying bills, and mowing the lawn — you probably don't look forward to these mundane chores, but when you're feeling pretty good, finding the necessary motivation isn't usually a major problem. Most days you just do what you need to do without giving it a second thought.

But when depression sets in, everyday living feels like walking in thick, gooey mud. A kitchen with a few dirty dishes may as well be a mess hall of an Army battalion, paying the monthly bills feels like doing three years of taxes, and taking out the garbage seems like scaling Mount Everest.

When you're battling depression, you're likely to neglect important duties. And that's perfectly understandable. However, putting off necessary chores can set off a cascade of additional negative thinking and guilt, which further saps motivation and deepens depression.

We call these thoughts *action-blocking thoughts,* and they include any negative thought concerning your inability to act or the futility of doing so. These thoughts stop you dead in your tracks, preventing you from getting started and making you feel even worse when you fail to act.

If you find yourself thinking action-blocking thoughts, take some time to subject these action blockers to scrutiny. If you carefully consider the distortions within these thoughts, you'll find that they're built on fundamentally flawed foundations. This type of examination can help you escape their tenacious grip and break the cycle of inactivity.

In the following sections, we shine some light on four common action-blocking thoughts one at a time to uncover their central flaws. Later in this chapter, we provide tools for overcoming inactivity.

I don't feel motivated to do anything

When you're feeling okay, you don't usually lack motivation — and on those occasions when you don't feel particularly motivated, sometimes the desire to get started just seems to come to you from out of the blue.

Motivation rarely shows up spontaneously in the midst of depression. You simply can't wait for motivation. *When you're depressed, actions almost always have to precede motivation.* Taking action actually creates motivation.

I'm too tired and depressed to do anything

This thought, like the previous one about motivation, essentially puts the cart before the horse. When you're fatigued, believing that rest will recharge your batteries is easy. Some people spend more and more time in bed, continuing to think that if they just get enough rest, they'll be ready to tackle jobs they put off for a long time.

But the imagined flow of vigor never comes, because excessive rest causes muscles to weaken and fatigue to deepen. Humans, unlike batteries, stay charged only by a healthy balance of activity and rest.

Activity (unless it's unusually excessive and prolonged) actually recharges the body with more drive and energy. The only cure for fatigue and inactivity is to work on revving up your engine — one small step at a time.

If I try, I'll just fail

Of course you'll fail! Everyone fails. We can't think of anyone we know that doesn't fail from time to time. So where's the flaw in this thought? No one, not a single person, fails at everything, every time. Depression invites negative predictions and failure is one of those predictions. But by starting small and breaking tasks into doable steps, you can minimize failure.

I'm just a lazy person

Assigning yourself the *lazy* label only makes getting started more difficult. The problem with labels is that they grossly overgeneralize and assign judgments about your character. When you're depressed, you truly feel tired and have far less enthusiasm for accomplishing necessary tasks.

Psychologists know that people don't fall into depression as a result of laziness. Out of the thousands of studies we've seen on depression, we can't think of a single one that implicated laziness as a cause. Getting started on tasks when you're feeling down is hard enough; don't add the burden of guilt and shame by sticking the *lazy* label on yourself.

Putting One Foot in Front of the Other: Activity Logs

Keeping an "Activity Log" is one of the best first steps you can take if you have severe depression and you're neglecting important responsibilities or chores. The technique is straightforward and fairly simple. (Check out Table 9-1 for a sample Activity Log.)

1. Get out your notebook and write down each day in a column on the left side of a page. (You can also use a day planner if you prefer.)

2. Schedule one neglected activity for each day — *make it a small activity at first!*

3. After you complete the activity, write down how it went and how you feel about accomplishing it.

Will simply tracking your activities increase motivation? Surprisingly, yes. We find that it focuses attention and typically helps get you moving.

Karlene's story gives you an example of how to keep an Activity Log. **Karlene** is sinking into depression slowly. For the past month, she's been spending most of her weekends in bed. Her mind fills with self-loathing. Although she makes it to work most days, the minute she gets home, she collapses. Her diet now consists of cold cereal and crackers because she doesn't have the energy to prepare anything or drive to the grocery store.

Karlene's best friend, Becky, notices her deteriorating mood and weight loss. Becky is worried about Karlene, so she stops by for a visit. She asks Karlene what she's been eating, because she sees that the refrigerator is almost bare. Karlene tells her, "Mostly just dry cereal." "So, what will you do when you run out of cereal?" Becky inquires. Karlene shrugs her shoulders and replies, "I guess I'll just stop eating. I don't really care."

Her friend suggests that Karlene start an Activity Log and briefly explains how to do it. Becky says, "I'm going to check back with you in a couple of days. I want to see food in the refrigerator. If you don't start moving a little and feeling better pretty soon, I'm taking you to your doctor."

Karlene reluctantly agrees, because she knows that Becky means business. At first, Karlene thinks that she can't muster the motivation to start an Activity Log. She also thinks that she's too lazy, and that if she tries, she'll probably fail. However, Karlene trusts Becky so she figures that she has little to lose by trying the exercise. Table 9-1 shows Karlene's Activity Log for the first week. Notice that the Activity Log in Table 9-1 doesn't feature huge projects.

Table 9-1		Activity Log
Day	*Activity*	*Outcome*
M	Go to a fast-food place and pick up something from the drive-through window.	Well, I did it. I didn't feel like eating, but I spoiled myself with a chocolate malt. That tasted pretty good.

Day	Activity	Outcome
T	Stop at the convenience store and pick up a couple of things for dinner, and some cereal just in case I don't feel like cooking.	This was a lot harder. I didn't want to get out of the car, but at least the line was short. When I got home, I didn't cook the food; I just ate cereal.
W	Go to the bank. I've been putting that off for a couple of weeks.	That felt surprisingly good to get off my agenda. I even decided to microwave what I picked up yesterday. It wasn't too bad.
Th	Go to the post office and get stamps so I can pay my bills.	This wasn't as hard as I thought it would be. I had to force myself to do it, but I guess that's okay.
F	Pay my bills.	I was just too tired; I couldn't get myself to do it. Maybe tomorrow.
Sa	Pay my bills. Shop for food at the grocery store.	I actually paid my bills on time this month! What a relief. I really get down on myself for accumulating late fees because of my procrastination. I felt so good. I actually went to the grocery store and shopped.
Su	Call my friend Becky with a report.	I have to admit I felt pretty good telling her I did a few things. I have a long way to go, but it's a start.

When you develop your Activity Log, select small, manageable goals. None of them should take more than 20 to 30 minutes at first. After you get started, you can consider taking on slightly larger tasks.

Karlene didn't do everything she set out to do each day. And don't worry if you don't complete everything. Celebrate your successes and forgive your failures. If you don't complete an item, consider putting it on the list for the next day. If you don't get to it the next day, the item may be more than you can handle right now. Try to hold that activity off for another week or so.

If you find yourself unable to get started on your Activity Log or don't feel a little better after using the log for a couple of weeks, consult a professional for assistance.

Conquering Can'ts

The human mind produces an almost constant stream of thoughts about the individual, other people, and the future. Whether you're depressed or not, many of these thoughts have about as much to do with reality as the idea that you're about to sprout wings and fly. In the following section, we review specific "can't" thoughts and ways to defeat them. Throughout this book, and especially in Chapters 5, 6, and 7, you can find more information about the myriad of other ways that thoughts warp everyone's vision from time to time and what you can do to change them.

Depression substantially magnifies the negativity of the mind's chatter. One of the most common thoughts we hear from our clients when discussing the idea of taking action is, "Well, I would, but I just can't." If you've ever had that thought, you most likely truly believe that you're incapable — whether due to basic inadequacy, incompetence, or depression itself — and the contemplated action lies beyond your ability.

Reviewing your thoughts

When you routinely tell yourself that you're incapable of accomplishing given tasks, we call this type of thinking "can't do-itis." Although this diagnosis may sound a bit whimsical, we assure you that its effects aren't. Through repetition alone, "can't do-itis" can become a mantra that you eventually view as a fundamental truth. Review the following common thoughts:

- I can't think clearly.
- I can't possibly clean out the garage; it's just too overwhelming.
- I can't concentrate on anything.
- I can't motivate myself to do anything.
- I can't even function anymore.

Do these thoughts sound familiar? They do to us! On some days, thoughts like these bellow through our minds. For example, although this is the fifth book we've written, some days we think, "We just can't write today!" Although we *choose* not to write on certain days, it simply isn't true that we absolutely *can't* sit down and write a little when that thought pops into our heads.

So when "can't thoughts" appear out of nowhere on our scheduled writing days, we usually try using a strategy for conquering them. Specifically, we put the "can't thoughts" to the test. We sit down at the computer for 30 minutes and see if we can write something — anything at all. Even a single sentence typed on the computer can disprove the we-can't-write-today thought. A sentence or two usually leads us to feeling like writing more. On rare occasions, the desire to write more doesn't increase, and we make a decision to take the day off. Nothing wrong with that: By writing just a sentence or two, we still refute the "can't thoughts."

Perhaps you're thinking that putting "can't thoughts" to the test may work for productive authors, but it won't work for you when you're terribly depressed. If so, you may want to know that the vast majority of our depressed patients also think that the strategy won't help. Nevertheless, when they try it, they almost always discover that testing out these "can't thoughts" helps.

Testing the waters

Try putting your "can't thoughts" to the test. You can prove each of these thoughts to be false with a single piece of disconfirming evidence. And after you find one contradiction, you can work on accumulating more. Here are some ideas you can use to test a few of the "can't thoughts" we list in the "Reviewing your thoughts" section, earlier in this chapter.

✔ **I can't even function anymore.** Breathing is practically all you have to do to refute this idea! You can test the idea by getting out of bed, pouring yourself a glass of water, and just picking up and actually doing a couple of small activities. If your "can't thoughts" start to interfere, ignore the thoughts by focusing only on moving your body to perform the task. Make a daily habit of refuting this kind of thinking: Construct an Activity Log that lists a new task each day (see the "Putting One Foot in Front of the Other: Activity Logs" section, earlier in this chapter).

✔ **I can't remember anything nowadays.** We have our colleague, Dr. Steve Hayes, to thank for this idea. Try remembering this number sequence — 1, 2, 3. Now pretend that we offer you one million dollars (don't forget that we said "pretend!") if you can remember "1, 2, 3." That's right, we're going to give you a million dollars if you can remember "1, 2, 3."

We're willing to bet that if a million dollars were on the line, you'd remember that sequence a few minutes from now. (If not, we suggest that you see your doctor, because something other than depression may be going on.) If you can pass this test, you can probably find many more examples of things you can remember. If you can remember something — anything — you can refute your "can't thought." At the same time, please realize that depression does cause some difficulty with memory. If you want more help with your memory, please see Chapter 8.

✔ **I can't possibly clean out the garage; it's just too overwhelming.** Clean out one very small item or space in your garage. After you accomplish that, consider cleaning another small area the next day. Perhaps in a few more days you can tackle two or three small spaces. Believe it or not, that's how insurmountable projects get done — a single piece at a time.

When you're depressed, your mind tricks you into focusing on the entire project that confronts you — as though you must accomplish it all at once. For example, if you picture all the miles you're going to walk in the coming year, and you believe that you must walk the entire distance today, you probably won't even feel like starting.

Break tasks down into very small, achievable chunks. You can conquer "can't do-itis" by choosing a small piece of what you think you can't do and then going ahead and doing it.

Charting Your Course through Negative Predictions

The mind maintains inaction in another clever way — by providing petrifying predictions for you to ponder. When depression sets in, these negative predictions usually seem more believable and monumental than ever. You may feel as though your horoscope consistently says, "Today is a horrible day for trying new things. Retreat, withdraw, and maintain a passive stance. Wait to take on any action." But the message never wavers; every day delivers the same forecast.

If you're hearing similar dire predictions from your mind's fortune-teller, perhaps the time has come to test out whether you should continue to pay for this "splendid" advice.

If you stall when it comes to tackling important tasks, try using our "Negating Negative Predictions" technique. Start off using it for one week. You just may find that it helps you get moving. We're not saying that this strategy will cure your depression, but it can help get the improvement process rolling. Follow these steps and check out the sample chart in Table 9-2.

1. **For each day of the week, write down one or two tasks you've been avoiding.**

Try to think of relatively small, doable projects. If you choose something larger, break it down into small pieces and then tackle one piece at a time.

2. Make a stress prediction for each task.

Predict (on a 0 to 100 point scale) how much stress the task is going to cause you. For example, do you envision that paying the bills is going to feel ponderously difficult? If so, you may want to predict the stress factor as 70 or above.

3. Make a "boost" prediction for each task.

Rate (on a 0 to 100 point scale) how much of a boost in satisfaction, confidence, and mood you predict you're going to feel by completing the task. For example, if you think that paying bills is going to give you a mild to modest boost in feelings of satisfaction, mood, or confidence, you may want to rate the expected boost as 25 or so.

4. Record the outcome (or your actual experience) on your chart for both the stress and "boost" categories.

After you complete the chore, write down how much stress and aggravation you *actually experienced* from doing the project, plus how much of a boost in satisfaction, confidence, and mood you actually felt.

Anise, a college professor, has been depressed for the past month. She starts arriving to work late and collapsing the moment she gets home. She drags herself to bed after watching mindless television all night. Important tasks, such as preparing lectures, grading exams, paying bills, and shopping for groceries start piling up. Anise decides to try the Negating Negative Predictions Technique. Table 9-2 shows you her chart.

Table 9-2	Negating Negative Predictions Chart			
Day	*Task*	*Predicted Stress*	*Experienced Stress*	*Predicted Boost*	*Experienced Boost*
M	Grocery shopping	50	25	10	20
T	Grade one exam	70	20	10	30
W	Do the dishes	45	10	5	20
Th	Finally call Thomas to talk	50	5	20	60
F	Pay bills	75	30	25	70

(continued)

Table 9-2 *(continued)*					
Day	*Task*	*Predicted Stress*	*Experienced Stress*	*Predicted Boost*	*Experienced Boost*
Sa	Mow lawn	50	50	15	50
Su	Plant flowers	40	10	25	60

As you can see in Table 9-2, Anise consistently predicted that activities would involve more stress and hassle than she actually experienced. The stress was as great as she anticipated in only one case — and that was because her lawnmower kept stalling. Although not every task gave her a huge boost in satisfaction, confidence, and mood, the boost that she actually experienced was always far greater than she imagined it would be. After one week, Anise still felt depressed, but she at least felt a little lift from the exercise. And that lift made it easier to take on new tasks.

If you're like most folks with depression, you'll likely experience results similar to Anise's. You'll predict activities to be more stressful and less rewarding than you actually find them to be. Try this simple strategy for a couple of weeks.

We didn't include any items that involve especially pleasurable, fun activities in the preceding exercise. Did we exclude these items because we think that you shouldn't or can't enjoy yourself if you're depressed? No. We excluded these items because we think that finding renewed pleasures is so important, that we devote all of Chapter 11 to the topic.

Giving Yourself Credit

Depressed minds can pull another cruel trick that can easily stop you dead in your tracks. What's the trick? Glad you asked. Consider this scenario:

You eventually manage to get yourself to accomplish something you put off for quite a while. Then your mind trashes the success with the thought, "Well, sure I did that, but so what? Any moron could have done that!" As this thought demonstrates, depression not only spoils quality of life but it also disrupts efforts you make on your own behalf to venture forward.

When you hear thoughts from your mind telling you to discredit your accomplishments, consider an alternative perspective. If you went grocery shopping in a normal mood, perhaps you wouldn't think too much of your achievement. But if you went grocery shopping with a broken leg, wouldn't you value the deed more highly?

Okay, you don't have a broken leg. But the effect of depression is rather similar. Depression makes everything harder to do than when you're in a good frame of mind. As we discuss in Chapter 2, depression depletes the body of energy; it saps enthusiasm, steals sleep, and creates mental confusion.

Given the wide array of physical and mental maladies that depression inflicts, accomplishing any task in this condition is a remarkable feat. Therefore, don't forget to give yourself a substantially greater amount of credit for getting things done when you're depressed. You give yourself credit by congratulating yourself for each effort you carry out.

Chapter 10

Working Out to Lift Depression

At 4 a.m., **Patricia** wakes up and can't get back to sleep. She knows that a lack of sleep affects her performance at work, which makes her even more upset, which makes getting back to sleep even more difficult. This early awakening has got to stop. Yesterday, her boss even commented that she looked tired. Patricia tosses and turns for the next two hours and then finally gets up at 6 a.m. What a miserable start to the day.

Depression runs throughout Patricia's family. She has been treated with medication off and on for about five years. Her physician tells her that she will likely need to take antidepressant medication for the rest of her life. But lately, medication alone just doesn't seem to work. Her depression intensifies. First, her doctor increases the dose; when that doesn't work, he suggests adding another drug to improve her response to the medication. Patricia, worried about both short- and long-term side effects, asks her doctor about other alternatives to consider instead of the additional medication. He suggests regular exercise. (And we agree!)

In this chapter, we tell you how jumping jacks, jogging, and gymnastics soar above anything else you can do to improve the quality of your life and health. Exercise exorcises depression. When depression tells you that you can't get going, we explain how to talk back to your depression and establish a plan for overcoming inertia. And we help you choose the type of exercise that's just right for you.

But as much as we advocate exercise, it represents just one piece of the puzzle. If you try and try, and you just can't get into exercise, don't beat yourself up. This book is filled with ways to defeat depression.

Introducing Endorphins into Your Life

Who doesn't want to feel good? All kinds of ways to feel good exist: laughter, a great meal, sex, or a walk on the beach are a just a few examples. But what about these activities actually make people feel good?

The answer lies, in part, in the brain. The brain has special receptacles that receive *opiates,* drugs such as heroin and cocaine that relieve pain and induce a heightened sense of well-being. The human body produces natural substances, called *endorphins,* that function like opiates in the brain. They produce the same sort of "high" that heroin and cocaine do. Except endorphins are legal. You can generate endorphins through exercise and pleasurable activities. Endorphins induce a feeling of pleasure and well-being that may counteract depression.

You can increase endorphins by having sex, eating chocolate, consuming spicy foods, and, you guessed it, engaging in exercise. You can try to increase your endorphin level by sitting around eating chocolate all day or having nonstop sex, but obvious factors make these approaches a bit difficult or unadvisable. So you're left with exercise.

Regular exercise not only stimulates endorphin production but it also tunes up your entire body. Exercise improves your cardiovascular system, reduces the risk of various cancers, decreases the risk of diabetes, and balances your cholesterol ratio. Furthermore, working out rids your body of excessive adrenaline that can cause anxiety and other problems. Flat out, exercise makes you healthier.

Endorphins: A miracle cure?

Science is very sure that endorphins reduce pain. Stories abound about soldiers who, after being injured in battle, manage to carry on heroically for hours, seemingly oblivious to the pain from wounds that would normally be incapacitating. Endorphins, released by the body in response to the demands of the battlefield, temporarily stop pain signals from getting through to the brain.

In addition, many have speculated that endorphins play a role in enhancing the immune system by activating natural killer cells that attack diseases. Endorphins may improve circulation and even keep brain cells young and healthy by neutralizing toxic substances. The endorphin system may provide a buffer against stress. And some have suggested that the body fails to produce sufficient endorphin levels during depression. In time, science is bound to clarify how and to what extent endorphins influence our body in beneficial ways. But we can be sure that endorphins at least provide a temporary boost in mood and well-being.

A growing body of research suggests that exercise alleviates depression. Of the various types of exercise, it isn't yet clear whether one form may be best at decreasing depression (or if they all work equally well). Although we don't recommend exercise as your sole answer to major depression, you will benefit enormously from regular workouts.

Always check with your doctor before beginning an exercise program — especially if you're overweight, over the age of 40, or have health problems. You also need to see your doctor if you experience serious pain, dizziness, nausea, or other troubling symptoms after exercising, because these symptoms don't normally occur after moderate exercise.

Conquering Couch Potato-itis

Exercise can help you feel better emotionally and physically, but there's just one problem: Depression tells you to withdraw, retreat, and hibernate. When you're depressed, paralysis can set in. Simple, everyday living takes extraordinary effort, and you may feel like staying in bed with the cover over your head.

Thus, the mere thought of starting to exercise may sound utterly impossible to you in the midst of depression. You can hardly put one foot in front of the other; how can we possibly suggest that you start working out? The depressed mind spins out thoughts that stifle initiative and motivation. These thoughts may be telling you that you can't possibly succeed in implementing an exercise regimen. We know you may feel this way. Please understand that we don't underestimate the difficulty of overcoming the inertia of depression. Nevertheless, we believe you'll find that the benefits of exercise outweigh the costs.

You *can* talk back to these dark thoughts that stifle activity. You don't have to allow them to take over your will. You can start by subjecting them to scrutiny and analysis. Ask yourself if there's an alternative perspective to your depressed mind's view. Is your mind exaggerating, distorting, or making negative predictions without any real basis? If so, try to replace the negativity with realistic alternatives. You need to short circuit any negative thoughts that come into your mind and start moving your body.

In the first column of Table 10-1, we list the five thoughts that most frequently get in the way of reasonable, alternative viewpoints and prevent you from getting going. If you find yourself thinking any of these de-motivating thoughts, argue back with motivating thoughts like the ones in the second column. (See Chapter 9 for other ideas on how to overcome action-blocking thoughts.)

Table 10-1	Defeating De-motivating Thoughts
De-motivating Thoughts	**Motivating Thoughts**
I'm too depressed to exercise.	Yes, that's how I "feel," but it doesn't mean that it's true. I can test this thought out by walking for ten minutes.
I can hardly get out of bed; I can't possibly exercise.	Another interesting thought. But I do get out of bed every day. And, if I can get out of bed, I can push myself to do a small amount of exercise.
Exercise isn't worth doing.	That's how it feels, but the evidence says otherwise. Exercise helps people feel better.
I don't like to exercise.	True. But I don't have to turn into a fitness buff. I can profit from even a small amount of exercise.
I don't have time to exercise.	I take time to brush my teeth every day. If something is really important, I can find a way to work it in a few days a week.

After you identify your de-motivating thoughts and dispute them, you may still feel unmotivated. And a few de-motivating thoughts will likely linger. Realize that thoughts are just thoughts — they're not necessarily true.

To show how thoughts aren't gospel, we have a brief exercise for you. (If you have a physical problem that prevents you from comfortably getting out of a chair, construct a similar scenario that affirms your ability to conquer de-motivating thoughts.)

1. **Sit down in a comfortable chair.**

2. **Say out loud, "I can't stand up!"**

3. **Forcefully say out loud, "I can't stand up!" ten more times.**

4. **Now stand up.**

Did you manage to stand up? Your mind said you couldn't stand up, but you did (or at least, we assume you did). The point of this admittedly silly exercise is to demonstrate that the negative thoughts people listen to aren't always inherently true.

People often think things that aren't true, and then act as though they are. For example, we bet that you've heard more than a few people say, "I can't stop smoking." Indeed, stopping smoking is incredibly difficult; at times, it may seem impossible. Yet *millions* of people who make that pronouncement eventually manage to quit. Of course, when smokers have the thought that they can't stop, they truly believe it. And when you're depressed, you fully believe the thought that says you just can't exercise.

Thoughts are just thoughts — many thoughts generated by a depressed mind have no more reality than "I can't stand up," or "I can't stop smoking."

Easing into Exercise

With any luck, you can convince yourself that you can start exercising. But that doesn't mean exercising will be easy. Depression truly saps your body of energy, so we suggest that you start your exercise program gently and ever so slowly.

Most exercise gurus preach the importance of exercising for at least 20 minutes, three to five times per week. You may have read recent guidelines recommending that exercise last for an hour or so each time. We don't know about you, but we certainly don't have an extra hour a day. Research shows that almost any exercise is far better than none, so even 10 minutes, three or four times a week, can help. And you can ease your way into the world of exercise with activities that barely seem like exercise at all:

- ✔ Park a little farther from your workplace.
- ✔ Take the stairs rather than the elevator.
- ✔ Do a few brief exercises during work breaks.
- ✔ If you use a cordless phone, walk while you talk.
- ✔ The next time you shop, walk a couple of laps around the mall.

Walking a little farther, taking the stairs, and moving around more make a good start for your exercise program. Then, if you want, you can add a little more motion to your daily routine. To obtain the maximum benefit from exercise, work your body a little harder each day.

The following list shows you three decisions you have to make when designing your exercise program. For each, start small and build up slowly. And remember that you're not competing with anyone, so don't compare yourself to others at the gym or on the track.

- ✔ **Frequency:** "How often am I going to work exercise into my life?" For starters, consider committing to twice a week.
- ✔ **Intensity:** "How fast am I going to walk or run? How heavy are the weights I'm going to use?" For starters, we suggest not very fast and not very heavy!
- ✔ **Time:** "How long do I want to exercise each time?" Again, try starting with ten minutes.

Vacuuming away depression?

Research has shown that exercise can help alleviate depression, but how about aerobic housework? Your spouse or roommate may urge you to increase your exercise by washing the dishes, sweeping floors, or dusting the furniture. Of course, their motives may not be all that altruistic — especially if it's their turn to tackle one of these chores.

But does housework alleviate depression the same way that exercise does? Apparently not. According to researchers at the University of Glasgow, domestic chores, unlike almost any other type of exercise, actually lowers mood. And the more housework you do, the lower your mood drops. So if you're depressed, start exercising, but it's okay to let the housework go for a little while until your mood improves.

On the other hand, we're not suggesting you totally let the house go. Doing a little housework may even provide you with a sense of accomplishment. But if you do get a small lift from doing housework, the lift comes from a sense of accomplishment, not the aerobic benefits.

But what type of exercise is going to work best for you? We can honestly say that we have no idea. And you may not know either. So, in the following section, we briefly discuss a few types of exercise that you can consider. If you want even more info on all the possibilities that are out there, check out a local health club or pick up a copy of *Fitness For Dummies,* by Suzanne Schlosberg and Liz Neporent (Wiley Publishing, Inc.).

Weighing Your Exercise Options

We recommend that you review the various exercise options and pick one that holds the most initial appeal to you — or at least the one that looks the least awful.

No matter what type of exercise you settle on, try it out for a couple of weeks. If you don't find yourself starting to like the exercise you chose, try another type of exercise. You may have to experiment a little, but you'll likely find an exercise that works well for you. In this section, we review strength training, aerobic exercise, and yoga — three of the most popular exercise options.

The goal isn't to become an accomplished triathlete; you only need to increase the intensity of your exercise slightly to start deriving benefits.

Pumping iron

Strength training involves building muscle. You can accomplish this build up through weightlifting with barbells, weight machines, or dumbbells. However, you don't actually need to use machines or weights at all. You can try the following strength-enhancing exercises that don't require any special equipment:

- Chin-ups
- Crunches
- Lunges
- Push-ups
- Squats

You may think that strength training is only for body builders or the younger set. Not so. Numerous studies have demonstrated that strength training provides incredible benefits at almost any age, perhaps even more so in older populations. Strength training appears to improve mood, reduce the risk of falls, enhance memory and thinking ability, and prolong life.

We had our son-in-law, a personal trainer, show us what strength training is all about. After the first week, we weren't so sure about our decision to work out. We discovered aching muscles that we didn't even know we had. But by the end of a month, we picked up a new, healthy habit.

Strength training can easily lead to injury if you aren't careful and don't know what you're doing. We recommend that you first either consult a trainer at a gym or pick up a book on the subject, such as *Weight Training For Dummies*, by Liz Neporent and Suzanne Schlosberg (Wiley Publishing, Inc.).

Revving up your heart and lungs

Aerobic exercise (or *cardiovascular exercise*) is one of the easiest exercise programs to start. This type of exercise increases your oxygen intake and speeds up your heart rate. (*Aerobic* means "with oxygen.")

Aerobic exercise has a positive effect on your body. In addition to improving your mood, it:

- Reduces bad cholesterol and raises good cholesterol
- Increases energy
- Reduces blood pressure
- Improves lung capacity
- Reduces anxiety
- Reduces the risk of breast and colon cancer
- Reduces the risk of diabetes

Walking is the most basic form of aerobic exercise. To participate in aerobic exercise, all you have to do is increase the pace of your walking so that your heart rate increases. Of course, you can also perform other aerobic activities, such as jogging, skating, bicycling, and — hold onto your hat — aerobics. Basically, an activity qualifies as aerobic if it revs you up to the point where you feel a little winded, but you can still say a short sentence without gasping for air.

Health care professionals often recommend that you establish a *target heart rate* for your aerobic exercise. You can determine your target heart rate zone by first subtracting your age from 220. That number represents your absolute maximum heart rate, a rate you want to avoid exceeding. Your ideal zone lies between 0.5 and 0.8 of your maximum heart rate, depending on your fitness level. Your physician can help you determine your fitness level and thus your ideal zone.

Yikes! Yoga?

When you think of yoga, you may conjure up images of bodies twisted up like pretzels. Or maybe you visualize rows of robed monks seated cross-legged on mats, chanting "Ommmm. . . ."

But today, you're more likely to find practitioners of yoga dressed in the latest gym attire, straining and sweating at a local health club. And although some people with highly advanced yoga skills may twist their bodies like pretzels, most yoga exercises don't require such awesome flexibility. We started practicing yoga some time ago, and we can guarantee you that we're not that limber.

You can take yoga classes at your local health club or YMCA. You can also learn yoga by reading a book, such as *Yoga For Dummies,* by Georg Feuerstein, PhD, and Larry Payne, PhD (Wiley Publishing, Inc.), or following along with a videotape, such as *Basic Yoga Workout For Dummies* with Sara Ivanhoe. As with many exercise routines, you won't know how you feel about yoga unless you try it.

Chapter 11

Rediscovering Healthy Pleasures

In This Chapter

▶ Feeling good all over

▶ Figuring out what's fun

▶ Giving pleasure busters the heave-ho

*W*hen you're depressed, nothing sounds appealing. Food doesn't taste as good, music doesn't soothe you, and comedy doesn't strike you as funny. Even the activities you used to enjoy seem flat, dull, and uninteresting. So, what can you do to bring back pleasure into your life?

In this chapter, we tell you about the surprising effects of pleasure on both your mood and body. Next, we help you rediscover a few of your favorite pleasures or find some new ones. We explain why pleasure is something you deserve, even if you don't think so. And you may not believe that you're capable of having fun, but we show you how to defeat your negative predictions.

Taking Fun Seriously

When depression sets in, you can hardly get through the demands of the day. You may not even feel like getting out of bed. Having fun feels both inconceivable and frivolous.

Nevertheless, we propose that you take a serious look at pleasure. Why? First, because pleasure lifts mood. The boost may be temporary and slight in the beginning. But with time and persistence, pleasurable activities can help defeat depression.

In addition to its positive effects on your emotional and mental state of affairs, pleasure may provide physical benefits, such as

✔ Alleviation of chronic pain

✔ Decreased risk of heart attacks

✔ Improved overall health

✔ Increased immune function

✔ Prolonged life expectancy

Pleasure also combats everyday stress. People who pursue enjoyable activities typically feel happier, more relaxed, and calmer. When you take all these factors into account, the pursuit of pleasure isn't a frivolous endeavor.

Making a List and Checking It Twice

When you're depressed, you may not even be able to remember what pleasure feels like. And generating a list of possible pleasurable activities may seem unimaginably difficult. Don't worry — we're here to help you get started.

If you're depressed, review the pleasurable activity lists in this section. Obviously, not all of these activities will appeal to you. However, we suggest that you circle each of the items that you either currently *or have ever* found enjoyable. Then think about which ones seem doable. For example, if you currently live alone, and you don't have a willing sex partner, having sex may not be a reasonable choice for you at this time. Try to start bringing as many of the doable items into your life as possible.

The following list contains the results of an international survey of what people find enjoyable. The Associates for Research into the Science of Enjoyment (www.arise.org) surveyed adults in a number of countries. They found that simple pleasures provide the most enjoyment. These activities include

✔ Drinking a glass of wine

✔ Drinking tea or coffee

✔ Eating chocolate

✔ Entertaining friends

✔ Exercising

✔ Going out for a meal

✔ Having sex

- Playing with children
- Reading
- Shopping
- Spending time with family
- Taking a hot bath or shower
- Watching television

If you've ever been to a French bakery, it probably won't surprise you to discover that the French have a particular fondness for indulging in pastries. Italians rank sex high on their pleasures list. The British apparently enjoy drinking tea as well as alcohol.

Perhaps the previous list doesn't capture your interests. If so, realize that you have many other sources of enjoyment to consider. Many of these other pleasures involve the senses, such as

- Eating spicy foods
- Getting a massage
- Listening to music
- Looking at beauty in nature or art
- Sitting by a lake or ocean
- Smelling fresh flowers
- Spending time in a sauna

You can seek pleasure through entertaining activities as well, such as

- Camping
- Dancing
- Hiking
- Hobbies
- Live plays, concerts, or comedy
- Movies
- Participating in sports
- Playing games
- Playing with pets
- Spectator sports
- Travel and vacations

Pain or pleasure? Some like it hot

In our great state of New Mexico, we consider pain a flavor! The pain comes from the hot chili sauce that chefs pour over just about everything. The hotter the better. A common question asked at a New Mexican restaurant is, "Red or green?" which refers to the color of the pepper used to make the sauce. The sophisticated diner often replies, "Which one is hotter?"

Newcomers and visitors don't understand this ritual. In fact, many plates remain almost untouched after the first bite or two. These visitors frantically search for something to quell the pain (which can be accomplished with sour cream or honey). They sit bewildered, watching other, more experienced chili enthusiasts wolf down huge quantities of fiery foods. But if they're willing to try the food again, many of these neophytes soon find themselves craving chilies as much as the natives do.

Science has discovered a cause for the strange eating habits of New Mexicans and others who crave hot, spicy foods. Chilies are actually addictive. Here's why: When you bite into something peppery, *capsaicin* (the portion of the chili that makes it hot) is released into your mouth. When capsaicin contacts the nerves in your mouth, pain signals rush to your brain. The brain responds by releasing a flood of *endorphins* (see Chapter 10 for more information about endorphins), which kill pain and induce a state of well-being and pleasure. The brain also releases endorphins when you engage in any of a variety of highly pleasurable activities, such as the ones we detail in this chapter.

Fighting the Pleasure Busters

When you're wrestling with depression, reincorporating pleasurable activities into your life isn't always as easy as it sounds. In fact, you may have the following negative reactions when trying to incorporate pleasurable activities back into your life.

- **Guilt tripping.** Guilt tripping occurs when you believe that pleasure is wasteful, frivolous, undeserved, inappropriate, unproductive, or even downright sinful. We explain more about guilt tripping in the next section.

- **Negative predicting.** Depression increases the likelihood that future events will be seen as bleak and joyless. See more about negative predictions in the "Expecting the worst" section later in the chapter.

You aren't going to get very far in your attempt to bring pleasure back into your life if either guilt or negative predicting are blocking the doorway to happiness. Therefore, we address each of these killjoys separately.

Guilt busters

Guilt can be a good thing. When you do something truly wrong, guilt tells you not to do it again. And knowing that you may feel guilty can prevent you from acting in ways that are either unhealthy or morally wrong. Guilt gives you a moral compass *when it's working right*.

When you wave a magnet around a compass, the needle spins every which way. In the same manner, too much guilt causes the needle on your moral compass to point you in the wrong direction. Out-of-control guilt grossly exaggerates the significance of any real or imagined transgressions. For example, excessive guilt may tell you that a single bar of chocolate represents uncontrolled gluttony. Furthermore, guilt may make you feel undeserving of any pleasure.

Excessive guilt is a prime feature of depression. So you get to feel down and blue, and guilty to boot. Guilt and depression make the pursuit of happiness excruciatingly difficult, because depression drains you of energy for pursuing pleasure, and guilt tells you that you don't deserve to feel good in the first place.

Increasing your awareness

Increasing your awareness of how guilt may influence your decision to undertake healthy pleasures is critical. We find that when guilt gets in the way of taking on the task of searching for enjoyment, certain thoughts may repeatedly run through your mind. See if any of these thoughts sound familiar:

✔ I'm not good enough; I don't deserve to be happy.

✔ I feel like pleasure is a frivolous waste of time.

✔ If I beat up on myself enough, I just may get motivated to do something more productive.

✔ I *should* have done things differently (there are about a million or so variants of this thought).

✔ I'm just a loser; pleasure is for winners.

Thoughts such as these induce powerful feelings of guilt. But how can you tell if your guilt indicates an appropriate, healthy response based on a well-functioning moral compass, or an out-of-control response, misdirecting you toward self-abuse and self-defeating thoughts and actions? Actually, identifying the type of guilt you're experiencing isn't that difficult.

Guilt is appropriate and reasonable only when it occurs following intentional, unnecessary acts that cause harm to you or someone else. And appropriate guilt has a time limit; it doesn't go on and on, because prolonging the bad feelings merely harms you by intensifying your depression. Holding on to guilt simply leads to unproductive rumination and self-abuse.

Breaking guilt's pleasure-denying power

Ask yourself if your pleasurable indulgences truly reflect conscious, maliciously motivated behaviors. If they do, perhaps a little short-term guilt will remind you to put on the "breaks" in the future. But before you reach that conclusion, be sure to ask yourself these "Guilt-Quelling Questions:"

- ✔ Was my indulgence primarily intended to harm myself?
- ✔ Is it possible that a little enjoyment can be a good thing rather than a bad thing?
- ✔ Is it possible that I'm magnifying the "awfulness" of my indulgences?
- ✔ Am I excessively blaming myself for something that actually has many causes?
- ✔ Am I berating myself merely for having human imperfections?
- ✔ Where is it written that I *should* have done something different?

Here's an example of how you can put these questions to use. **Connie** works as a nurse practitioner at a busy hospital clinic. The stress of working long hours (which are filled with handling the urgent needs of patients) piles up on her. The shortage of health care workers in her community pushes her to accept extra work shifts on a regular basis. She has little time for friends or fun. Her fatigue and loneliness gradually meld into depression.

A few coworkers notice Connie's deteriorating mood. They tell Connie that she needs to do something for herself once in a while. Their suggestions include

- ✔ Eating chocolate
- ✔ Drinking wine
- ✔ Getting a massage
- ✔ Going to a comedy show

As Connie contemplates her possible pleasures, negative thoughts churn in her mind. She thinks, "Great, I'm already ten pounds overweight, just think of how fat I'll get eating chocolate and drinking wine all day. And I'd feel horribly guilty spending my hard earned money on something so self-indulgent as a massage. Massages are for the rich. So that leaves going to a comedy. In my mood? Not a chance I'd like that."

Connie feels guilt *in advance* of indulging in a few simple pleasures such as eating a couple of chocolates, drinking an occasional glass of wine, or getting a massage. After she answers the Guilt-Quelling Questions we list earlier in this section, her feelings may change:

- ✔ **Was my indulgence primarily intended to harm myself?** Connie's response: "Well, actually I haven't even done it yet. But my intent is to enjoy something, not to harm myself."

- ✔ **Is it possible that a little enjoyment can be a good thing rather than bad?** Connie's response: "I guess I rarely give myself latitude to indulge in much of anything. What's so horrible about a little pleasure? I'm starting to sound like my mother! I've read that pleasure actually is good for the body and mind."

- ✔ **Is it possible that I'm magnifying the "awfulness" of my indulgences?** Connie's response: "I suppose an occasional chocolate, glass of wine, or massage doesn't exactly equate with being a mass murderer. Ben Franklin had a point when he advocated the benefits of taking all things in moderation."

- ✔ **Am I excessively blaming myself for something that actually has many causes?** Connie's response: "Well, in the case of my weight, I realize it's caused by so many things — genetics (most of my relatives are over-weight), too little exercise, food dropped off by the pharmaceutical sales reps almost every day, processed foods, too much fast food, and on and on. A few carefully selected candies or a glass of wine has relatively little to do with the problem."

- ✔ **Am I berating myself merely for having human imperfections?** Connie's response: "Hey, at least I'm good at beating up on myself! I guess if I think about it, everyone has their flaws. Ten pounds of extra weight isn't exactly the worst thing I could imagine."

- ✔ **Where is it written that I *should* have done something different?** Connie's response: "I use that word *should* on myself a lot. Maybe I *should*, oops, I mean maybe it *would be better if* I rethought that word. Although diet books don't exactly promote eating chocolate and drinking wine, most of them advise modest indulgences and recommend that almost no foods should fall under an 'absolutely never' category."

We hope that you can seriously review these Guilt-Quelling Questions and come to Connie's conclusions about healthy pleasures. We believe that you deserve a reasonable balance of pleasure in your life. You don't need to earn the right to pursue happiness — indulging in a few joys can be a powerful tool in fighting depression if you give yourself the right to do so.

Guilt: The world tour

The Associates for Research into the Science of Enjoyment conducted an international survey to look at the relationship between guilt and enjoyment. They found that guilt destroys the experience of enjoyment. Apparently, the Dutch like to have fun, and they don't feel guilty when they indulge in pleasurable activities. On the other hand, Germans feel more guilty about having fun than other Europeans, and thus they land at the bottom of the pile in terms of their overall enjoyment.

Although the researchers didn't conduct a survey on enjoyment and guilt in the United States, had they done so, we surmise that they would have discovered high levels of guilt and relatively low levels of enjoyment. We believe that the so-called work ethic that is so heavily promoted in the United States may lead to these feelings of guilt. For example, most American companies dole out vacation time with all the generosity of Ebenezer Scrooge. We also believe that guilt thrives in the United States because of the constant stream of contradictory, yet sensational headlines that admonish the citizenry to stop drinking as well as to drink moderately, to eat low fat diets as well as eat high fat diets, or to eat carbohydrates as well as avoid carbohydrates. You may get the impression that, no matter what you do, it's the wrong thing.

If you answer the Guilt-Quelling Questions we list earlier in this section, and guilt still blocks you from seeking enjoyment, please read Chapters 3, 5, 6, and 7 for more information about tackling the guilt that rides along with your depression and robs you of a basic human right — the right to experience pleasure.

Expecting the worst

You select a variety of potentially pleasurable activities to try, and then as you contemplate actually doing them, your mind fills with dread. You begin to picture the so-called pleasurable activities as distasteful, dreary duties. Depression forms a cloud of dismal thoughts that obscure your ability to think about the future clearly.

Lucas graduates with a degree in architecture and immediately finds work he loves with a small firm in Seattle. However, when the economy tanks, his firm downsizes and lays him off. Around that same time, Lucas breaks up with his girlfriend of the past four years. Understandably, he finds his mood miserable, his energy low, and his sleep disturbed. Lucas' counselor suggests that Lucas make a list of activities that he has found pleasurable in the past. He comes up with:

✔ Spending time with friends

✔ Camping

✔ Joining a softball league

✔ Going to clubs

But his mind immediately floods with negative thoughts. He predicts that his friends are going to find him boring because of his bad mood. He envisions having a miserable time camping because of all the hassle involved, and he believes that he has no spare money for going to a club.

If you're experiencing even a mild depression, beware. Your predictions of the future are likely to be as unreliable as a cheap used car from a sleazy car lot. Because pleasure seems impossible when you're down, anticipating enjoyment is particularly difficult to do. Press on and try to ignore your mind's pessimism.

If you find it difficult to simply ignore dire mental predictions concerning activities that are meant to be fun, you can combat your mind's gloomy forecasting with an activity called "Firing Your Mind's Faulty Forecaster." Put down your umbrella, pick up a pen and some paper, read the following steps, and construct a chart similar to the sample in Table 11-1. You may be surprised how helpful this activity can be.

1. **Pick three or four small, potentially pleasurable activities.**

   You don't have to view these activities as truly pleasurable yet. However, you should choose items that either seem relatively "unawful," or that you enjoyed in the past.

   If you have solid reasons for not engaging in a particular activity (other than low expectations of pleasure), don't select that item.

2. **On a point scale of 0 to 10, rate the amount of pleasure or fun you anticipate feeling from the activity.**

   Zero indicates that you expect absolutely no fun, five means that you anticipate a moderate amount of enjoyment, and ten suggests that you anticipate total ecstasy. We doubt that you're going to have many nines or tens if you're depressed.

3. **Perform the activity.**

   This is the hard part. Even if you rate an item as zero or one, push yourself to do it anyway. Your mind may resist with negative thoughts. Short circuit those thoughts and move your body.

4. **After you complete the activity, rate how much pleasure you actually experienced and briefly describe your reaction in words.**

If you complete this exercise, you're likely to find that you experience more fun and enjoyment from activities than you predicted. Discovering that your predictions were inaccurate may spur you on to try more pleasurable activities. And the more pleasure you experience, the less depressed you will be.

Checking back in with Lucas, he has four items on his pleasure list. None of them sound satisfying to him, so he tries the "Firing Your Mind's Faulty Forecaster" exercise. Table 11-1 provides his results.

Table 11-1	Firing Your Mind's Faulty Forecaster	
Activity	*Forecasted Fun*	*Experienced Fun*
Spending time with friends	3	6 — It was a good experience.
Camping	2	4 — It was a hassle, but I did like getting away.
Softball	3	5 — I was pretty rusty, but it was nice to be with the guys.
Going to a club	4	2 — I felt horrible about spending the money.

Notice that in three out of four cases, Lucas experienced significantly more fun and pleasure than he anticipated. In one case, however, he actually had a pretty rotten time. Experiencing less pleasure than you originally anticipate can result for any number of reasons. For Lucas, his concerns about finances actually were somewhat realistic.

Also notice that Lucas didn't have the greatest time in the world with any of the activities; this is normal, because depression mutes joy. However, if Lucas continues to pursue pleasurable activities, the amount of fun he feels will very likely increase slowly over time.

Like Lucas, you may have less pleasure than you anticipate occasionally. For example, you could go camping on a rainy weekend. Or going to a club, you could feel uncomfortable or awkward. But realize that the more pleasurable activities you attempt, the more your odds go up of experiencing pleasure.

Depression is a formidable foe. Adding pleasure to your life is but one small step in the fight. Give fun a chance, and realize that rediscovering healthy pleasures takes time and patience.

Chapter 12

Solving Life's Headaches

Depression pours sludge into your brain's problem-solving machinery. The resulting diminished capacity for finding solutions causes every difficulty you face to grow in size and complexity. Problems that may look like minor molehills to someone in a normal mood suddenly loom larger than mountains. And when you're depressed, big problems induce a state of paralysis and hopelessness. This bleak discouragement in turn increases your depression and further clouds your ability to see a way out.

Nevertheless, we have some good news for you. Learning more effective problem solving strategies helps defeat depression. This approach has received increased attention from professionals in the past few years. Furthermore, a number of studies have validated that problem solving works. You'll find that our take on problem solving is easy to get the hang of; you can readily find ways to apply it to your real-life problems.

In this chapter, we present a comprehensive game plan for unraveling dilemmas that come in a wide variety of shapes, colors, and sizes. Adele's story is just one of the numerous types of problems that people with depression face. But getting the hang of something new is always easier if you have examples, so we use her story throughout this chapter to provide further insight into how to follow our formula to solve your problems.

Adele married her husband Eddie, a self-described computer geek, at the age of 19. On their 25th wedding anniversary, Adele realizes that she's fallen into an oppressive boredom. She and Eddie don't seem to talk to each other anymore, and their life together feels stale and boring. She tries to discuss her feelings with Eddie, but he's uninterested and distant. As the months go on, Adele slowly slides into a deepening depression. She contemplates getting a divorce or having an affair, although neither option appeals to her. She feels stuck, and she's unable to see a way out.

Drawing Up the Problem-Solving Game Plan — S.O.C.C.E.R.

In recent years, the problem-solving approach to combating depression has gained wider popularity due to increased research efforts that have demonstrated its effectiveness. The primary goals of this approach, when applied to depression, are to

✔ Uncover life problems that may be contributing to depression

✔ Figure out how depression decreases coping

✔ Teach effective problem solving techniques

✔ Prevent relapse as a result of improved skills

To make our problem-solving plan easy to remember, we base it on the acronym S.O.C.C.E.R. S.O.C.C.E.R. guides you through a series of steps. These steps will help you find effective solutions to your problems and help you implement these solutions.

✔ **S** stands for the *situation,* or the problem itself. The situation includes the nature and cause(s) of the problem, your feelings about the problem, and your beliefs about trying to solve it. For example, you may believe that the problem is insurmountable. That belief is part of the situation or problem.

✔ **O** stands for any and all possible *options* for approaching the problem creatively.

✔ **C** stands for the likely *consequences* that carrying out each option entails.

✔ **C** involves making a final *choice* about which option you want to try.

✔ **E** stands for your *emotional plan* for carrying out your option, because some choices require a bit of courage.

✔ **R** stands for *run it* and *review.* This step calls for you to implement your plan and then review the outcome in terms of whether your solution worked. It also includes figuring out what to do next if your plan doesn't work.

S.O.C.C.E.R. problem-solving game plans don't guarantee success. But the approach does give you a better way to think through your problems. A thorough analysis helps improve your chances of discovering and implementing the best possible solutions. S.O.C.C.E.R. helps alleviate depression by increasing your confidence and competence.

In the following sections, we explore each of the steps in the S.O.C.C.E.R game plan individually. Like many of the exercises throughout this book, most of the steps involve putting pen to paper (or fingers to keyboard), so get out a notebook (or turn on your computer).

If you currently view the problems in your life as utterly hopeless, and you can't imagine even attempting to tackle them, please seek professional help prior to using our problem-solving plan. The plan may still help you, but you'll need professional assistance to carry it out.

Assessing Your Problem Situation (S)

The first step in our S.O.C.C.E.R problem-solving approach entails a careful observation of the ins and outs of the current conundrum. You need to consider a number of issues:

- ✔ **Come up with a description of the problem.** Carefully consider what the problem actually involves. If a problem seems to entail a variety of issues, try to zero in on one important aspect first. After you zero in on a key issue, write down as much about the nature of the problem as you can.

  Adele (who we describe at the beginning of the chapter) reflects and decides that the quality of her marriage is a larger problem than boredom — although the latter still plays an unwelcome role. She decides to zero in on her marriage. She also realizes that she and her husband don't share any common interests; they rarely have sex anymore, and their evenings usually consist of her watching mindless television for several hours while he works on the computer. She wants a change, but she doesn't know what to do.

- ✔ **Reflect on your feelings about the problem.** Reflecting on all the feelings you have regarding a given problem is important. Doing so helps you understand the impact of the problem on your life.

  Adele realizes that boredom is one of the feelings she is experiencing. She has to work hard to figure out the rest of her feelings, because she has a habit of thinking that she doesn't deserve much from life and that she has no right to have certain types of feelings, such as anger. However, Adele eventually concludes that, in addition to boredom, she feels resentment and anger toward her husband and anxiety about the possibility of leaving her marriage.

- ✔ **Consider the causes of the problem.** Depression may mislead you when it comes to figuring out the causes of your problem. Depressed minds often make the assumption that the person who has the problem is also the cause of the entire problem. Although you may be partially responsible for the problem, considering any and all causes of the problem is important. Sometimes an understanding of all the causes can point the way toward certain solutions.

In Adele's case, she first blames herself for being an inadequate, unexciting wife. As she ponders the situation further, she realizes that she has made attempts to improve things and her husband Eddie has rebuffed her. She concludes that another cause may lie in the emptiness they've both felt since their second and last child chose to attend an out-of-state college six months ago. Finally, she speculates that she and Eddie were left feeling like they have no social outlets after their friends Beverly and Tom took jobs in Cincinnati last year.

✔ **Search for information about the problem.** Odds are, you're not the first person to ever experience a problem like the one you're having. Look around for books and articles on the subject. Whether the problem lies in the area of finance, relationships, career, sex, in-law troubles, difficulties with your kids, or whatever, books and articles on the subject probably exist in abundance. Read. In addition, consider talking to an expert in the area for further advice.

Adele picks up *Making Marriage Work For Dummies,* by Steven Simring, MD, MPH, Sue Klavans Simring, DSW, and Gene Busnar (Wiley Publishing, Inc.), and *The Seven Principles for Making Marriage Work,* by John M. Gottman, PhD, and Nan Silver (Three Rivers Press).

✔ **Consider the importance of the problem.** Ask yourself how much this problem matters to you and your life. Will solving it help you? If so, how much? You can rate the problem on a scale of 0 (no importance to you whatsoever) to 100 (nothing in the world could be more important). This rating may tell you how much effort to put into the project.

Adele realizes that the quality of her marriage matters a great deal to her. She rates the issue as 75 on a 0 to 100 point scale. She decides that it's worth putting some work into.

✔ **Check out solution-interfering beliefs.** After you've described the preceding aspects of the problem, a crucial step remains. You need to ask yourself if you have any beliefs that may interfere with your attempts to solve the problem. These beliefs can stop you from even attempting to do something about your problem. Therefore, they form part of the problem itself.

Adele realizes that she has five major beliefs that may put up a barrier to her problem-solving attempts. Her interfering beliefs happen to be the one's we encounter most often when we teach problem solving to our patients.

Table 12-1 lists the five beliefs that most commonly interfere with problem solving (in our experiences) and provides positive alternative ways of looking at those beliefs to facilitate solutions.

Table 12-1	Common Solution-Interfering Beliefs and Some Facilitating Views
Solution-Interfering Belief	**Facilitating View**
My problems are too big to solve.	Sure my problems are large, but they don't have to be solved all at once. People solve big problems all the time. It just takes persistence.
I don't think my problem is solvable.	Of course, it's always possible that my problem isn't solvable, in which case I'll have to work on figuring out how to cope with it. However, I won't know if it's solvable unless I try everything I can first.
I'm not a good problem solver.	Well, I haven't always tackled big problems easily in the past, but that doesn't mean I can't learn. The S.O.C.C.E.R. problem-solving plan looks pretty straightforward. Besides, what do I have to lose by trying?
I prefer to let problems solve themselves.	Oh sure, I guess that could happen — probably when pigs fly. My experience has been that problems usually just stick around or get worse if I don't do something about them.
If I try and fail to solve my problem, I'll just feel like an even bigger failure. It's better not to try	And of course if I don't try, I'll ensure failure. Besides, if my attempts fail, I just may learn something from the failure and make another run at the problem, armed with additional information.

If you discover that you have beliefs standing in the way of your attempt to solve the problems in your life, put them in a table like Table 12-1 and see if you can come up with facilitating views that counter those interfering beliefs. If you attempt this strategy and come up short on alternative views, consider reading Chapters 5, 6, and 7 for more information on dealing with problematic thoughts and beliefs.

Foraging for Options (O)

Step two in our S.O.C.C.E.R. problem-solving plan helps you find possible solutions for your problem. At this point, you need to suspend all judgment while searching far and wide for these solutions. Write down anything your mind comes up with; don't listen to your internal critic saying, "That's a really stupid idea!" We ask you to evaluate your ideas later, not now. Sometimes the most absurd solution leads to another idea that's more grounded in reality.

Creative solution searching without judgment is also known as *brainstorming*. We've found three ways to improve your brainstorming ability — "letting go," "thinking visually," and "permitting playfulness." After your brainstorming session, you can review all the options you come up with.

Letting go

Believe it or not, if you try too hard to solve a problem, you're likely to hit a wall. Too much intensity can stifle creativity. You need to give the process time; don't push yourself. You've probably been working on the problem for quite a while, so taking a little more time to solve it isn't going to hurt anything — in fact, it just may help.

First, we suggest relaxing your mind and body as a means for unleashing your creative potential. We have a quick relaxation technique you can use for this purpose:

1. Place your hand on your abdomen.

2. Take a slow, deep breath, and watch your abdomen expand.

3. Hold that breath momentarily.

4. Slowly breathe out and let your shoulders droop.

5. As you exhale, say the word *relax*.

6. Repeat this exercise ten times.

If you practice this relaxation technique several times a day for five days in a row, you may find it helps to calm your mind and body. If it doesn't work for you, or even if it makes your tension worse, you may want to read Chapter 18 for more ideas on how to let go. Also, if you suffer from anxiety in addition to your depression, you may want to also read another book of ours, *Overcoming Anxiety For Dummies* (Wiley Publishing, Inc.).

You may profit from other letting-go strategies when attempting to search for options to your problem. We often find our best ideas for writing or other problems when we take our two dogs out for a long jog. Somehow the rhythm of the running and the obvious pleasure the dogs experience help distract us from any worries or concerns. Thus, our minds feel free to wander and consider new possibilities without pressure.

You can try jogging, too. However, feel free to experiment. Other exercises like walking, weight lifting, or yoga (see Chapter 10) are also good ideas. Or you can try a recreational activity that you enjoy as a means to let go (see Chapter 11 for interesting and distracting healthy pleasures to consider). Of course, hot tubs aren't bad either.

Letting go as a way of finding creative solutions works best if you don't force your mind to find answers.

Thinking visually

Many people find that their creative juices start flowing more easily when they get into a visual mode. You can start by relaxing (you may want to use the quick relaxation procedure we describe in the "Letting go" section) and picturing your problem in your mind. Picture, in your imagination, the various ways you can tackle the problem; do so without the expectation of necessarily carrying any particular idea out.

Some people find that flow charts and diagrams help them find better options for solving their problems. Try picturing all the components of your problem in separate boxes. Draw possible solutions to each component in these separate boxes, and then draw arrows to the relevant component of the problem.

Adele put her marital problems on a flow chart. She put each component of her problematic marriage in a box, and then she developed solutions for each one. Take a look at Figure 12-1 to get your juices flowing; it contains one of the components of Adele's situation as well as ideas for attacking the problem.

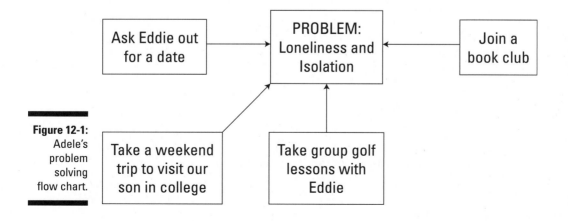

Figure 12-1:
Adele's problem solving flow chart.

Permitting playfulness

Yes, we realize the seriousness of your problem. However, allowing yourself to play with ideas is important. Realize that rigidity merely keeps you stuck. Play with the most absurd solutions imaginable. Play allows you to forget about the usual rules and break out of the box.

One way to play around is to consider solutions that appear to be the total opposite of your first ideas. For example, Adele (who we describe at the beginning of this chapter) has a difficult marriage. One solution she considers is having an affair. Then she thinks of the opposite — having an affair with her husband. "How absurd," she initially thinks to herself.

But then she realizes that it just may be worth a try. She can imagine that he's a man who she just met and finds attractive (after all, she did find him very attractive years ago, and he hasn't changed all that much). Then she can plot how to seduce him.

Reviewing your options

As you brainstorm options for dealing with your problem, list everything that you come up with. Don't leave any ideas out at this point. After you finish writing your list down, review it and see if a little pondering leads to more ideas.

Adele lists options for handling her marital problems. As you can see, Adele's options list contains possibilities that range from probably productive to downright destructive:

- Have an affair.
- Have an affair with my husband.
- Get a divorce.
- Ask for a temporary separation so that I can clear my head.
- Seek marital counseling if I can convince Eddie to go.
- Simply work on my own to improve our marriage by showing more caring and affection, as well as by working on being non-defensive (see Chapter 14).
- Go on an exotic trip to Asia and not tell anyone.
- Focus on making myself happy in ways that aren't related to my marriage, such as developing new hobbies, looking for a more interesting career, expanding my social circle, finding volunteer work, and so on.

> ✔ Drink more.
>
> ✔ Quit my whining and try to forget about this issue!

We expect that your list of possible solutions may contain options ranging from really helpful to pretty destructive. Good brainstorming avoids judgment of even the wildest options. The evaluation phase comes next. In this phase, you don't evaluate yourself for having good or bad ideas; instead, you merely evaluate the likely consequences of your ideas.

Contemplating Consequences (C)

Take the options you cook up in the preceding "Foraging for Options" section of this chapter and list them in the "Options" column of a two-column table, as shown in Table 12-2. Next, label the second column "Likely Consequences and Probabilities." Then contemplate each option, one at a time. For each option, list possible outcomes or consequences. Write down each outcome and rate the probability of that outcome happening with a 0 (almost totally impossible) to 100 (almost completely certain) point scale.

Table 12-2 lists Adele's options and the outcomes she deemed most likely for each one. This example can give you an idea of how to begin your table.

Table 12-2	Likely Consequences of Adele's Options
Options	*Likely Consequences and Probabilities*
Have an affair.	Fun and excitement (55); Guilt (95); Sexually transmitted disease (5 or less if I'm careful); Eventual ruination of my marriage (60)
Have an affair with my husband.	Fun and excitement (65 because of no guilt, but it may be less intense than a real affair); Possible enhancement of my marriage (55); Utter rejection from my husband (60)
Get a divorce.	Some relief from the struggle (75); Sadness and loss (80); Eventually, a new and better relationship (30)
Temporary separation.	Clear my head to see what I really want to do (35); Increased distance from my husband (55); Increased chance my husband will have an affair (35)

(continued)

Table 12-2 (continued)	
Options	**Likely Consequences and Probabilities**
Seek marital counseling if Eddie will go.	Improvement in the marriage if he agrees (65); Anger and rage from Eddie because he's always opposed this idea (50); Rejection from Eddie (30); Divorce if it doesn't work (55)
Work on my own to improve marriage.	Improve marriage (30); Harm marriage in some way (10)
Go on an exotic trip and not tell anyone.	Fun and excitement (85); Guilt (99); End my marriage (99)
Increase my own happiness through a new career.	Be happier (70); Become more distant from my husband (40)
Drink more.	Temporary decrease in pain (65); Become addicted to alcohol (50); Increase pain in the long run (75)
Quit whining and forget the problem.	Increased dissatisfaction (90); Marriage will improve on its own (1)

Sometimes this exercise points the way to a single, simple solution that stands out as the obvious option. But all too frequently, the best options aren't so obvious. So, in the next section, we help you dive in and make a choice.

Choosing Your Poison (C)

After you go through the first three steps of the S.O.C.C.E.R. problem-solving plan, you can choose your option(s). Make a commitment to yourself. (And hopefully your choice won't feel like poison.)

Even when you decide not to choose an option for dealing with your problem, you're still making a choice — you're choosing to live with your problem "as is."

The fourth step in the S.O.C.C.E.R. problem-solving plan requires you to carefully reflect on each and every option. You may be able to quickly zero in on the one, two, three, or perhaps four best possibilities simply by reviewing the likely consequences of each. Tune into your feelings about each option. Does the option make you feel hopeful, distressed, anxious, calm, angry, sad, relieved, eager, or some combination of these feelings? Your feelings may provide you with additional information.

Please realize that the option you choose for dealing with your problem can entail a combination of several options; they don't have to be mutually exclusive.

Adele picks three options that look like they have the best chance of helping her distressed marriage:

- ✔ Do everything I can on my own to improve the marriage.
- ✔ Increase my own happiness by exploring a new career.
- ✔ Seek marital counseling.

After further reflection, Adele decides not to choose the option of having an affair with her husband — he has seriously rebuffed her sexual advances in the past, and she doesn't want to risk rejection again. She decides that the first two options from the previous list could improve her happiness without incurring great risk. Even though she initially believed that exploring a new career could create distance from her husband, she believes that it won't do so if she combines it with the first two ideas.

Adele has just one problem. She greatly fears that she'll incur Eddie's wrath if she brings up marital counseling one more time. And if it doesn't work, she fears an increased chance of a gut-wrenching divorce. Is this the choice she really wants to make?

If you find yourself stuck with indecision about one or more of the options you've chosen, we have two more strategies that may help — "consulting the friend within" and "choosing sides." You'll need a couple of chairs for both of them. Yes, chairs — just go with us on this one.

Consulting the friend within

You have a friend that you can call on for another perspective. That friend resides in you! This technique may be one of the simplest you find in this book. But don't be fooled by the simplicity.

We find the "Consulting the Friend Within" strategy to be surprisingly useful. To use this strategy, sit down in a chair and place an empty chair opposite from you. Imagine a close friend of yours is sitting in that chair. Your friend happens to have pretty much the same problem you do; she came up with the same choice for a solution, but dreads carrying it out. Start talking to your friend. Talk out loud. When you're done, ask if the advice sounds good for you, too.

You may not only think that this idea sounds simplistic, but you may also wonder how it could possibly help you when you failed to choose an option up to now. Well, frankly, we aren't entirely sure why it works, but it does. We suspect that it's because the procedure helps give you a little emotional distance from the issue, which frees up your stuck mind-set.

Adele tries this strategy. Here's her imaginary monologue with her friend:

> "Well, you know, as much as working on your marriage on your own sounds like a great idea, I doubt it will work unless you combine it with marital therapy. Sure you're scared! But do you really have anything to lose by trying? What are the odds that your marriage will work out on its own if marital therapy fails? Pretty low I would guess. Your husband gets angry, but he's never beaten you. If he gets angry, so what? It happened plenty of times before, and you lived through it. If he totally rejects the idea, try again. Then again, if he still won't go at the end of the day, maybe you need to listen to that information and consider other options. Stop avoiding the issue!"

Adele finds this exercise helpful, but she doesn't quite feel ready to implement her decision to ask Eddie to go to marital counseling. She needs one more technique — "choosing sides." You can give it a shot, too.

Choosing sides

The "Choosing Sides" strategy, like the preceding "Consulting the Friend Within" technique, requires you to place two chairs facing each other. Label the first chair as representing one side of your argument and the second chair as representing the other position. Sit in Chair No.1 and imagine the other side of your argument is sitting in Chair No.2. Argue with the other side out loud and as forcefully as you can. When you run out of steam, switch chairs and argue the other side of your argument.

Are you going to feel a little silly? Maybe. But do this technique by yourself and have a go at it. You may be surprised at how useful you find it to be. Psychologists have recommended this approach for many decades, and clients continue to report that it helps them reach difficult decisions.

Here's what Adele's dialogue sounds like when she tries the "choosing sides" strategy to help her determine if her option of marital counseling truly is the best option for her. She labels Chair No.1 "Get Counseling" and Chair No.2 "Don't Do It."

> **Get Counseling chair (Speaking to the Don't Do It chair):** "Look, you know that counseling has the best chance of succeeding. You made a few attempts on your own, but they didn't work. You reviewed the likely

consequences, and you know that getting help looks better than anything else."

Don't Do It chair: "Okay, sure. I thought about it carefully, but the bottom line is that I don't think I could stand it if therapy failed and I ended up divorced. The loneliness and sense of loss would feel overwhelming to me."

Get Counseling chair: "Oh, so that's what's holding you back! First, who says marital therapy will fail? The odds aren't that bad if you combine it with your own efforts. You already found those ideas in the books you've read encouraging. With the help of a trained professional, it just may work."

Don't Do It chair: "Sure, but if Eddie rejects it, I'll just feel more frustrated and angry. That would increase the odds of divorce. Bottom line is — I don't think I could stand it."

Get Counseling chair: "So you think that ignoring the problem has a better chance? I doubt it! If your marriage is headed for divorce, it's better you find out now than later. And who says you couldn't stand it? People get divorced every day, and most manage to get through it."

Don't Do It chair: "But I'd hate it."

Get Counseling chair: "Of course you wouldn't like to get divorced! I don't know many people who do. But stop saying you couldn't stand it. You were okay on your own before you met Eddie, and you could do it again. Furthermore, dating may not sound too great right now, but other men are out there you know."

Don't Do It chair: "Okay, I get your point. I wouldn't like it, but life would probably go on. Somehow I'll find the courage to carry this option out . . . I think, anyway."

Adele feels more resolute in her decision to seek marital counseling after trying the Choosing Sides technique. Nevertheless, she quivers and trembles at the thought of approaching Eddie.

Some options for solving problems can cause unexpected reactions. You can be quite certain that your decision is the right one but still feel fearful. If that's the case for you, you may need an emotional plan for helping you proceed. And we just happen to have one for you in the "Handling Your Emotions" section that follows.

Handling Your Emotions (E)

Assuming that you chose the option or options that look as though they have the best possible chance of helping to solve your problem, troublesome emotions may sabotage your best intentions. This step in the problem-solving process is best viewed as a crutch for helping you implement your choice.

If you feel great uncertainty about your selection, go back through the suggestions on the topics of foraging for options, contemplating consequences, and choosing your poison in the earlier sections of this chapter. If you come up with the same solution and still feel uneasy, rest assured that your uneasiness represents normal feelings that can be handled with this problem-solving step.

Most solutions to difficult problems require a little courage to carry out. If that weren't so, the solutions would probably pop into your mind more easily. After all, we did say "difficult" problems.

Two fairly simple techniques can help quell the queasiness that lies in the pit of your stomach as you anticipate acting on your solution — rehearsal and self-talk.

Holding the dress rehearsal

Imagine the quality of a Broadway musical if the musicians, actors, and actresses never attended rehearsals. The performers' stage fright would then make good sense, because no one would know what to do. The production would likely result in disaster. And it probably wouldn't take long for the audience to start throwing tomatoes. Rehearsals not only enhance performance, they also help to decrease stage fright.

If your problem-solving option involves a confrontation with someone or stirs up anxiety, rehearsal may help. You can rehearse your plan

- ✔ In your mind
- ✔ In front of a mirror
- ✔ Through role-playing with a trusted friend
- ✔ By writing out a script

Talking to yourself

You may be thinking, "Talk to myself? Do you guys think I'm crazy?" Actually, most people talk to themselves. However, people don't often try to control the content of their self-talk; they merely go on autopilot. And if they feel anxious or depressed, their self-talk usually contains negative predictions and self-defeating statements.

The short positive self-statements in the following paragraphs are no cure for depression, nor do they work for long-term issues and problems. However, they can serve as a temporary band-aid for getting you through difficult moments.

You can decide to select new, more productive content for your self-talk. In order to push out negative thinking, you may first need to rehearse the script out loud. Write down short, simple, positive statements. Possibilities include

✔ What I'm about to do is the right thing to do.

✔ This is really hard, but I can do it.

✔ I considered all the options.

✔ I have the right to do this.

✔ Just do it.

Good ol' Adele decides to ask her husband Eddie to see a marital counselor as a means for solving her problem — the state of her marriage. She makes an appointment on an evening that's free on both of their calendars. First, she rehearses how she's going to approach Eddie with the idea. Then she chooses the self-talk coping phrase, "I can handle whatever reaction he has." She uses this phrase like a mantra, repeating it over and over in her mind as she approaches her husband.

Running and Reviewing (R)

Okay, at this point, you've gone through all the problem-solving steps but the final one. You've described the problem situation, chosen an option, and you're ready to roll. The time has come to take a run at your problem and execute your plan.

The chances of your problem working out are higher because you've done your homework. Nevertheless, S.O.C.C.E.R. doesn't come with an unconditional guarantee. After you implement your solution, review how it worked. Carefully consider what worked and what may not have. Perhaps all went well and the problem has been resolved. But if the problem or a remnant remains, go back to the drawing board and start a new S.O.C.C.E.R. game plan.

Here's how Adele's S.O.C.C.E.R. plan works out:

> Adele repeats, "I can handle whatever reaction he has," in her mind repeatedly as she enters the study where Eddie is sitting at the computer. "Eddie, could we talk for a couple of minutes?"

Eddie swivels to face her and replies, "Okay, but not too long, I'm in the middle of something."

"This won't take long. I've been concerned about our marriage; neither of us seems very happy," Adele begins.

Eddie interrupts her, "Speak for yourself. I'm not unhappy. Women, they're never satisfied. What more could you want? This isn't paradise; it's real life."

Adele, who is now close to tears, continues, "I'm not asking for the moon, Eddie. I want us to be closer. And I've made an appointment with a marriage counselor. It's for next Thursday at 6 p.m. I want you to come with me."

"Forget it. I'm not going to some touchy-feely, nosey therapist," Eddie's voice rises, "Here's another way you've found to throw my hard-earned money away. I'm not going to waste my time talking about this!" Eddie turns back to his computer and ignores Adele.

Ugh. Adele went through all the steps and received a lousy outcome. It takes her a couple of days to recoup, but she goes through a new S.O.C.C.E.R. game plan. This time she decides to go to counseling by herself and explore other options with the counselor. After several sessions, the counselor helps Adele find a better way to ask Eddie to attend at least a few sessions with her.

Over a period of months, Eddie realizes how much he values Adele. Both commit to making their marriage stronger.

If you or someone you care about is depressed, problems loom larger than life. And solutions seem amazingly elusive. Take the time to prepare a game plan. See how S.O.C.C.E.R. works for you.

Part IV
Rebuilding Connections: Relationship Therapy

The 5th Wave   By Rich Tennant

©RICHTENNANT

"I sense that you're becoming more defensive and unapproachable lately."

In this part . . .

Interpersonal therapy is another widely researched approach to the treatment of depression. That research means that you can believe us when we tell you that interpersonal therapy works. In this part, we cover key elements of interpersonal therapy, including how to deal with change and transitions, grief, and loss.

Depression also interferes with important relationships with friends, coworkers, family members, spouses, and partners. Therefore, we give you tips and tools for enhancing your relationships. We review ways to build bridges with others and communicate more effectively. With these tools, your relationships can become a source of support rather than just another set of problems that drag you down.

Chapter 13

Working Through Loss, Grief, and Mourning

*H*ave you ever stood at the kitchen counter with tears welling up in your eyes as you quickly cut onions? If so, you've experienced your body's response to irritants. Tears help clear out the noxious molecules released by the sliced onion.

As you're also probably aware, your body produces tears in response to another stimulus — strong emotions. The two types of tears have different chemical compositions. Given the nearly universal reports of relief following emotional crying, scientists speculate that crying somehow cleanses the body of emotional toxins and brings it back to a more relaxed state.

Grief and crying are normal reactions to loss. However, sometimes grief lingers and disrupts life in major ways. Mourning can trigger depression (see Chapter 2 for a description of the types of depression). Loss may cause depressed feelings without your awareness. Sometimes events in the past continue to plague you far longer than you realize. Even if you haven't experienced a major loss in decades, looking at unresolved grief as a possible cause of your current depression may yield fruitful insight.

In this chapter, we explore the uniquely human response to loss. We discuss the various types of losses people experience and how they react to them. If you're depressed, consider whether any of your problematic feelings stem from one of these losses. Working through your grief may help relieve your depression, so we give you a variety of ways for working through grief, whether it's a normal, uncomplicated grief or a profound, traumatic experience.

Losing What You Care About

All people experience loss of one kind or another during their lives. People grieve about all different types of losses. Yet the response to each particular loss varies from person to person. We don't have any easy way to tell how someone will react when something bad happens. And there's no right or wrong way to handle loss. Some people seem to bounce back quickly, while others remain in a prolonged state of intense grief.

If your grief stretches over many months without letup, if you're overwhelmed by thoughts of yearning and loss, if you have thoughts about the futility of the future, or if you feel worthless and excessively guilty, you may have a complicated grief and/or a major depressive disorder (see Chapter 2 for more information about grief and various types of depression). If you have any of these symptoms, seek professional assistance. Both of these conditions require prompt treatment.

We can't possibly give you a complete list of the types of losses that lead to grief, but the three major categories are

- ✔ Death
- ✔ Life transitions
- ✔ Relationship loss

In the following sections, we discuss these categories of loss at length. There's no right or wrong way to deal with such losses. Understanding how each event affects you is what's important. With awareness, you can draw on your resources for coping. In the "Working Through Grief" section, later in this chapter, we give you ideas for handling these losses effectively.

Losing someone

Death is never easy to deal with. Even people with strong religious convictions feel great sadness upon the loss of a loved one. Unexpected death generally is more difficult to accept than death following a prolonged illness. But the period of anticipation before the loss isn't the only factor that affects the response to death. For example, the person's age, the difficulty of the dying process, whether there was an opportunity to say goodbye, and the remaining resources and connections available to the griever all contribute to the reaction in complicated ways.

Your relationship to the individual also plays a large role in how the loss affects you:

- **Death of a life partner:** This type of loss is often thought to be one of the most difficult to get through. It requires major adjustments.

- **Death of a child:** Most experts believe that this loss probably involves the most painful, lengthy recovery. Somehow it feels as though it's against the laws of nature for a child to precede a parent in death.

- **Death of a parent:** The difficulty of this loss hinges on many factors, such as the age of the parent and child at the time of the death, the nature of the relationship, and unresolved issues. Sometimes the grief is actually intensified if the relationship was stormy and conflicted.

- **Death of friends and relatives:** Again, the difficulty of dealing with departed friends and relatives varies considerably.

- **Death of a pet:** The attachments people form with their animals can be very strong. Pets become special family members. Sometimes other people don't fully appreciate or understand the intensity of the bereavement that the loss of a pet can evoke. Such a lack of understanding by others can compound the sense of isolation.

- **Death of others:** Sometimes a traumatic event witnessed by uninvolved parties can cause grief reactions. For example, when a drunk driver kills a child, it may re-traumatize a family that lost a child years before. Or witnessing a violent crime may also cause the observer to mourn.

Are there stages of grief?

Elisabeth Kubler-Ross, MD, is a psychiatrist that devoted the majority of her professional career to the care of the dying. Her widely cited book, *On Death and Dying* (Scribner), proposed that people go through a series of stages when they face terminal illness:

- **Denial:** No way, I'm not sick; it can't be me!

- **Anger:** Damn it! Why me?

- **Bargaining:** God, help me! I'll do anything to get out of this.

- **Depression:** I just can't go on, I can't stand it. I give up.

- **Acceptance:** This is the end; I'll try to go in peace with dignity.

These stages have been extended to include reactions to other types of loss, such as death of a loved one, loss of physical health, or relationship breakups. However, each person is a unique individual, and it appears that not everyone goes through all the stages reported by Kubler-Ross. And people may bounce from one stage to another, skipping some or even returning to an earlier stage. In that sense, they really aren't best thought of as stages so much as states of emotional reactions that people frequently experience.

Yet some mental health counselors erroneously believe that resolution of grief only comes about after experiencing all these stages of grief in sequence. But no single, healthy way of going through the grief process exists. Each person grieves in a unique way. Kubler-Ross's work has helped people around the world handle difficult transitions. However, grief is complicated, diverse, and not easily categorized.

Transitioning through life

Nothing ever remains completely the same. People have a variety of roles to play in life. For example, people are parents, employees, employers, students, husbands, wives, or partners. Much of the way people define themselves comes from such roles.

People also define themselves according to their self-visions, such as seeing yourself as a person who is consistently healthy, safe, prestigious, attractive, and so on. Yet, roles and self-visions frequently change due to unavoidable circumstances. When these changes take place, the transition can be smooth or rocky.

People routinely fail to appreciate the impact that transitioning from one role or self-vision to another can have on their sense of self and well-being. When the transition involves a loss (and many transitions do), grieving or depression can result. Sometimes the transition is obvious, such as when you lose a job; other times the transition is more subtle, such as losing a feeling of safety because of an increase in the crime rate where you live.

No one responds in exactly the same way to these life transitions. As with death, no right or wrong answer exists. The types of transitions that frequently cause trouble include

- ✔ **Leaving home:** Adolescents and young adults often look forward to the day when they can leave home. However, when they actually do leave, they experience loss, as well, and they're generally quite surprised. No longer can they turn to their parents for instant advice and support. They may feel a loss of connection, and they may sense a loss of the free, irresponsible aspects of childhood. Another related loss comes at graduation time. The young person must move on from the familiar routines and friendships of high school or college and onto new, unexplored responsibilities.

- ✔ **Getting married:** You may wonder why we include marriage as a troubling transition. For most people, marriage is a joyous but nerve-wracking time in life. Yet marriage includes losses, which occasionally lead to unexpected feelings of depression. When you get married, you give up your identity as a single person. You may lose contact with single friends. Like leaving home, marriage requires giving up the irresponsibility of childhood.

- ✔ **Having a baby:** Another joyous occasion! But bringing a newborn into your life causes a loss of freedom and ushers in new stress. When you have a baby, you find yourself having to spend more money, and you lose the opportunity to sleep in on Saturday mornings.

Experiencing some minor distress after having a baby is normal for both parents. However, depression in women after childbirth can become serious: This condition is referred to as *postpartum depression*. See Chapter 2 for details about this disturbing condition that requires prompt treatment.

✔ **Changing jobs:** Whether you're starting your first job, getting a promotion or demotion, or going through a layoff or firing, changing what you do everyday entails stress and loss. A first job leads to a loss of free time. A promotion can lead to overwhelming responsibilities. Demotions, layoffs, and firings cause a loss of both money and status.

✔ **Going to jail:** Being convicted of a crime and subsequently incarcerated entails numerous losses. Duh.

✔ **Experiencing major economic and political changes in society:** All stock markets decline. Everyone knows a few people who had to postpone retirement or had problems sending their kids to college when stocks plummeted. Most of the time, no one feels enduring disappointment when political leadership changes hands. However, in some countries, new regimes can bring on the loss of freedom, economic hardship, or possibly war. These changes can disrupt families and lives in devastating ways.

✔ **Moving:** Moving to a new home, whether in the same city or somewhere else, is exciting, but it comes with losses. You may lose connections with friends, the simplicity of your former residence, or the sense of history with a place you cared about for a long time.

✔ **Dealing with an empty nest:** Parenting is the only loving relationship in which the goal is to foster independence and eventual departure. Do your job well and your children leave you. You may feel not only the loss of the kids but your role as a mother or father, as well.

✔ **Going through a chronic illness:** The diagnosis of a chronic illness shakes up your world. You lose a measure of control over your life; suddenly the health care system takes charge of significant aspects of your daily living. You encounter the loss of invincibility. In addition, your financial situation, freedom, and status may suffer.

✔ **Aging:** You'd probably rather be old than the alternative. Nevertheless, aging inevitably illuminates the certainty of death. Along with the threat of loss of life itself comes the loss of function, loved ones, independence, appearance, status, and good health.

These changes are expected over the course of a lifetime. But depression may be an unexpected consequence. If you feel intense sadness or depression, and you can't figure out why, review the recent transitions in your life. Ask yourself if any of the issues we discuss in the previous list may be part of the problem.

Breaking up is so hard to do

Losing someone through a breakup or divorce can also lead to severe mourning. Unfortunately, society tends to provide much more support to those who lost a loved one through death than to those who lost someone through the end of a relationship. The typical expectation is that people will regroup and get on with their lives in a fairly short period of time. The intensity of grief that is felt after a breakup may catch people by surprise and overwhelm them. After a relationship ends, feelings of loneliness and isolation take hold.

Yet, when people consider breaking up, they too often fail to comprehend the magnitude of the disruption and loss. Thus, they make cavalier decisions about leaving loved ones. Anger, lust, or boredom may drive the choice to end the relationship.

When you break up with your partner, you potentially incur many types of losses:

- **The relationship:** Companionship, affection, mutual goals, support, a sense of history accumulated with the partner, love, and sex.

- **A vision:** Most people who begin a serious relationship together have an expectation concerning the future of the relationship. In the case of partners with children, the vision of an intact family disintegrates when the relationship ends.

- **Family and friends:** Bonds with the family of the lost partner often vanish. Mutual friends sometimes choose sides.

- **Finances:** Whether the money is spent on lawyers, therapists, or establishing two households, divorce or the breakup of live-in partners costs major dollars.

- **Status:** Sometimes people derive prestige from the connection with their partner.

- **Ego:** Your ego may suffer, especially when you feel like you are being rejected. However, even the person making the decision to leave is sometimes surprised by feelings of failure and guilt, and by the other losses we cover in this list.

There's not a right or wrong way to handle grief after a breakup or divorce. Giving yourself permission to feel whatever feelings come up can help you deal with the loss. If those feelings engulf you or endure, we provide strategies for helping you deal with your distress in the remaining pages of this chapter.

Working Through Grief

The loss of people, roles, and self-visions, as we describe earlier in this chapter, usually leads to feelings of grief. That's to be expected. However, such grief sometimes digs in and continues to disrupt happiness and well being well beyond the typical 6 to 12 months. When grief endures far longer, people often fail to realize the source of their unhappiness. So, if you're currently depressed, we suggest you consider if any losses in your life, whether recent or old may be contributing to your melancholy. (And see Chapter 2 for more information on the differences between simple bereavement and depression.)

Long-standing or complicated bereavement frequently requires professional assistance. Seek professional help if your efforts at self-help like the ones in this book don't bring substantial relief or if you have severe depressive symptoms (see Chapter 2 for a discussion of the symptoms of depression).

If you determine that unresolved grief is part of your life, you need to think about how you can lighten your load. Explain your situation to trusted friends and family. Let them know that you'll need some extra consideration during this period of time by asking for their support and help. Consider delegating or even letting go of a few responsibilities. Even if you're not physically ill or sick, you should give yourself the same considerations you'd give someone who is.

When you're ready to approach friends and family for their assistance and understanding, you may wonder how they're going to give you a break if your grief involves a loss from long ago. You may want to explain that your grief work is a temporary project, and that if you don't improve, you intend to seek professional help. Tell them you realize that it's been a very long time, and that you too were surprised by the discovery that grief was still causing you trouble.

Bereavement saps you of energy. Getting better takes effort and time — you can't push the process. While you're at it, don't forget to take care of your body:

- ✔ Eat healthy foods.
- ✔ Exercise on a regular basis.
- ✔ Make sure that you're getting enough rest.

Before you tackle the job of untangling your grief, you should understand that the goal of this work isn't to make you forget about your painful losses. Nor is it designed to make you give up caring about the absent person or other losses. Rather, the goal is to help you get back to the business of living a productive, happy life.

People sometimes say that they would feel consumed by guilt if they got over their grief. Again, working through grief isn't about "getting over it" *per se.* You'll always feel the loss, but you can refocus and renew your spirit. You deserve to love and laugh again.

Working through grief may actually lead to an increase of negative feelings for a short time. These feelings are natural. If you experience significantly increased depression with feelings of hopelessness or thoughts of suicide, you need to get an immediate evaluation from a professional.

In the following sections, we discuss ways of coping with the loss of people, roles, and self-visions discussed in the "Losing What You Care About" section earlier in this chapter. The next section deals with the loss of important people in your life, whether from divorce, death, or separation.

Reconstructing the relationship

When grief endures or involves complex issues, people often focus on only the details of the loss they endured. In other cases, they fixate on some specific aspect of grief, such as the emptiness they feel. Having such a narrow focus can block your ability to process all the effects of the loss. It can also prevent you from experiencing difficult feelings.

We suggest broadening your field of vision to help you reconstruct all aspects of the lost relationship and what it meant to you. Appreciate the fact that no person consists of all positive or negative qualities. Then ask yourself the following "Grief Exploration Questions." You may want to write down your answers to these questions in a notebook.

- ✔ What was my life like with this person?
- ✔ What did I value in this person, and what did I struggle with?
- ✔ What did I learn from this person (both good and bad)?
- ✔ How has my life changed as a result of this loss?
- ✔ What do I feel resentful for with respect to this person?
- ✔ What things do I feel grateful for with respect to my relationship?

Take your time answering these questions. They may require some careful pondering. And they may evoke unexpected pain. After you thoroughly exhaust your review, you may want to discuss and possibly compare your feelings with someone you fully trust who knew this person well.

When you complete this portion of the task, you may want to compose a letter to the person you lost. This letter can help you more fully process the meaning of the relationship and the nature of your loss.

When you avoid feelings, you keep them stirring inside you. Expressing your feelings can help with healing.

Bruce's mother died when he was a child. Now, many years later, Bruce is a father. He discovers himself having sad feelings. Bruce concludes that he has unresolved grief. Bruce answers the Grief Exploration Questions, and then he processes his grief in the letter to his deceased mother in Figure 13-1.

Dear Mom,

   Guess what? My wife and I have a baby. A girl — we named her after you. I've got a job and a house. And I'm doing pretty good. But after the baby, I started having some really sad times. I did some reading and I think it's about never really dealing with your death. I know it happened a long time ago, but I guess I never got over it.

   I was only 12 years old when you left me. I was outside playing and a police car drove up. I ran up to the porch. Dad was standing there, already crying. I never saw him cry before. Mom, things changed so much after you died. Dad never got over it; he was sad or drunk most of the time. I started getting into more and more trouble. My life was pretty hard. I even spent some time in jail. I never talked about you to anyone. I wouldn't even let myself think about you. It hurt.

   I knew I was sad, but I didn't realize until now how mad I am. I'm mad because I remember when you were home, you'd usually be in the bedroom. Somehow, I thought it was my fault you were always crying. I was lonely and scared. I'm mad, Mom, because you were so depressed but you didn't get help. I'm mad because Dad didn't get you help. Mom, if you cared about me, you wouldn't have killed yourself.

   Now, I've said it. I am mad. But over the years I've learned that depression is an illness. And that you and Dad probably didn't realize that people could get help and get better. So, Mom, I forgive you for leaving me. And I promise to not let my own sad feelings hurt my little girl.

Love,
Your son, Bruce

Figure 13-1:
Bruce's attempt to process his grief.

Eileen left her husband two years ago. She experienced unexplained sadness, guilt, and anger. Her therapist helped her connect unresolved feelings about her divorce as the cause of these emotions. She first answers the Grief Exploration Questions we list earlier in this section. Then she constructs the letter in Figure 13-2.

After you complete your reconstruction of the relationship, you'll be more prepared to deal with the next issue.

When you're ready, ask yourself how you can begin the process of replacing as much of what you've lost as possible. You may want to think about active alternatives, such as:

- ✔ **Dating:** This can feel scary, but ultimately you can learn to love again.

- ✔ **Grief support groups:** You may find comfort in commiserating with others who've experienced similar losses. You can find support groups for bereavement as well as for the loss of a relationship.

- ✔ **Recreation:** People who are filled with grief typically pull away from pleasurable activities and then fail to pick them back up again when their grief subsides. (See Chapter 11 for more information on rediscovering pleasure.)

- ✔ **Religious congregation groups:** These groups can provide support, connections, and spiritual guidance.

- ✔ **Volunteer work:** This can be a great way to reestablish connections and obtain a sense of renewed purpose.

Rolling through roles

As we discuss in the "Transitioning through life" section earlier in this chapter, circumstances can compel you to give up one or more of the roles you occupy in life, such as the role of parent, employee, student, or child. Because these roles encompass much of how people define themselves, the loss can feel devastating.

Society hasn't clearly defined the transition type of loss. But at times, the grief involved feels almost as intense as the grief you feel after a death or divorce. It can also leave you feeling bewildered by what to do next. If a role transition seems to be causing you trouble, we recommend that you ask yourself "Role Exploration Questions." Again, consider writing your answers down in a notebook.

✔ What did I enjoy about my old role?

✔ What did my old role allow me to do?

✔ What did I dislike about my old role?

✔ What freedoms and limitations did I feel in my old role?

✔ What were the negative and positive feelings I experienced when I gave up my old role?

✔ What did I resent about my old role?

✔ Do I feel grateful for having had my old role?

Your answers to these questions will help you more fully appreciate and understand the nature of your loss. If you've been idealizing the position you used to occupy, answering these questions should help you see your old role in a more realistic light. And when you review exactly what you feel was important in the loss, you can start to search for alternatives. The alternatives may lie in finding a new role, looking for new ways to meet your needs, or even exploring new interests and meanings. See Chapter 19 for information on using findings from the field of positive psychology to facilitate this exploration.

Dear Henry,

Why did I leave you? I was afraid. Your rage was carefully hidden at times, but I never knew when it would surface. Henry, you never hit me, but the punishment was worse than being beaten. You tortured me with silence — silence that seemed to last forever. Silence for the holidays, on trips, for birthdays and graduations. Silence at the dinner table and after we made love.

We never played with ideas or worked on compromise. You were always right; you knew the truth. I feared expressing my thoughts, feelings, or emotions, because if they differed from what you wanted to hear, you were angry. When you got angry, I was punished. The more critical you were with me, the more I withdrew from you. I couldn't properly plant tomatoes or fold the laundry. After losing self-confidence, self-worth, and self-control, I got help. And I became more independent and more ambitious — so that I could stand alone, and so that I wouldn't need you.

I know you were deeply hurt as a child. I understand how my own overreactions to your criticism stemmed from my childhood issues. Now, from a distance, I remember the good times. You are a brilliant man and generous to a fault. You care about people. I hope you are happy.

Take care,
Eileen

Figure 13-2:
Eileen's letter to her ex-husband.

Mike retires from his position as a high school English teacher. He was counting the days until his retirement. He plans to travel, read books he never had the time to read, and go fishing. Four months into his retirement, he starts waking up at 4 a.m., unable to go back to sleep. He puts off his travel plans and fishing trips. Those books he was going to read remain on the shelf. Mike is suffering from the consequences of his role change. His wife suggests that he answer the Role Exploration Questions. Here's what Mike came up with:

- ✔ **What did I enjoy about my old role?** "I liked the interaction with the kids. I loved getting through to an unmotivated student."

- ✔ **What did my old role allow me to do?** "I could make a difference in a few kids' lives. That was fantastic."

- ✔ **What did I dislike about my old role?** "I hated the endless paperwork. And the boring meetings drove me crazy."

- ✔ **What freedoms and limitations did I feel in my old role?** "I loved the freedom to develop new ways to teach. But as the years wore on, there were more and more requirements. We lost most of the freedom to choose materials."

- ✔ **What were the negative and positive feelings I experienced when I gave up my old role?** "I couldn't wait to start fishing! And seeing new places excited me. I felt relief from the day-to-day grind. And I felt happy and joyous. Later I felt a deep sense of loss. I miss working with the kids. And I miss thinking of myself as a teacher."

- ✔ **What did I resent about my old role?** "The salary, of course. I also resented the increasing pressure from administration to dole out passing grades even when undeserved. I resented the lack of respect from some parents — that seemed to get worse over the years."

- ✔ **Do I feel grateful for having had my old role?** "Not many people get a chance to make a difference in other people's lives. I know I did that. And despite the pathetic salary, I feel quite grateful for the excellent retirement benefits."

After he reviews his answers, Mike more fully appreciates where his grief has been coming from. And he realizes that he can replace some of what he's lost by volunteering at an adult reading clinic near his home. He can use his skills as a teacher to make a huge difference in the lives of illiterate but enthusiastic students.

Your depression could be coming from a change in your life. Remember, sometimes the change can be good, such as getting married, starting a new career, or having a baby. Nevertheless, all adjustments take a little time, energy, and planning.

Chapter 14

Relationship Enhancement

. . . .

In This Chapter

▶ Viewing the connection between depression and rejection

▶ Improving your relationship with positive behavior

▶ Overcoming defensiveness

▶ Enhancing your communication skills

. . . .

Depression extracts a heavy toll on friendships and intimate relationships. But all isn't lost! You can do much to improve the quality of your relationships whether you're depressed or not. That's the purpose of this chapter — to show you how to outwit the deviousness of depression's handiwork when it starts to harm your relationships.

In this chapter, we discuss the ways that depression insidiously affects important relationships. But don't despair — we wouldn't present that information without giving you ideas for what you can do to turn things around. We offer some good tools for improving your relationship skills.

If your relationship is suffering, you may want to ask your friend or partner to read this chapter, too.

You can use the tools we present in this chapter to enhance the way you relate with friends, co-workers, family members, and intimate partners. However, we focus our discussion and techniques on intimate relationships here because problems in these relationships create more distress than difficulties with friends and acquaintances. Depression can cause problems in close relationships, and those problems can deepen depression.

Abusive relationships sometimes cause depression. If you believe that your partner has been emotionally or physically abusive, you may need to terminate the relationship. However, when you're depressed, making that decision can be especially difficult. Seek professional guidance if you have any doubts.

The Depression-Rejection Connection

Depression feels terrible — you experience sadness, fatigue, pessimism, and feelings of worthlessness. These feelings can be difficult to deal with in their own right. Yet one of the cruel tricks that depression inflicts on its sufferers is an increased likelihood of rejection. Rejection hurts, and it can intensify your depression.

When people get depressed, friends and family initially respond with offerings of empathy and support. But after a while, and as much as they want to help, friends and family struggle to sustain their support — for a number of reasons:

✔ Spending lots of time with someone in the throes of depression can be difficult.

✔ Depressed people don't have the energy to respond positively to others, so they typically retreat from interaction. Friends and family, who may begin to feel rejected themselves, eventually decrease their support and show less caring and engagement.

And to add to this increased likelihood of facing rejection, depression causes people to deal with communications from others in three self-defeating ways. First, they magnify the negative intentions of others. Second, they look for negative feedback even if it doesn't exist. And finally, they tend to get angry and defensive in response to legitimate criticism. All these tendencies lead to more interpersonal trouble.

Exaggerating the negative

When depressed people receive negative feedback, they usually see more negativity than there actually is. In other words, they magnify the degree of any rejection they receive.

Keith's story illustrates how depression clouds the vision of its victims. **Keith,** who is from Southern California, chooses a college in Upstate New York. His freshman year begins unremarkably. However, as fall draws to a close and the days shorten, Keith's mood deteriorates (see Chapter 2 for information about seasonal affective disorder). He has trouble getting out of bed and starts missing his morning classes. His roommate makes a number of efforts to help him — offering to wake him up, suggesting that he talk to a counselor, and inviting him to social events.

But Keith responds with sullen withdrawal. One morning, feeling at his wit's end, his roommate snaps, "Look, I've done what I can for you. Stop feeling so sorry for yourself and get out of bed, or at least get help."

Rather than understand his roommate's frustration, Keith concludes that his roommate despises him. His roommate's remark was negative, but it came from concern and worry. Keith magnified and personalized the message into total rejection.

See Chapters 5, 6, and 7 for more information about how depression insidiously distorts peoples' perspectives about events in their lives.

Looking for negative feedback

Depressed people actually ask for disapproval and disparagement from other people. A series of studies conducted by Dr. William B. Swann and other colleagues demonstrated that depression leads people to seek negative feedback from others. And when they get that poor feedback, they feel even worse.

Do these findings mean that depressed people may actually *desire* feeling bad? We don't think so. Considerable evidence exists that says most humans are highly motivated to *self-verify;* in other words, people actively seek information that confirms whatever it is that they believe about themselves and reject information that runs counter to those self-beliefs. Thus, people with positive self-views work to maintain their rosy outlook, while people with negative self-views labor just as diligently to sustain a sinister, dark take on themselves.

Sometimes depressed people seek positive reassurance from their partners. If they receive a dose of support, more often than not they find a reason to reject and deny their partners' positive efforts (due to the drive to self-verify). Not surprisingly, their partners then feel rejected. And a rejected partner typically withdraws and provides less support. This pattern can evolve into a vicious cycle of rejection and increased depression.

Billy has a chronic, low-level depression known as dysthymia (see Chapter 2 for more information). He complains to his wife that he's a failure at work, expecting reassurance. When his wife tells him that he's very successful, his depression causes him to reject her support by saying, "You don't know what you're talking about." His wife feels hurt and withdraws.

Fighting off constructive criticism

Seemingly contrary to the info we present in the preceding sections, some people with depression occasionally attempt to fend off criticism. However, their depression rarely allows them to do so constructively. Instead, depressed minds sometimes dictate a defensive response that either denies the feedback or counterattacks. Again, a cycle of negativity and rejection ensues.

Pursuing Positives

Depression encourages withdrawal, avoidance, and isolation. The depressed mind tells you to not only expect negative reactions, it also guides you to elicit them. Therefore, many of your relationships may suffer. Overcoming those dark messages from your mind requires considerable effort. And mustering effort isn't easy when you're depressed. But you can ignore your mind's chatter and start reaching out to the ones you love, one step at a time.

If you've been depressed for quite a while, you've probably fallen into some bad habits in your relationships. Even if you don't seek negative feedback, you probably don't feel like building positive interactions. And your depressed mind may be telling you that if you do something positive, others will only reject you.

Repeating the same old behaviors isn't going to improve your relationship. You have to do something different. What do you have to lose? Infusing positive interactions into a relationship rarely causes trouble! If you don't get an overwhelmingly positive initial response from your partner, keep at it. Persistence is the key.

Everyone likes an occasional pat on the back. When you're depressed, you don't pat yourself on the back, and you don't pat anyone else on the back either. After a while, no one wants to pat you on the back, either. But the glue that holds relationships together is based on positive interactions.

We think that "pats" are a way to improve relationships. When you infuse your relationships with pats, they inevitably improve. And improving your relationships will help decrease your depression.

"Pats" come in four forms — giving compliments, doing nice things, planning positive times together, and introducing "nice" into your daily routine. If you're depressed, we fully realize that you probably don't feel like putting forth the effort to perform these good deeds. That's why we make them simple for you.

Giving compliments

Receiving appreciation, thanks, gratitude, and compliments feels good. Make a goal of giving your partner one or more of these expressions of your feelings each day. Find a way to remind yourself to do so. Perhaps you can write a note in your day planner or put a sticky note on your mirror. Don't forget that, when you're depressed, your memory can defeat your best intentions (see Chapter 8 for more information on depression and memory).

Keep just a few things in mind when giving compliments and appreciation:

✔ **Be specific.** Don't merely say, "I appreciate you." (Although it's okay to say it sometimes.) Try to single out reasons why you feel appreciative, such as your partner's help with cooking, cleaning, shopping, or finances. Or compliment your partner about specific aspects of his or her appearance, problem-solving ability, or special talents.

✔ **Avoid "buts."** Avoid the temptation to give a compliment and then take it back. Don't tell your partner, "I appreciate your attempt to balance the checkbook, but you made an error."

✔ **Be sincere.** Don't give false flattery. Only say things you really mean. You can find something positive to appreciate. If you can't, don't make something up. However, if you can't think of anything positive to say, you want to consider getting expert help.

Doing nice things

Compliments can be very useful, but actions speak louder than words. Again, depression may make doing nice things difficult, so here's a list to get you started. Having a list can inspire you to take action even if you don't feel like it (see Chapter 9 for information about how action creates more motivation). So, circle the items you think your partner will like, and feel free to add some of your own. Make a goal of doing one positive action two or three times a week. We call this plan "Making Nice."

✔ Bring home flowers.

✔ Cook a romantic meal.

✔ Express how much you care.

✔ Give a hug.

✔ Hold hands.

✔ Make a short phone call to express caring.

✔ Offer your partner a backrub.

✔ Prepare a breakfast in bed.

✔ Put a love note in your partner's lunch.

✔ Run an errand.

✔ Send a card.

- ✔ Take over a task your partner usually does, such as the laundry.
- ✔ Tell your partner to take a hot bath while you do the dishes.
- ✔ Wash your partner's car.

Making Nice isn't a quick fix. Don't expect instant returns, and don't keep score. Over a period of weeks, the exercise will likely improve the emotional tone of your relationship. If it doesn't, consider seeking relationship counseling.

Planning positive times together

Many busy couples devote time to pleasing others — they shuttle their kids to and from after-school activities, they take care of their elderly parents, and they work long hours to impress their bosses. But they neglect devoting time to their relationship. If one member is depressed, this neglect almost always increases.

You can improve your relationship by planning positive times together. These activities don't have to involve elaborate vacations or expensive outings. Rather, simple pleasures can work wonders. The key is to sit down to plan pleasures and then make sure that they happen. Be creative; make sure the activity is something you'll both enjoy. Here are some suggestions to help you get started:

- ✔ Buy a couple's massage at a day spa.
- ✔ Get an ice cream sundae.
- ✔ Go dancing.
- ✔ Go for a scenic drive.
- ✔ Plan a date.
- ✔ Plant a garden.
- ✔ See a movie and hold hands.
- ✔ Spend the night together in a motel.
- ✔ Take a walk together.

If you're depressed, these outings may not sound very appealing. However, depression causes you to have a bleak outlook on future activities. See Chapters 9 and 11 for more info about this process of negative predicting and how to overcome it.

Introducing nice into your everyday routine

One of the best ideas for doing something nice is to suggest having a conversation with your partner at the end of every workday. And if your schedule just won't permit a daily talk, try to at least schedule it in three times a week. We call this exercise "The Daily News." The purpose of The Daily News is to build closeness with your partner. The Daily News consists of a number of important components:

- **Avoiding conflict.** Only discuss items that don't involve conflict between the two of you. In other words, discuss things that occur outside of your relationship.

- **Expressing empathy.** Tell your partner that you understand how he feels. Try to endorse or validate his emotions. You can say, "I think I'd be stressed by that too," or, "I can see why you'd be upset." Stay focused on your partner's perspective; don't find fault. For example, if your partner is complaining about someone else's behavior, it's not a good time to point out that the other person may be right.

- **Listening.** Listening means asking questions for elaboration and better understanding. It means focusing on your partner and showing interest through head nods, light touches on the arm, and brief comments such as, "I see," "Oh," "Uh huh," and "Wow." You can also enhance listening by demonstrating affection and approval. For example, you can say, "I really like your thinking on that," or offer a hug if you see distress.

- **Staying away from advice.** Don't give advice unless your partner specifically asks for help with an issue. Even if your partner asks you for advice, give it sparingly and merely as a possible option to consider.

- **Talking one at a time.** Let your partner talk for 10 to 20 minutes, and then you take a similar amount of time.

You may be surprised by how much The Daily News can enhance your relationship — sometimes in a matter of days.

April and **Tasha** have been together for eight years. Their relationship starts to suffer from April's depression. April is in the midst of a difficult menopause complicated by a prolonged depression. Tasha, her partner, is years away from menopause. Although she sympathizes with April, Tasha's patience wears thin after months of withdrawal, moodiness, and irritability. The women, who were once almost inseparable, find themselves becoming more and more distant.

April begins to talk to a counselor and realizes that her withdrawal from Tasha is a normal response to her depressed feelings. The counselor tells

April about a technique similar to The Daily News that she can use as a tool to combat depression and improve her relationship. April values her relationship and vows to make it better. Despite feeling momentarily unenthused, she explains, "Tasha, depression has tried to come between us. I can't promise an instant recovery, but having positive time together every day could help. Let's sit down with a cup of tea and talk."

Tasha, feeling relieved that her partner is making an effort, responds with renewed empathy and compassion. Their daily conversation becomes a ritual that helps close the gap between them.

Defeating Defensiveness

When relationships begin heading downhill, people start making what we call *malicious assumptions* about their partners. In other words, they reflexively interpret potentially ambiguous or even caring statements as coming from someone who has malicious, hostile motives. Depression, with its inevitable gloomy outlook, can increase the frequency of malicious assumptions.

After the malicious assumption takes over, people typically do something that is especially self-defeating — they get defensive in response to the perceived attack. And defensiveness pretty much assures that the other party will become hostile, even if hostility wasn't originally intended!

Ed notices that his wife, **Sheila,** has been lethargic and depressed for the past few weeks. The bills that she normally pays begin to stack up, unopened on her desk. Sheila, who is usually meticulous about her appearance, recently stopped wearing makeup. Ed cares deeply about her and worries that she may be ill. One Saturday morning, he approaches her and asks, "Sweetheart, I'm worried about you. You haven't been taking care of things like you always do. Are you feeling all right?"

Sheila erupts sarcastically, "So, great, you think I'm not measuring up. Thanks for being so supportive. I do the best I can; I work ridiculous hours; all I ever do is work. On top of everything else, I don't need your criticism."

"But Sheila, I'm not being critical. It's just, you've changed, and you don't seem to be your old self. I'm not trying to start an argument, I just want to help," Ed pleads.

"If you want to help, just leave me alone. Can't you tell that I work myself to the bone already? Of course some things aren't getting done! I'm not a machine after all." Sheila stomps away in tears.

So just what constitutes a defensive response? Basically anything you may say to absolve yourself of any blame or responsibility for a perceived criticism. And you may wonder what could possibly be wrong with that; after all, you may have done nothing wrong whatsoever. Well, defensiveness is a problem for two reasons:

- ✔ It absolutely assumes that your partner intended to be hostile in the first place.
- ✔ Adding spice to your defensiveness in the form of criticism and hostility is all too easy to do.

So what can you do to keep from falling into a defensive, critical mode when you feel that your partner may have said something scornful to you? The following sections discuss two particularly useful strategies — "Checking It Out" and "Depersonalizing."

Checking it out

The best way to counteract malicious assumptions that lead to defensiveness is to use the "Checking It Out" strategy. This two-step technique is basically what it sounds like:

1. Stifle your urge to get defensive or attack.

2. Make a gentle inquiry about your partner's meaning and intent.

In the previous section, Ed says to Sheila, "Sweetheart, I'm worried about you. You haven't been taking care of things like you always do. Are you feeling alright?" Sheila responds defensively and sarcastically, "So, great, you think I'm not measuring up. Thanks for being so supportive. I do the best I can; I work ridiculous hours; all I ever do is work. On top of everything else, I don't need your criticism."

Sheila obviously interpreted Ed's comment as critical and malicious. But she could have checked out her assumption by saying, "Ed, are you upset that I'm not dong enough? If you are, I'm willing to talk about it."

Likely, Ed would have replied with something like, "No, not at all. I've just been worried that you look a little rundown lately. Is anything wrong?"

Generally speaking, if you take the time to check out the meaning of what you perceive as critical, you'll find that the intent wasn't as vicious as you had thought. Feeling a bit defensive when you "think" that you've been criticized is perfectly natural. But take the time to take a deep breath and check it out.

On the other hand, sometimes you may discover your partner has a real complaint. If so, try to maintain a non-defensive posture. Keep asking questions and consider using the buffering and defusing techniques that we discuss later in this chapter.

Don't attempt to use Checking It Out, or even the other communication techniques we discuss later in this chapter, if you're feeling hostile and significantly upset. If you rate your upset as higher than 50 on a 100 point scale, the odds of you thinking of anything useful or productive to say are about one in ten billion. Ask for a timeout and come back to discuss the issue when you feel relatively calm — perhaps in 30 minutes, a few hours, or even a day or two. But don't put off talking for much longer than that, because resentments may build. And taking time to get into a better frame of mind on your own isn't a license for avoiding communication altogether.

The Checking It Out technique requires you to block out your malicious assumption while you inquire gently about your partner's meaning and intentions.

Depersonalizing

Personalizing occurs when you attribute your partner's tantrums, tirades, and upset remarks as being about you. For example, **Patrick** spills a glass of water on the computer keyboard. And his partner **Beth** explodes. Patrick, already deeply embarrassed by the accident, feels even worse about himself after hearing Beth explode. Patrick, perhaps naturally, assumes that Beth's explosion is all about him and his clumsiness. Not so.

In actuality, Beth came from a highly abusive family in which accidents were treated as catastrophes. Yelling at Patrick was a habit learned long ago. Someone else may have responded with a little annoyance or even empathic concern.

Depersonalizing means figuring out when your partner's reactions have less to do with you and more to do with previous upbringing or learning that formed core beliefs about the meaning of certain types of events.

Everyone has core beliefs, instilled during childhood, that continue to exert a huge influence on how they perceive and feel about events. (See Chapter 7 for more information about these beliefs and how they work.) Core beliefs lie behind your hopes, dreams, and fears — in other words, all the issues you have strong feelings about. And you don't have to be depressed for one or more of these core beliefs to generate a lot of emotion. Table 14-1 shows a few of the common core beliefs, or hot buttons, that interfere with relationships.

Table 14-1	Relationship Hot Buttons (Core Beliefs)	
Hot Button	*What It Means*	*Common Origins*
Vulnerability/ Pessimism	Expecting the worst and having intense worries about issues such as health, money, or safety.	An impoverished childhood, pessimistic parents, and traumatic events during childhood.
Abandonment	Fearing that anyone close to you will eventually leave.	A parent who was emotionally unavailable, parents that divorced at an early age, and other serious losses of people close to you.
Dependency	Thinking that you need more help than you really do.	A parent who stepped in to help whenever things got frustrating, or critical parents who gave messages that you were incapable.
Perfectionism	A driven need to make everything you do perfect, or believing that something just isn't good enough.	Highly critical parents, or parents who excessively focused on accomplishments.

Stan grew up in a very unstable and poor family. He developed a core belief of pessimism and vulnerability. **Norma's** father abandoned her when she was 6. After he left, Norma's mother became seriously depressed and withdrew from her. Norma developed the core belief that people who love her will eventually abandon her.

Stan and Norma are now married. Stan opens a credit card bill and discovers that Norma spent slightly more money this month than their paychecks can cover. He confronts his wife. "Norma, we can't afford to pay the credit card bill this month. We're getting deeper and deeper into debt. If you keep this up, we'll end up having to declare bankruptcy! Stop this wild spending at once!" Norma starts to cry and says, "Fine, if you want a divorce, just do it now. I knew this marriage would never work out."

Are Stan and Norma crazy, or just irrational? Neither. Stan's exaggerated response comes from his childhood, when his family often had to scramble to put food on the table. Stan's hot buttons concerned vulnerability and pessimism. And Norma's abandonment hot button comes from the physical loss of her father and the emotional loss of her mother. Both reactions may be excessive, but they make sense if you understand their backgrounds.

If your partner consistently gets upset, distraught, or passionate about an issue in a way that seems either excessive or possibly irrational, odds are that one or more core beliefs is at work. Doing some detective work can help you find out which core belief may be affecting your partner's perspective. You can start by determining your own core beliefs (see Table 14-1 and Chapter 7). One of *your* core beliefs may help explain why your partner's feelings seem excessive or irrational to you.

After you figure out what your hot buttons (and those of your partner) are about, you may still disagree. However, you can at least appreciate that much of the emotional charge isn't about you. Step back and depersonalize. Realize that the conflict has more to do with either your own or your partner's early upbringing than it does with you. Doing so can help reduce your own negative feelings.

Getting Your Message Across

Poor communication can rip your relationship apart. On the other hand, using the right communication style can help keep your relationship together. Communication matters most when you're talking about difficult issues and conflicts. And communication techniques aren't that difficult to master.

We've found that certain people resist using these techniques. For some depressed people, asserting their concerns may seem too difficult to accomplish. But the alternative of stuffing their concerns and avoiding the expression of their views only leads to resentment and hostility.

Other folks always want to express themselves with brutal honesty. Yet doing so frequently leads to hostile rejection. We urge you to give these techniques a try; they can improve your communication with friends, family, coworkers, and loved ones.

Three strategies are particularly helpful for improving communication whether you're depressed or not — "I Messages," "Buffering," and "Defusing." These techniques are particularly designed to help you communicate about difficult issues while preventing the discussion from deteriorating into conflict.

Using "I Messages"

When two people disagree, the language they use to express themselves can do much to add fuel to the fire. A simple technique called "I Messages" can help prevent the disagreement from getting out of control. The idea is to state how you're feeling rather than accuse or criticize your partner. This technique is an alternative to using blaming messages. Table 14-2 shows some examples of blaming messages and their more productive I-message equivalents. Read the examples of both types of messages. Then, when you feel tempted to blame your partner, try rephrasing your concerns in terms of I Messages.

Table 14-2	The I Message Technique
Blaming Messages	*I Messages*
You never show affection.	I wish you would hug me more often.
You spend too much money.	I feel worried about our finances, can we talk about it?
You are so critical about everything I do.	I feel like I'm not pleasing you.
You make me so mad.	I'm feeling a little upset right now.
You never do the things you say you're going to do.	I feel unhappy when you forget to follow through on something you promised.

Creating buffers

"Buffering" gives you a way to add a spoonful of sugar to distasteful messages. This technique involves finding ways to soften any criticism you want to communicate. You add a phrase to acknowledge the possibility that your position may not be entirely correct. After all, can anyone ever truly be 100 percent certain that they are correct in their views about a particular event? Not often.

Buffering offers the opportunity to discuss your concerns and opens the door to compromise. The following list provides some good buffering phrases:

- ✔ "I could be wrong here, although I have a concern that . . ."

- ✔ "I may be making too much out of this, . . ."

- ✔ "Please correct me if I'm off base; I feel a little upset that . . ."

- ✔ "Help me understand your take on what I have to say."

If you use such phrases prior to talking about your concern or criticism, your partner will be less likely to go into a defensive or attacking mode. The technique increases the likelihood that you'll be heard rather than dismissed.

Defusing criticism

The "Defusing" technique helps prevent a criticism from escalating into a full-blown argument. This technique helps you deal with criticism from your partner (instead of defending or fighting). In a sense, it's the opposite of Buffering. With the Defusing technique, you find *something* about the criticism to validate or agree with. And apologizing for any valid portion of the agreement doesn't hurt, either. Here are some examples of responses you can use to help defuse an argument:

- "I'm sorry, you could have a point about that."
- "Sometimes what you're saying is probably true."
- "I can see why you think that."
- "I can agree with part of what you're saying."

Excuses actually convey the idea that you care more about saving face than you do about your partner's concerns. When you provide a partial agreement and a sincere apology (Defusing), you indicate that your interest lies in repairing your partner's hurt feelings. When you make excuses, you demonstrate that you're more interested in repairing your own ego.

When you're depressed and your self-esteem is low, you may feel like making excuses in order to prevent further erosion of your self-esteem. If you work hard to avoid that temptation, you'll be rewarded in the long-run.

Putting the techniques to work

Now that you've seen what Buffering, Defusing, and I Messages look like, you may want to see how they look in action. That way, you're more likely to appreciate the value of these communication strategies. But first, we show you how gruesome communications can sound when you don't use these techniques. **Aretha and Dennis** are having a disagreement about housework. Here's their conversation without the Buffering, Defusing, and I Messages techniques.

> **Aretha:** You never help me with any of the housework. I'm really getting sick and tired of it.

> **Dennis:** Yes I do. I mowed the lawn last week. Just what do you want out of me?

> **Aretha:** Mowing the lawn is your job. I'm talking about laundry, cooking, shopping, dishes. You don't do any of those things. If it weren't for me, this place would look like a pigsty.

> **Dennis:** Look, I make more money than you, and I'm beat when I get home. When we got married, you said if I was the main bread winner, you'd take care of the house. This isn't fair!
>
> **Aretha:** Fair? What are you talking about? I work too, you know. You can't even talk about a simple thing like housework without shouting!

Not a very productive discussion, is it? Both Dennis and Aretha resort to criticism, defensiveness, and anger. Nothing is solved, and bad feelings escalate. Now we're going to take the same conversation and insert the Buffering, Defusing, and I Messages strategies.

> **Aretha:** Help me understand your viewpoint (Buffering). I feel a little overwhelmed with the housework (I Message), and it kind of seems like you're not pitching in as much as I'd like.
>
> **Dennis:** Well, I agree that you do more of the housework (Defusing). I'm sorry that I've made you feel so overwhelmed. I guess I come home so tired that I often don't think about housework, but maybe I should (I Messages). What do you need?
>
> **Aretha:** Sometimes I feel like I do everything (I Messages). And maybe I'm overreacting (Buffering). Still, if you could help with the dishes after dinner, that would feel better.
>
> **Dennis:** (Defusing) I can see why you'd like that; after all, we do have a large family and a whole lot of dishes (Defusing). I'm just so tired after dinner (I Message). How about I take on the laundry on the weekends instead? And maybe we can start getting the kids more involved with the dishes. They're getting old enough.
>
> **Aretha:** Well, that's not a bad compromise I suppose. Thanks for listening to my concern.

That turned out a little better, didn't it? When you use the Defusing technique, you focus more on finding something to agree with (or even apologize for some aspect of the complaint), and you pay less attention to conjuring up defensive excuses. Buffering allows you to express concerns in a gentle, non-confrontational manner. I Messages keep the focus on your concerns and prevent you from blaming your partner. All three of these techniques can be applied to communicating with intimate partners as well as other important relationships.

After you've read the dialogs between Aretha and Dennis, consider writing out a dialog that you have with someone that doesn't go too well. Then rewrite the conversation inserting as many Defusing, Buffering, and I Messages as you can. With a little work and practice, you'll find yourself gradually communicating better over time.

Who to turn to: People or pets?

Many studies suggest that improving the quality of your relationships and social support can help you cope better, decrease the severity of your depression, and even prevent future bouts with depression. That's why we devote this chapter to giving you advice on enhancing the quality of your important relationships. Of course, we now realize that we left out one important type of relationship — the relationship you have with your pet.

A study by Karen Allen, PhD, and colleagues at the State University of New York found that pet owners have lower blood pressure, slower heart rates, and appear to handle stress better than people who don't have pets. We know that chronic stress leads to a host of problems, including depression. So if you currently have no one else to turn to, it actually makes sense to find a furry friend. By the way, the researchers found that dogs and cats work equally well for reducing stress and battling depression.

Part V

Fighting the Physical Foe: Biological Therapies

The 5th Wave   By Rich Tennant

"Is there an herbal remedy for acute option shock?"

In this part . . .

Year after year, new medications for depression hit the market, and getting a handle on all your options can be overwhelming. We bring you the latest information about medications for treating depression. More importantly, we help you make a decision as to whether medications are the right choice for you.

Other alternatives for treating depression also exist. In the pages that follow, you can read about natural alternatives such as herbs or light therapy. And finally, we discuss electric shock treatment and other biologically based strategies for treating difficult cases of depression.

Chapter 15

Prescribing Pleasure

● ●

In This Chapter

▶ Deciding how to deal with depression

▶ Looking into medication

▶ Figuring out how medication works

▶ Describing drugs

● ●

"**D**oc, I feel terrible," **Bryce** complains. "I can't stand to be around my family, and I get irritated by the smallest things. I'm having trouble sleeping; I wake up at 4 a.m. and usually toss and turn the rest of the night. I feel restless inside; it's hard to describe. I feel pain, but I can't tell you where. All I can tell you is that it hurts. I don't know what's wrong with me. Maybe I have a brain tumor."

After a complete physical and more discussion, Bryce's doctor concludes that he suffers from major depression. His doctor prescribes an antidepressant and explains to Bryce that he has a "chemical imbalance." Slightly puzzled as to how his brain chemicals got out of whack but willing to try out the medication, Bryce agrees to fill the prescription.

At the drug store, the pharmacist encourages Bryce to look over the literature about the popular antidepressant his doctor prescribed. When Bryce starts to read about possible side effects, he worries. Headaches, dry mouth, dizziness, stomach upsets, and oh no — sexual dysfunction. He wonders whether or not he should just pitch the drugs and tough his depression out. After some pondering, Bryce decides to give the medication a try because his depression feels so awful. Besides, he reasons that if he experiences bad side effects, perhaps the doc will know of a different medication that won't affect him in that way. Bryce made a good decision; his depression began to lift within a couple of weeks.

Until recently, many people believed that depression resulted from a character flaw or weakness. Because of that belief, those suffering from depression often didn't seek treatment. Feeling embarrassed, guilty, and worthless, they suffered in horrible silence. Or worse, ended their pain with suicide.

Medication for depression has alleviated suffering for millions. And maybe even more importantly, it encourages treatment. If a pill indeed can change your mood, then it would seem there really must be a physical cause for depression. Those afflicted can declare, "Depression isn't our fault."

Depression is an illness of the body and mind. Left untreated, it not only robs you of happiness, but also takes a lasting, physical toll as well. (For a complete rundown, check out Chapter 1.) Please get help if you're depressed. Toughing it out is not an option. Take a look at this chapter to help select the best treatment for you — therapy, medication, or a combination.

In this chapter, we help you decide for yourself whether medication is an option for you. We provide a guide for making that important decision. Then we tell you about where to get help, how long you may have to take medication, and when mixing talk therapy with drugs may give you even more relief. Finally, we provide some guidance to the most popularly prescribed pills.

Hammering Depression: Choosing the Right Tool for You

You've probably heard the saying that if the only tool you have in your toolbox is a hammer, you're likely to treat everything like a nail. Well, physicians and psychiatrists have prescription drugs in their toolboxes, and psychologists and therapists hammer away with talk therapy. So it's no wonder that each group tends to recommend their treatment as the best treatment for depression.

We've spent the vast majority of this book giving you methods to improve your mood and defeat depression. Most of these tips are based on techniques borrowed from the fields of cognitive-behavioral therapy (a combination of cognitive therapy reviewed in Part II and behavior therapy discussed in Part IV). Honestly, we want to encourage readers to adopt healthy thinking and behavior to battle the blues as their first line of defense against depression. Is that because the only tool is therapy? Certainly not!

But we've reviewed the latest research. And a huge body of studies pits prescription medications against psychotherapy for the treatment of depression. Most studies concur: Cognitive-behavioral therapy is at least as effective as medication for the treatment of depression. Better still, therapy may help prevent relapse.

And just in case you're skeptical, a study completed at the University of Pennsylvania and Vanderbilt University looked at people with severe depression and compared how they reacted to treatment with cognitive therapy and medication. This study included both physicians and psychologists and was funded through the National Institute of Mental Health and a major pharmaceutical company.

The results were impressive. Cognitive therapy worked at least as well as medication for the long-term treatment of severe depression (in this study, *severe* didn't include people with psychotic symptoms). Realizing that relapse in depression is a serious problem, scientists looked at what happened to these folks a year later. They found two groups less likely to have relapsed. The first group still took their antidepressant medication and the other group had completed cognitive therapy. In fact, 75 percent of participants who had therapy didn't experience relapse compared to 60 percent who continued taking medication. Remember that cognitive therapy adds an additional boost to any treatment of depression. (See Part II for more information about cognitive therapy.)

For some people with depression, the combination of medication and therapy appears to give them a slight edge over using just one or the other. Sometimes antidepressant medication helps a person make better use of therapy.

Ultimately, the decision as to whether or not to take medication is up to you. If you choose to stick with self-help or therapy, work seriously through the exercises provided in this book or with your therapist. Don't expect to get better without considerable effort. With work, you can expect that the skills you pick up can help inoculate you against future struggles with depression. But for many folks, medication is part of the solution — and for good reason.

Exploring the Medication Option

Given all of the evidence that therapy works, why would anyone take medication? Well, for about 90 percent of depressed people, a single medication or a combination of medicines can be found that will either decrease symptoms or completely cure depression. Opting for the medication route is often advisable when

> ✔ **You have serious suicidal thoughts or plans.** You need help now. First, get checked out by a mental health professional to determine the best treatment for you. Sometimes antidepressant medication can work a few important weeks faster than cognitive therapy.

> ✔ **You have bipolar disorder or depression with psychotic features.** Usually medication is the best answer for folks with bipolar disorder or

people whose depression is so severe that they hear voices or see things that aren't really there (see Chapter 2). However, therapy often helps stabilize and keep people from discontinuing medication and suffering relapses.

✔ **You've given cognitive therapy or interpersonal therapy a good try and your depression keeps reoccurring.** Evidence indicates that untreated depression becomes more severe, frequent, and resistant to treatment. If your depression keeps returning, you should probably consider adding long-term use of medication to your other efforts.

✔ **Your symptoms of depression are mostly physiological.** For example, you have problems with your appetite or sleep, you feel overwhelming fatigue, forgetfulness, and poor concentration. *Caution:* Not everyone with the physical symptoms of depression will respond better to medication, and some of those with physical symptoms may be trying to stuff feelings and thoughts inside. So, if medication doesn't work, a visit to a therapist may be a very good idea.

✔ **Depression takes control of your life.** If severe symptoms cause you to neglect the important tasks of everyday living, you may need medication to get you going again. But, after you're feeling a little bit better, consider self-help or cognitive therapy to keep you healthy.

✔ **Medical conditions cause your depression.** Sometimes people with other illnesses become depressed. (See Chapter 2 for more on causes of depression). Doctors aren't sure how that works, but many believe that one disease causes the other. Medication may be the quickest way to overcome this type of depression.

✔ **Panic or anxiety accompanies depression.** You may have too much on your plate to wait for the benefits of therapy. Again, when the medication starts taking effect, you may have more mental energy available to tackle anxiety and depression in therapy or with the help of books like this one or another of our titles, *Overcoming Anxiety For Dummies* (Wiley Publishing, Inc.).

✔ **Therapy doesn't work.** A few people just don't seem to benefit from therapy. Or they may need long-term therapy because of complicated issues. In this case, medication may be a good adjunctive choice.

✔ **Your depression has lasted most of your life.** Some evidence suggests that extremely chronic depression (such as *dysthymia,* see Chapter 2) may benefit a great deal from medication in addition to therapy.

✔ **You don't have time for therapy.** For a few folks, therapy is too time consuming. If your schedule is already too full, we hope you at least take a few minutes out of your busy day to read through this book.

✔ **You don't have insurance coverage for psychotherapy.** Some insurance companies don't cover psychological services. We hope this will change, but if your insurance covers only medication, and you can't afford therapy, finances may dictate that you go the medication route for defeating your depression.

Many of you may choose to take medication. Don't worry that you're taking the easy way out. If you have an infection, you take an antibiotic. If you have depression, taking an antidepressant often makes sense.

Taking medication the right way

Antidepressant medications are powerful drugs. They affect the body in numerous ways. That's why they're not sold over the counter. Therefore, keep these tips for taking antidepressant medications the right way in mind should you decide to give antidepressant medication a try.

- ✓ **Tell your doctor about any other physical conditions you have.** Discuss all your current health concerns with your doctor, especially liver disease, hepatitis, diabetes, high blood pressure, or kidney disease.

- ✓ **If you think you may be pregnant, intend to try to get pregnant, or are breastfeeding, let your doctor know.** Certain medications may not be safe.

- ✓ **Tell your doctor what other medications you're taking.** Antidepressants may interfere with other medications, or other medications may interfere with antidepressants. Be sure to include non-prescription medications in your discussion.

- ✓ **Tell you doctor about any herbs or supplements you take.** Again, there may be interactions with antidepressants. For more about herbs and supplements, please see Chapter 16.

- ✓ **Hang in there.** Antidepressant medication usually takes at least a week to begin working and may take as long as six weeks for a maximum benefit to occur. And you may not respond to the first attempt. Give your doctor a chance to help you. You may have to go through months of experimentation to find the right drug or drug combination. The good news is that after you find what works, that drug will likely keep working to alleviate your depression.

- ✓ **Talk to your doctor about side effects.** Although many of the bothersome side effects go away after a couple of weeks, don't suffer in silence. Your doctor may be able to help you manage the side effects with either a change in the dose or by adding another drug to the mix.

- ✓ **Talk to your doctor about *all* side effects.** Okay, one of the most common and somewhat embarrassing side effects of antidepressant medication is a decrease in sexual pleasure. Some experience a decrease in desire. Others may undergo a frustrating inability to achieve orgasm. Tell your doctor. Treatments for this side effect are available.

✔ **Don't drink alcohol when you take antidepressants.** Drinking alcohol can boost the mood temporarily, but its overall effect is that of a depressant. Alcohol may interact with antidepressant medication increasing fatigue or blocking its effects. An occasional drink is probably harmless.

Whatever you choose, remember that depression is a highly treatable illness. If the method you choose doesn't work, don't give up hope. Be patient, get help, and try something different.

Opting out of medication

If taking a pill can cure you, why not? You may be one of the lucky people who begin taking antidepressant medication, enjoy a reduction of symptoms, have few side effects, and go merrily on with your life. Why then doesn't everyone fill up at the drug store?

✔ **Side effects can be very bothersome.** More than a third of people prescribed antidepressant medication discontinue taking their medications. Most stop because of side effects. Side effects can include nausea, headaches, insomnia, dry mouth, weight gain, feelings of apathy, and sexual dysfunction.

✔ **Not generally safe for pregnant or breastfeeding women.** Research about the effects of antidepressant medication on the fetus or infant comes from animal studies or case examples. What woman would risk the health of her baby to participate in a drug trial? Not enough information is available to judge the safety of most antidepressant medications. So, talk to your doctor if you're planning on getting pregnant, might be pregnant, or are nursing a baby. In most cases, psychotherapy is a better choice than medication.

Depression after the birth of a baby is a common problem that can become serious if left untreated. Please get help if you experience more than a couple of days of baby blues (see Chapter 2 for more on postpartum depression).

✔ **Worry about long-term effects.** If you have one bout of depression, your risk of relapse or recurrence increases. If you have more than one major depressive episode, if depression was severe or long-lasting, if you have bipolar disorder (see Chapter 2), or your depression never completely lifted, your physician may recommend lifelong medication. Although long-term treatment appears to have little risk, some experts have expressed concern regarding the lack of knowledge about lifelong use of antidepressant medication.

✔ **Just say no.** Some people don't want to take medication, for religious or philosophical reasons. If you choose this path, please get help for your depression through cognitive-behavioral or interpersonal therapy techniques (see Parts II, III, and V). Depression requires treatment. If your mood doesn't improve within a few months of self help or if your depression feels very deep, please find a mental health professional for assistance (see Chapter 4 for information on finding professional help).

Working with Your Doctor to Find the Correct Medication

A positive, collaborative relationship with your prescribing health care practitioner (your primary care physician, psychiatrist, or another practitioner such as a physicians assistant; see Chapter 4) may be the most important ingredient for successful treatment of depression. You and your health care provider must openly discuss your unique symptoms of depression, your response to the medication, and any side effects you may experience.

Unfortunately, science hasn't yet figured out which particular antidepressant medication is likely to work for any one individual. Some people respond to the first drug prescribed; others will make changes in their medications. The drug your doctor chooses depends on several factors:

✔ **Depressive symptoms:** Your doctor will want to know all about your symptoms before choosing a medication. The doctor may want to know the answers to the following questions. Do you sleep too much, or too little? Have you gained or lost weight? Do you have aches and pains? Do you feel anxious as well as depressed? Do you find yourself unable to concentrate?

✔ **Side effects:** For most people, the first choice in medication is the drug with the fewest side effects. But side effects of a drug can sometimes be used advantageously. For example, people with sleep problems may do better with a medication that has a side effect of sedation. Again, no one knows how bothered you will be by side effects. Sometimes a change in medication, or a change in the dose, or even the addition of another drug is used to manage side effects.

✔ **History of depression:** If you have had previous depressive episodes and have been successfully treated with a particular antidepressant, the same one will likely be used again. And, the doctor may well decide to continue the medication for a much longer period of time.

✔ **Family response to antidepressant medication:** Although the evidence is scant that genetics affect how different antidepressant medications will work, if a member of your family had a favorable response to a specific antidepressant medication, let your provider know. Depending on many factors, that antidepressant may be a good first choice.

Less than a quarter of people treated with medication for depression get adequate treatment, meaning that they receive a reasonable number of psychotherapy sessions with treatments found to be effective for depression (see Chapter 4 for an overview of those treatments) or take an adequate dose of medications for a sufficient length of time. About 10 percent of people with prescriptions for antidepressants fill the prescription but stop taking their medication within the first week! Many more stop the minute they feel a little better. If you choose to be treated for depression with medication, follow through. Your risk of having a relapse grows when you don't get completely better.

Brushing Up on Biology

Scientists continue to study the mystery of depression and biology. Researchers know that the brains and bodies of depressed people look and even work differently than those of people without depression (see Chapter 1). However, we also know that the biological aspect of depression isn't as simple as a mere chemical deficiency. If that were the case, an IV infusion of an antidepressant would create instant joy. Doesn't happen.

To understand how antidepressant medication apparently works, you need to understand some basics about your brain and body. We promise to keep this simple. And don't worry — no final exam!

Knowing the nervous system

The human nervous system senses activity in your body and outside of it. The brain takes in the sensory information and plans a response. The nervous system then responds with action. For example, when you touch a hot stove with your hand, pain messages surge to your brain. Your brain reacts almost instantly with the information that touching something hot caused the pain. Your brain sends a message to your hand to quickly pull away. Hopefully, your brain will remember the experience so that next time you won't touch the stove.

The nervous system consists of the central nervous system (CNS) and the peripheral nervous system (PNS). The CNS includes the brain and the spinal cord. The CNS takes in information and tells the rest of the body what to do. The PNS contains nerves that carry information to and from the CNS. The PNS acts as the go between with the CNS and skeletal muscles, sense receptors, smooth muscles, cardiac muscles, and glands. Antidepressants primarily affect the CNS.

Dueling theories

Why does antidepressant medication take so long to work? One theory is that when the neurotransmitters aren't up to snuff, the receiving cells beef up the sensitivity of their receptors. When the antidepressants increase the available neurotransmitters, the receptors eventually calm down and become less sensitive. This process takes about the same amount of time that it takes for a person to feel the beneficial effects of the medication.

Another hypothesis has to do with what kinds of messages the neurotransmitter gives to the receiving cell. Some speculate that despite normal amounts of chemical messengers, the communication between cells and their genetic responses have somehow become deficient. With new research, scientists hope to find better ways to predict responses to medication, quicker avenues to treatment, and drugs with fewer side effects. Stay tuned.

The brain is packed with nerve cells called *neurons*. Neurons take in information about the state of the world both outside and inside the body and react to these internal and external happenings. Basically, neurons are the backbone of the *nervous system,* which controls all actions, thoughts, and emotions (see the "Knowing the nervous system" sidebar in this chapter). Neurons allow you to walk, talk, and smell the roses. Neurons give you the ability to love, to remember, to learn, and to feel. But to do this, neurons have to communicate with each other. Depression somehow disrupts communication among neurons.

So how do the 100 billion neurons in your brain talk to each other? They send chemical messengers back and forth. Scientists estimate about 100 trillion different lines of communication exist between all those neurons. But to save some time, taking a look at just one neuron conversation will do.

Pretend that Ned and Nellie are neighbor neurons (see Figure 15-1). Nellie Neuron has an important message to get to Ned, so she sends a jolt of energy down a long tube called an *axon*. When this burst of energy reaches the end of Nellie's axon, chemical messengers, or *neurotransmitters,* are released into a tiny space, called a *synapse,* between Nellie and Ned, her next door neuron.

The neurotransmitters hang out in the synapse. But then Nellie becomes anxious (as all good neurons do) that she let out so many chemicals, so she gets out a pump and pulls some neurons back in from the synapse. But Ned the neighbor welcomes some of the chemical messengers with open arms called *dendrites.* After they're inside, these neurotransmitters talk to Ned and may even start bossing him around. So, in the end, some of the neurotransmitters are taken in by the neighboring neuron and some return to the original cell.

Depression occurs when the chemical conversations between neurons break down. When neurons can't communicate well, the mind is unable to use all its resources to deal with events such as stress. The fact that this depleted state leads to a breakdown in the form of depression seems rather natural.

Some experts believe that depression results when there aren't enough neurotransmitters to get the message out. Others think that depression may stem from neurotransmitters that aren't working properly. Different drugs act on different neurotransmitters in different ways. The bottom line is that no one is entirely certain exactly why antidepressant medications work, other than the fact that they do seem to improve communication among neurons (see the "Dueling theories" sidebar in this chapter).

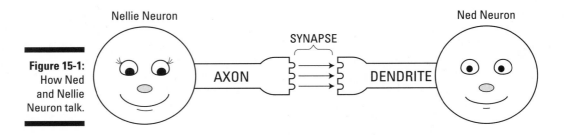

Figure 15-1:
How Ned and Nellie Neuron talk.

Deciphering Drugs for Depression

Although pharmaceutical companies spend billions of dollars searching for the next hot treatment for depression, interestingly, no one really knows exactly how antidepressant medication works. Nonetheless, most experts believe that antidepressant medications somehow increase one or more of the neurotransmitters in the brain and that doing so improves communication among neurons and ultimately reduces depression (see the "Brushing Up on Biology" section earlier in the chapter).

The relationship between the various neurotransmitters and depression isn't yet completely understood. However, the three neurotransmitters that are targeted by most antidepressants appear to have different symptoms associated with them.

- **Serotonin:** Problems with serotonin are associated with depressed mood, anxiety, insomnia, obsessive compulsive disorder, seasonal affective disorder, and even violence.

- **Dopamine:** Disruptions in dopamine seem to be related to problems with attention, motivation, alertness, increased apathy, and difficulty in experiencing pleasure.

- **Norepinephrine:** Disorders in norepinephrine are correlated with lack of energy, decreased alertness, and lethargy.

Your particular symptoms will give your health care provider clues on which antidepressant to start with. However, current science hasn't yet developed a precise way of predicting which symptoms will be best ameliorated by which medications.

Antidepressant drugs are classified by how they affect one or more of these neurochemicals. In this section, we present the most commonly prescribed antidepressants and explain their actions, common uses, problems, and side effects. The following discussion can give you practical information about each class of antidepressant drug. Remember that new antidepressants are constantly being developed.

We believe that knowledge helps you get the best medical care for your depression. The information we give you below will help you communicate with your health care provider. Working together, you can find the right medication.

Selecting SSRIs

Ever since Prozac came on the market in the late 1980s, *selective serotonin reuptake inhibitors* (SSRIs) have been the most popular antidepressants. One reason for their popularity is that their side effects are less severe than older antidepressants and the consequences of overdose are also much less severe.

An SSRI is often the first choice of antidepressant medication. These drugs are used for the treatment of major depressive disorder, dysthymia, and seasonal affective disorder. (For more about these disorders, see Chapter 2.) SSRIs are commonly used when depression and anxiety are mixed. (These medications are also used for treating anxiety-related disorders that aren't accompanied by depression: premenstrual syndrome, eating disorders, and some types of chronic pain.)

SSRIs fight depression by increasing the available levels of serotonin. Here's basically how they work. Remember Nellie the neuron from the "Brushing Up on Biology" section earlier in this chapter? Imagine that Nellie sends out a burst of serotonin into her synapse. Normally, some of the serotonin goes visiting at Ned's, the neighbor neuron, but Nellie pumps some of the serotonin back into her cell. An SSRI antidepressant clogs Nellie's pump so that she can't get her serotonin back home. More of the serotonin hangs out in the synapse for Ned to draw on.

SSRIs usually take about one to four weeks to become effective. Side effects may include increased anxiety, fatigue, upset stomach, insomnia, apathy, lack of sexual interest, or inability to obtain orgasm. Other side effects include dizziness, sweating, tremors, dry mouth, headache, and weight loss or weight gain. Side effects are worse during the first couple of weeks and generally decrease over time.

SSRIs may present some additional complications and problems. Keep these things in mind:

- If you have bipolar disorder, SSRIs may be dangerous. Occasionally, these drugs activate manic states, which can involve dangerous or risky behaviors (see Chapter 2 for more information about bipolar disorder).

- Abrupt discontinuation of SSRIs (or for that matter, any antidepressant medication) can produce flu-like symptoms such as nausea, headache, sweating, fever, and chills. Sudden withdrawal can also cause vivid dreams and problems with sleep. Talk to your doctor if you decide to stop taking SSRIs for advice on how to do so safely.

- The FDA recently announced that the popular SSRI medication Paxil may be associated with an increased risk of self-harm in children (which could potentially lead to suicidal attempts). Whether other SSRI medications will demonstrate this problem is unknown at this time. Because much less is known about the effects of antidepressant medications with children (especially on a long-term basis), special caution should be exercised in considering their use with kids.

- Taking SSRIs with another class of antidepressant called MAO inhibititors (discussed more fully later in this chapter) can trigger life-threatening interactions. Other drugs may also interact negatively. Tell your doctor about all of the medications you take.

Table 15-1 shows you the six SSRIs currently available on the market. We've put typical dosage ranges for your information. However, your doctor will work with you in determining what's appropriate for you.

Table 15-1	Selective Serotonin Reuptake Inhibitors (SSRIs)		
Brand Name	*Generic Name*	*Usual Dosage (In Milligrams)*	*Comments*
Celexa	Citalopram	10–60	May have fewer inter-actions with other drugs. Not particularly stimulating or sedating.
Lexapro	Escitalopram	10–20	A chemical cousin of Celexa, which may work faster.

Brand Name	Generic Name	Usual Dosage (In Milligrams)	Comments
Luvox	Fluvoxamine	50–300	Generally more sedating than the others. The first to be approved for obsessive-compulsive disorder.
Paxil Paxil CR	Paroxetine	20.0–60.0 12.5–62.5	Somewhat sedating. May be associated with more weight gain and more pronounced withdrawal symptoms.
Prozac	Fluoxetine	10–80	Stimulating, may cause insomnia if taken late in the day. Some report increases in anxiety. Clears out of body very slowly and therefore has the least withdrawal symptoms if abruptly stopped.
Zoloft	Sertraline	50–200	Not as stimulating or sedating as some of the others.

Untreated depression often decreases interest in intimacy. And SSRIs can interfere with sexual arousal, pleasure, and interest. If you're in a relationship in which sexual intimacy has already been disrupted, tell your health care provider about your concerns.

Getting more bang for the buck

Antidepressant medication likely works by increasing the amount of certain neurotransmitters in the brain. SSRIs target serotonin, but some antidepressants increase more than one such chemical messenger or act on the neuron and its neurotransmitters in more than one way.

In the following list, we take a look at these medications, noting which neurotransmitter system the medication affects and how it acts on them. You don't need to know the complicated terminology represented by the initials, but we include it in case you run across the terms in other literature. Take a look at Table 15-2 for more information on the following drugs:

✔ **SNRIs (Serotonin/Norepinephrine Reuptake Inhibitor):** Boosts both serotonin and norepinephrine

✔ **NDRIs (Norepinephrine/Dopamine Reuptake Inhibitor):** Boosts both norepinephrine and dopamine

✔ **NRIs (Norepinephrine Reuptake Inhibitor):** Selectively boosts norepinephrine

✔ **NaSSAs (Noradrenergic/Specific Serotonergic Antidepressants):** Enhances the release of norepinephrine and serotonin while blocking certain serotonin receptors

✔ **SARIs (Serotonin-2 Antagonists Reuptake Inhibitors):** Blocks the reuptake of serotonin while also blocking one specific type of serotonin receptor

Other older antidepressants also targeted multiple neurochemicals (see the section "Next choice: Tricyclics" later in this chapter). However, these newer versions appear to have fewer side effects and are more specific in their actions on the neurotransmitters than the older tricyclics.

Table 15-2	More Antidepressant Choices		
Brand Name	*Generic Name*	*Usual Dosage (In Milligrams)*	*Classification/Comments*
Desyrel	Trazadone	150–400	SARI. Sedating side effects. Used mostly along with other antidepressants as a sleep aid.
Effexor Effexor XR	Venlafaxine	75–375 75–375	SNRI. May have quicker action so good for severe depression. Fewer drug interactions than most antidepressant medications. Can elevate blood pressure in higher doses.
Remeron	Mitrazapine	15–45	NaSSA. Helps when insomnia is a problem. It may also cause weight gain.

Brand Name	Generic Name	Usual Dosage (In Milligrams)	Classification/Comments
Serzone	Nefazodone	100–600	SARI. May be sedating. May help decrease anxiety.
Vestra	Reboxetine	2–8	NRI. Can improve attention, increase energy. May also increase anxiety. (**Note:** Not available in the United States.)
Wellbutrin Wellbutrin SR	Bupropion	150–450 150–450	NDRI. Less likely to cause weight gain or sexual dysfunction. May initially increase anxiety. Not for people with seizure disorder.

Next choice: Tricyclics

This class of antidepressant medication was the most widely used for many years. *Tricyclic* medications are thought to have more general effects on neurotransmitters than the newer, more refined medications (the ones we cover in the "Selecting SSRIs" and "Getting more bang for the buck" sections earlier in the chapter). The name is based on their chemical structure rather than the way they exert their effects, which vary somewhat from one type of tricyclic medication to another.

The primary reason they're now out of favor is that an overdose can be fatal. The newer antidepressants are much safer. Tricyclics are also associated with a host of side effects. These medications can cause dizziness from *orthostatic hypotension,* a sudden drop in blood pressure upon standing. Therefore, tricyclics are usually not prescribed for people at risk for falling, such as the elderly. Other side effects include weight gain, dry mouth, blurred vision, constipation, sweating, and sexual dysfunction.

Nevertheless, tricyclics are often prescribed when other medications haven't worked or when anxiety mixes with depression. Take a look at Table 15-3 for more information.

Table 15-3	Tricyclic Antidepressants	
Brand Name	**Generic Name**	**Usual Dosage (In Milligrams)**
Anafranil	Clomipramine	75–300
Asendin	Amoxapine	150–600
Elavil	Amitriptyline	75–300
Ludiomil	Maprotiline	75–225
Norpramin or Pertofrane	Desipramine	75–300
Pamelor or Aventyl	Nortriptyline	50–150
Sinequan	Doxepin	150–300
Surmontil	Trimipramine	75–300
Tofranil	Imipramine	75–300
Vivactil	Protriptyline	15–60

Figuring out MAO inhibitors

The first drug to treat depression was discovered in the early 1950s, totally by accident. Scientists were experimenting with a new treatment for tuberculosis. Unfortunately, the drug had no effect on TB, but surprisingly, the patients taking the drug became quite cheerful. Thus, the first antidepressant was born — a *monoamine oxidase inhibitor* (MAO inhibitor).

MAO inhibitors work by zapping a substance that destroys neurotransmitters. Because fewer neurotransmitters are destroyed, this action increases levels of serotonin, norepinephrine, and dopamine. MAO inhibitors are *infrequently* prescribed because of serious side effects when combined with common foods or medications. Side effects can include dangerous spikes in blood pressure that can result in cerebral hemorrhage or death.

People taking MAO inhibitors should avoid food with *tyramine* (a natural substance found in the body that also forms as proteins breakdown as they age) such as sausages, beer, red wine, avocados, aged cheese, and smoked fish. Drug combinations to avoid include any other antidepressant medication, most drugs for colds and asthma, drugs for the treatment of diabetes, blood pressure medication, and some pain killers.

More about MAO inhibitors

Newer types of MAO inhibitors are under development. The original drugs can cause deadly side effects when mixed with common foods or over the counter drugs. The newer models may not have the same risk of hypertensive crisis.

Called Reversible inhibitors of MAO A or RIMAS, they will have the same antidepressant effects as their parent drugs without the risks of dangerous interactions.

Despite all of the problems with MAO inhibitors, they're still used to treat some forms of resistant depression. When safer medications haven't helped, these drugs can be effective. They're especially useful for the treatment of atypical depression, which often involves overeating, sleeping too much, and irritability. Take a look at Table 15-4 for more information.

Table 15-4	MAO Inhibitors	
Brand Name	*Generic Name*	*Usual Dosage (In Milligrams)*
Marplan	Isocarboxazid	10–40
Nardil	Phenelzine	45–90
Parnate	Tranylcypromine	30–60

Looking Beyond Antidepressants

For most people with depression, an antidepressant medication alleviates symptoms. You may have to undergo some initial experimentation, but usually one or more of the drugs we discuss in the "Deciphering Drugs for Depression" section earlier in the chapter eventually works. However for some people, another type of medication will need to be tried or added to a mix.

When several different classes of antidepressant medication haven't worked, other types of drugs may be used to augment or enhance the treatment. These pharmacological mixes are usually best prescribed by a *psychiatrist,* a specialist trained in the medical treatment of mood disorders.

Depression is a deadly disease. Get treatment. If the first trial of medication doesn't work, hang in there with your health care professional. Another drug or a drug combination will almost certainly help you.

Smoothing out moods

A group of drugs called mood stabilizers don't directly impact serotonin, dopamine, or norepinephrine — the neurotransmitters that antidepressant medications target (see the "Deciphering Drugs for Depression" section earlier in the chapter). No one really knows how mood stabilizers work, but many of these drugs seem to affect two other neurotransmitters, glutamate and gamma-aminobutyric acid (GABA). Usually the first choice in treating bipolar disorder, mood stabilizers are also used in combinations with antidepressants for treating resistant depression.

When taking some mood stabilizers, you'll need to have periodic blood tests to find out the concentration of the medication in your system. These drugs can have serious side effects when levels get too high. Toxic levels can be deadly, so follow your doctor's instructions.

Some of the drugs described in Table 15-5 haven't yet been officially approved for the treatment of depressive disorders. However, specialists have safely and successfully used many of them in their practices.

Table 15-5		Mood Stabilizers
Brand Name	**Generic Name**	**Comments**
Eskalith, Cibalith-S, Lithane, Lithobid, or others	Lithium	Used primarily for bipolar disorder but can be added in small doses to antidepressants to enhance treatment. Side effects can include weight gain and tremor. Increased tremor, disorientation, and slurred speech may indicate a dangerous toxic reaction that can result in seizures or death.
Depakene Depakote	Valporic Acid Divalproex	An anticonvulsant, may be useful for treating persons with mood swings or mixed states. Toxicity or overdose less common than with lithium.
Tegretol Carbitrol	Carbamazepine	Also an anticonvulsant and used to treat those with mood swings. Can be fatal in overdose. Interferes with the effectiveness of birth control pills.
Lamictal	Lamotrigine	Found to be useful for some with bipolar disorder. There are worries about skin reactions that can potentially be fatal.

Brand Name	Generic Name	Comments
Neurontin	Gabapentin	Fewer side effects, less toxic. Generally ineffective by itself for mania. Used for anxiety and peripheral nerve pain. Needs more study.
Topamax	Topiramate	Has been used both as an anticonvulsant and mood stabilizer. Unlike many other choices, this drug is associated with weight loss.

More help for severe depression

For people with severe symptoms, a new class of medication, called atypical antipsychotics may help. In addition, these medications are sometimes given to those who don't benefit sufficiently from the other antidepressants discussed in this chapter. Take a look at Table 15-6 for more information. Antipsychotics may help when individuals suffer from psychosis, paranoia, or delusional thinking (see the sidebar in Chapter 2 for more information about these severe depressive symptoms). These drugs may also be used when people with depression have problems with controlling their temper, tend to over-react to small frustrations, or swing back and forth from depression to mania.

Antipsychotic medication may cause disturbing side effects. The newer atypical antipsychotic medications have a significantly decreased risk of a long-term side effect known as tardive dyskinesia. *Tardive dyskinesia* involves involuntary movements, often in the face. When tardive dyskinesia appears, it usually does so after long-term treatment. Other serious side effects may include an intense feeling of agitation or restlessness, muscle spasms, muscle stiffness, shuffling gait, sedation, dry mouth, blurred vision, and hypotension. Weight gain is also particularly common and problematic.

Table 15-6	Atypical Antipsychotics	
Brand Name	Generic Name	Comments
Abilify	Aripiprazole	Has minimal tendency to cause sedation, weight gain, or movement disorders.
Geodon	Ziprasidone	This drug may cause less drowsiness and less weight gain than some of the others.

(continued)

Table 15-6 *(continued)*

Brand Name	Generic Name	Comments
Risperdal	Risperidone	Helps decrease agitation and behavioral disturbances, can cause movement disorders in higher doses.
Seroquel	Quetiapine	Low risk of movement disorders, can cause weight gain and sedation.
Zyprexa	Olanzapine	Improves mood in bipolar disorder. Can cause weight gain.

A few more for the road

Your physician may prescribe other drugs for the treatment of depression or for the treatment of the side effects of antidepressant drugs. Here are a few examples:

- **Stimulant medications:** These medications can be used to decrease fatigue, help with sexual drive, and improve attention.

- **Hormones:** Sometimes hormone therapy is indicated because of abnormalities or as an augmenting agent.

- **Sedating medications:** These drugs can help calm agitation or help with sleep.

Chapter 16

Hype, Help, or Hope? Alternative Treatments for Depression

- -

In This Chapter

▶ Keeping your health care provider informed

▶ Getting help at the health food store

▶ Turning on the lights

▶ Electrifying help for depression

- -

*W*hen depression takes over, optimism fades into pessimism, and despair replaces hope. Depression hurts, and getting better seems almost impossible at times. Then you read about a treatment that offers hope in the form of a supplement, pill, new therapy, change in diet, light bulb, or complicated medical procedure. With hope comes a lightening of mood, a little relief, and a small seed of optimism. Hope can be a powerful tonic for depression.

But a general sense of hope in a future free of depression and in a treatment path that you know little about or that may be dangerous are two different matters. If you follow a certain course of treatment, you may get a little better because you truly believe that the treatment is going to help you. There is nothing wrong with that — if the treatment is harmless. But, at the same time, we want you to be careful and not get taken advantage of by false promises. That's our purpose for writing this chapter.

Some treatments for depression can be expensive and possibly harmful. The real harm comes from postponing legitimate, evidenced-based treatment. Remember what your mother said, "When something sounds too good to be true, it usually is."

In this chapter, we give you the information you need to decide whether one or more of these alternative treatments may be for you. We present the latest research on treatments you can find at the health food store. Next, we explain what the diet gurus have to say about eating and moods. Finally, we describe electric shock therapy and other advanced medical treatments.

Keeping Your Doc in the Loop

We consider treatments for depression to be *alternative* if they're either not widely accepted as effective by conventional mental health and medical professionals or if these professionals don't use the treatments as first-choice approaches for most cases of major depression.

The *alternative* label certainly doesn't mean they're a secret: A report in the February 2001 edition of the *American Journal of Psychiatry* provided the results of a survey that indicated that well over half of the people with cases of severe depression sought out alternative treatments such as herbs, spiritual healing, vitamins, and special diets. Furthermore, most of the people who used these alternative treatments found them to be helpful.

However, those individuals surveyed also said that they typically didn't inform their doctors about these therapies. That's something of a problem, because certain alternative treatments, such as herbs, may interact badly with some medications. Most of the depressed individuals who sought alternative treatments also used conventional mental health or medical treatment, which is a good thing, because these approaches have the support of a large body of research.

Doctors today are becoming increasingly accepting of alternative treatments. Thus, we urge you to let your health care providers in on any alternative treatments you're using for depression. They may be able to tell you whether a particular alternative treatment is known to work, or whether it may interact badly with a medication they're prescribing for you. Either way, this information is important to know.

If you or someone you love suffers from severe depression or has thoughts of suicide, you need to get professional help immediately. Remember, most clerks at health food stores don't qualify as licensed mental health professionals.

Swallowing Supplements and Herbs

Many folks who suffer from depression walk into a health food or supplement store looking for a natural solution to their problems. They walk up to a touch-screen computer, enter the word *depression,* and get five pages of herbs, supplements, and vitamins that promise relief. Some of these promises may pan out, but others won't. And some choices can be dangerous.

You may believe that taking herbs and supplements for depression is a relatively harmless and natural alternative. The problem: Most people take these potent pills without medical supervision. Many of these "natural" substances can significantly interact with other medications you're taking and lead to dangerous results. So, if you're considering using these alternatives, including the ones we discuss in this section, you need to first consult with your doctor.

St. John's wort

Hypericum perforatum, better known as St. John's wort, is a small woody perennial that has been used since ancient Greece for a variety of medicinal purposes, from curing stomach problems to healing wounds. In recent years, it has been extensively used for depression. This plant has been widely studied throughout Europe and the United States.

Here's the scoop: Some studies show St. John's wort to be as effective as some antidepressant medications, while other studies show it to be about as effective as a placebo A *placebo* is a pill that has no physical effect on the person taking it. Good studies make sure that the people giving and the people receiving the drug or medication have no idea whether they're taking the actual drug or a placebo. Interestingly, in most studies, a significant number of people taking the placebo get better too. Why? Hope.

The conclusion you can make from these studies as a whole is that St. John's wort is probably an effective treatment for mild depression for some people.

If you decide to take St. John's wort, buy it from a reputable company. Make sure that it has at least 5 percent hyperforin, which is thought to be the active ingredient in St. John's wort. Side effects sometimes include gastrointestinal upset, over-sensitivity to sunlight, and agitation. St. John's wort appears to work by increasing chemicals in the brain — such as serotonin, norepinephrine, and dopamine — that affect mood. (See Chapter 15 for more information about how these brain chemicals work.)

SAM-e

S-adenosylmethionine, or SAM-e (a compound found in human cells), is a newer dietary supplement that appears to have a variety of good effects on the body (from treating liver disease to combating memory loss and arthritis).

A growing body of research supports the usefulness of SAM-e for treating mild depression as well. SAM-e seems to boost mood and even improve effectiveness of medications when given with other antidepressants. Because SAM-e is associated with fewer side effects than prescription antidepressants, it has also become a popular alternative treatment for depression. Nevertheless, more research is needed before it can be determined exactly how effective SAM-e is. And it does have its downsides:

- ✔ Health insurance doesn't cover it, so it can be quite expensive.
- ✔ People with bipolar disorder should never use it because it may trigger an episode of mania (see Chapter 2 for more information about bipolar disorder and mania).
- ✔ It can cause heart palpitations, gastrointestinal upset, and headache.

Tryptophan and 5 HTP

Tryptophan is an amino acid found in many common foods such as milk, potatoes, turkey, sunflower seeds, and chicken. Tryptophan in the body can be converted into *5 HTP* (another type of amino acid), which can then be converted into *serotonin,* a chemical messenger that seems to have a positive effect on mood.

Tryptophan as a dietary supplement was removed from the United States market after a contaminated batch caused severe illness and death. Thirty-seven people died and about 1,500 people were permanently disabled after taking tryptophan in the late 1980s. They contracted the disease EMS, or eosinophilia myalgia syndrome, which resulted in paralysis, neurological problems, fatigue, and heart problems. Almost all the people who were affected had taken a supplement from one Japanese company that was believed to have contaminated a batch of the supplement.

However, 5-HTP is still available as a dietary supplement for the treatment of depression. Because many antidepressants increase levels of serotonin, it is believed that 5-HTP can be an effective antidepressant.

But the U.S. Food and Drug Administration (FDA) is concerned that 5-HTP may carry the same risk as tryptophan. Because the safety of 5-HTP hasn't been firmly established, we think that getting your serotonin boost from turkey or sunflower seeds is a better bet at this time. Make sure that you get advice from your doctor before taking any type of dietary supplement.

Omega-3 fatty acids

Omega-3 fatty acids play a role in the function of dopamine and serotonin — critical neurotransmitters (see Chapter 15 for more information about neurotransmitters) that affect mood. Omega-3 fatty acids can be found in flax seed, soybeans, avocados, tofu, and fish. They can also be found in supplement form.

Some intriguing research shows that increased levels of omega-3 may help decrease depression. Furthermore, studies clearly indicate that increasing your intake of omega-3 helps reduce the risk of cardiovascular problems and may even help lower cholesterol levels. So make sure that you include foods that are rich in omega-3 in your diet or consider taking a supplement.

Herbs with more hype than help

Visit any health food store or herbal Web site and you'll find a cornucopia of suggestions for herbs that ostensibly decrease your depression. Some of the wilder recommendations we've found include

- Basil
- Black Hellebore
- Clove
- Ginger
- Oat straw
- Rosemary
- Sage
- Thyme

Hold on to your pocketbook before you invest heavily in herbs like these. You may be able to concoct some interesting and tasty dishes, but the research showing that these and many other herbs and tonics may be effective at treating depression remains elusive. Stick to what's known to work.

Vibrancy from Vitamins and Minerals

If you suffer from moderate to severe depression, taking extra vitamins and minerals isn't likely to cure you. But a lack of certain vitamins and minerals does seem to be related to depression and memory problems. The research seems to clearly show that when people have a deficiency of B vitamins (especially B6, B12, and folic acid), depression is often present. These critical vitamins help keep neurotransmitters firing (see Chapter 15 for more information about neurotransmitters).

Deficiencies in calcium, magnesium, potassium, iron, selenium, zinc, and sodium also seem to be associated with depression. However, most people who are depressed don't suffer from deficiencies in these vitamins or minerals.

Take a complete multiple vitamin supplement. Be sure that the vitamin contains at least the recommended daily values of the B vitamins. Increasing your intake of folic acid may also help improve the effectiveness of some anti-depressant medications. Between 400 to 800 milligrams of folic acid is recommended daily. However, you need to remember that more isn't better.

You don't need to take megadoses of vitamins and minerals; doing so won't likely help your depression. And too much of certain vitamins can be down-right dangerous. Rather than increase your good mood, too many supplements will merely increase your credit card balance.

Happy Foods

Depression can cause a decrease in appetite and lead to weight loss. It can also stir up cravings, which cause weigh gain. In either case, nutrition may suffer. Poor nutrition depletes the body of the nutrients needed for proper brain functioning. When the brain is malfunctioning, the intensity of depression increases. Therefore, when you're depressed, maintaining a healthy diet is especially important. We recommend that you

- Eat sensible, well-balanced meals
- Don't skip meals
- Drink alcohol only in moderation, or not at all
- Don't beat yourself up if you occasionally indulge in a chocolate chip cookie

In addition, you should know about the important role carbohydrates play in regard to moods. Put simply, carbohydrates boost moods. Have you ever craved something sweet when you felt sad or upset? Yum — the smell of fresh baked chocolate chip cookies. This craving for sweets may be your body's way of telling you that it needs a carbohydrate fix. Carbohydrates are broken down and converted to *glucose* (sugar), the fuel that keeps you going.

Two different kinds of carbohydrates exist: simple and complex. The body quickly converts simple carbohydrates (such as white rice, bagels, cookies, crackers, beer, wine, and most pastas) into sugar. The spike in your blood sugar level that results when you eat simple carbohydrates may cause a temporary lifting of spirits.

The problem with simple carbohydrates is that the quick conversion into sugar also signals your body to produce excess insulin. The insulin then causes your blood sugar level to fall. For many, the drop in blood sugar then leads to a lowered mood, irritability, and more cravings for sugar. Doctors believe that these rapid peaks and valleys in insulin levels aren't good for you for numerous reasons, such as a real possibility that they may contribute to the development of diabetes and heart disease.

Complex carbohydrates represent a good alternative method for improving moods. These carbohydrates are found in whole grains, beans, vegetables, roots, and whole fruits. Complex carbohydrates break down into sugar more slowly, allowing your insulin levels to remain more stable. They don't increase cravings or lower moods. Some nutritionists contend that complex carbohydrates also raise serotonin levels. Therefore, consuming complex carbohydrates may be a useful way of improving moods without the peaks and valleys that occur with simple carbohydrates.

If you have depression, what you eat can either make you feel better or worse. Therefore, pay attention to your diet. Make sure it's balanced and contains complex carbohydrates.

Lighting Up the Darkness

If winter consistently brings on the blues, you may suffer from *seasonal affective disorder,* or SAD (see Chapter 2 for more information). Most people feel a little down when the sun rises late and sets early day after day, and the clouds dampen the daylight. However, people with SAD experience symptoms of a major depressive disorder (see Chapter 2 for more information), such as loss of pleasure and interests, reduced energy, and so on.

SAD can be treated with all the usual treatments for depression that we discuss throughout this book, but light therapy has become a highly popular treatment. With light therapy, a person is exposed to bright light that is from 25 to 100 times more powerful than a standard 100-watt light bulb. Thus, the lighting used with light therapy is much more intense than the lighting you find in a well-lit room.

Studies generally have shown that the treatment works better than no treatment and placebos. However, the effectiveness of light therapy remains somewhat controversial, and a few studies haven't shown any more improvements than those obtained with a placebo. Many practitioners recommend a daily walk outside during the brightest part of the day as an alternative to light therapy.

With light therapy, exposure to the light box typically lasts from 30 minutes to two hours per day. A light box can be purchased for around $200 to $500. A few insurance companies will reimburse you for this expense, so you should check your medical insurance before making your purchase. Here are some advantages of light therapy:

- ✔ It often works quite rapidly (sometimes within a week).
- ✔ It has fewer side effects than most medications.
- ✔ After the initial purchase of the equipment, it is inexpensive.

On the other hand, light therapy does have a few, usually mild side effects, which can include headache, nausea, eye strain, jumpiness, sleep disturbance, and agitation. Studies have found that patients who use light therapy for many years don't suffer from any ill effects on the eye. However, the extremely long-term effects of the therapy still remain unknown. And if you suffer from significant eye problems, check with an ophthalmologist prior to using light therapy.

Treating Severe Depression

Unfortunately, some cases of depression are unusually difficult to treat. Medications and psychotherapy occasionally fail to alleviate the pain and suffering of these difficult cases. The following alternative treatments are used specifically for treating especially stubborn depression. We call these treatments alternative largely because they're not used for the vast majority of depressed persons.

Shocking depression

In April 1938, Italian doctors in desperation administered shock to a severely psychotic man. He apparently lived a normal life after receiving the treatment. Thus, *electroconvulsive therapy* (ECT), popularly known as *shock therapy,* was born. The interest in ECT for the treatment of depression blossomed through the 1950s. Soon after, the emergence of antidepressant medication decreased the popularity of ECT. However, ECT is still in use, particularly for treatment-resistant cases of serious depression.

ECT may conjure up images of patients who are strapped down on a table and thrashing wildly, with electrodes glued to their scalps. The reality of modern day ECT contrasts sharply with that image.

Edison suffers from major depressive disorder. Severe depression haunts both sides of his family. He lost his eldest brother and two uncles to suicide. Edison takes several different antidepressant medications and has participated in extensive therapy. Yet, after a particularly stressful month, his medication regime seems to be ineffective. He is plagued by suicidal thoughts; his psychiatrist suggests ECT as an alternative. Desperate for help, Edison agrees.

Edison's doctor runs several tests, checks his heart, and declares him fit for the procedure. The doctor then administers general anesthesia and muscle relaxants. Edison isn't going to feel a thing. The doctors hook him up to monitors and attach electrodes to the right side of his head. The treatment lasts for about 30 seconds. Edison's big toe wiggles a bit. He wakes up confused, muttering, "Where am I, what's going on?"

Edison doesn't remember anything about the procedure, but as he leaves the hospital, his mood already starts to brighten. Edison remarks to his wife that the procedure was less uncomfortable than a trip to the dentist. (We'd like to apologize for this story to any of our readers who are depressed dentists!)

Today, if your doctor recommends ECT, your experience will likely be similar to Edison's. However, you should know that some patients complain about varying kinds of problems with their memory. Others complain of headaches. Generally these side effects are mild and short term, but they can be more serious.

Most ECT treatments take place in a series of sessions, such as two to three times a week for a month. Patients typically respond to ECT shortly after receiving treatment. Overall, ECT appears to be somewhat more effective in the short term than drug therapy, especially for difficult, severe cases of depression. In that sense, ECT can be considered a mainstream treatment for depression. However, we include it in this chapter on alternative treatments because it's utilized much less frequently than medications and therapy for depression, with the important exception of especially severe cases.

More about ECT

The brain is divided into two hemispheres: left and right. One hemisphere is considered dominant over the other. The dominant hemisphere is more responsible for language. For most right-handed people, the left hemisphere is dominant. Sometimes doctors will attempt to administer the ECT to the non-dominant hemisphere in order to reduce the side effects of the treatment, including fewer memory impairments. However, a review of the ECT literature appearing in the journal *Lancet* in 2003 concluded that so-called *unilateral ECT* is less effective for improving depression than *bilateral ECT* administered to both hemispheres. Researchers also determined that higher-dose ECT is more effective than low-dose ECT. Therefore, there seems to be a trade-off: The more effective types of ECT treatments cause more cognitive impairments such as memory loss.

Unfortunately, relapse rates (see Chapter 17 for more information about relapse) are relatively high with ECT, probably because of the severity of the depression in the people who undergo the treatment. But the relapse could be due to something about the ECT itself. Patients often require antidepressant medication, psychotherapy, or more ECT to remain free of their depression. And like drug therapy, the effects of receiving ECT over many years are uncertain. That's because long-term studies of these patients don't yet exist.

Stimulating nerves

Scientists are constantly searching for new treatments for depression. Much of their motivation comes from the fact that a small percentage of people with depression have exceptionally stubborn, treatment-resistant cases. In the past, ECT was one of the few approaches to work for these cases. However, ECT has some potential for serious side effects and is frankly scary to many people.

One of the newest treatments currently under investigation is vagus nerve stimulation. The *vagus nerve* is one of the 12 nerves that run through the head. The vagus nerve controls your heart rate, vocal cords, bronchial constriction, and movements within the digestive tract. Vagus nerve stimulation was first found to be effective in preventing seizures during the 1980s. More recently it has been applied to the treatment of serious, resistant depression.

The procedure involves implanting a device, which intermittently emits a mild electrical impulse to electrodes woven around the vagus nerve, in the upper part of the chest. Patients who undergo this procedure report mild side effects, which include

- Facial muscle weakness
- Shortness of breath
- Mild sore throat
- Hoarseness or cough

These side effects are worse while the stimulation is being applied, but they usually decrease over time. Stimulation is typically applied for about a half minute every three to five minutes, 24 hours a day. Patients are given a means for shutting the device off if they find it to be too uncomfortable.

Early evidence suggests that vagus nerve stimulation may result in great improvement in a significant number of patients. And the vast majority of those who improve don't experience early relapse. The treatment takes quite a while to work. It may also improve in effectiveness the longer it continues.

Vagus nerve stimulation treatment is expensive: It currently costs as much as $25,000. Furthermore, the evidence for its effectiveness is very preliminary. This approach must still be considered experimental. Thus, only those with extremely resistant cases of depression should consider this therapy.

Magnetizing depression

Since the close of the 20th century, a flurry of research has started to emerge on a new treatment for depression known as *transcranial magnetic stimulation* (TMS). This therapy involves putting an electrical coil, which produces a strong magnetic field, on the scalp. The magnetic field is aimed, at varying frequencies, at certain areas of the brain. This treatment has shown promise as an alternative to ECT for treating stubborn, resistant forms of depression.

TMS has two different approaches: one involves inducing a seizure (like ECT), while the other doesn't. No one knows for sure which strategy works best. However, the real advantage of TMS is that it doesn't appear to create either short- or long-term cognitive impairments. And patients report tolerating the procedure quite well.

On the other hand, the evidence isn't yet sufficient enough to recommend TMS as a replacement for ECT. Although the research has been promising, some studies have failed to show that TMS is significantly more effective than a sham, placebo procedure. Perhaps in a few years, more data will roll in and help your doctor determine whether this may be the best procedure for you. In the meantime, it must be considered rather experimental in nature.

Searching Further

We searched the literature for additional alternative treatments for depression. Trust us, you don't want to see everything that anyone has ever suggested. (We would have to fill another book the size of this one, and it probably wouldn't be very productive.) However, we will tell you about a small number of other intriguing possibilities.

New alternative treatments, as well as new medications and refinements in psychotherapy techniques, are continually being investigated for the treatment of depression. We urge you not to give up hope. We know many people who failed to receive help from a variety of medications and therapies, only to eventually discover a formula that works for them.

Air ionization

You can find devices that have been designed to increase the negative ion concentration in the air. These devices have been suggested for treating SAD, because negative ions appear to increase serotonin levels (see Chapter 15 for more information about serotonin), which decrease in the fall and winter. According to two controlled studies, this type of device may actually help alleviate SAD (see Chapter 2 for more information on SAD). These machines truly need additional supporting research before we can give them a strong recommendation. As of yet, they haven't been tested for any form of depression other than SAD. However, they have shown potential, and they may actually have little or no side effects.

Massage

Massage therapy, when delivered by a trained therapist, involves the manipulation of the body's soft tissues. Most people know that a massage can feel pretty good, but can it alleviate depression? Two controlled studies have actually suggested that repeated massages may help treat depression. However, these studies didn't assess the long-term outcomes of massage therapy. Again, more research is clearly needed. However, massage probably won't hurt you, and it just may have some short-term benefits.

Relaxation

Various techniques exist for teaching people how to relax their muscles. We discuss several of these in detail in another book of ours, *Overcoming Anxiety For Dummies* (Wiley Publishing, Inc.). A half dozen or so small, controlled studies suggest that relaxation may be effective for treating depression. Once again, however, more research is called for, and studies haven't yet shown whether relaxation training reduces depression over the long run. Nevertheless, relaxation has a very low potential for negative side effects, and it may actually help alleviate depression.

Part VI
Looking Beyond Depression

In this part . . .

Save reading the chapters that comprise this part until after you've succeeded in defeating your depression. The bad news about depression is that it has a nasty habit of returning. The good news is that you can take action to reduce the chances of that happening. And if depression should return, we give you other ideas on how quickly to recover. But we want you to feel *better* than *good* again. And positive psychology offers ideas for finding true happiness. We take a page from the positive-psychology book to provide suggestions that can help you find renewed purpose and meaning in your life.

Chapter 17

Reducing the Risk of Relapse

In This Chapter

▶ Understanding the nature and risks of relapse

▶ Protecting yourself against relapse

▶ Handling relapse when it shows up

*T*he information in this chapter is especially important after you experience improvement with your depression. If your mood hasn't yet substantially improved, we suggest that you work on your depression before you worry too much about relapse. Parts I through V of this book can help. If you put in a lot of personal effort, and your depression still hasn't improved much, seek professional help. But if you've seen substantial improvement in your symptoms — or if you don't suffer from depression but you want to find out more about it — keep reading.

Craig took a new position as a high school principal last year. He hasn't felt like himself for six months. Craig usually tackles problems head-on, so he makes an appointment with his primary care physician. His doctor prescribes an antidepressant medication (see Chapter 15 for information on antidepressant medications). After just six weeks of faithfully taking his prescribed medication, Craig feels on top of the world again. He has no remaining symptoms of depression. Although his doctor recommended continuing the medication for at least six months, Craig chooses to ignore his doctor's advice and stop. Craig "knows" that he'll be alright; after all, he hasn't felt this good in years. Besides, he slowly tapers his medication consumption down so that he can avoid the withdrawal effects that he was warned about. Five weeks later, Craig suffers a relapse and crashes into a bottomless pit, feeling more depressed than he did before he started the medication.

In this chapter, we discuss what is currently known about relapse and depression. *Relapse* refers to a fall or slip back into depression after having largely or completely recovered. We explain how often relapse occurs, and we tell you what you can do to reduce the risk of relapse. We also give you ideas for dealing with relapse in the event that it happens to you.

Risking Relapse with Depression

In writing this book, we choose to shoot straight. That's why our approach to cognitive therapy (see Part II) recommends that you use objective, evidence-based thinking rather than delude yourself with simplistic positive self-affirmations as a cure-all for your depression. We want you to see yourself and the world as they are, not as a fairy tale. Denial only makes things worse.

So when it comes to the treatment of depression, we give you the good news and the bad. The good news is that, with the wide array of both established and new therapies and medications available today, the vast majority of people with depression can be successfully treated. By successful treatment, we mean that the majority of their depressive symptoms can be eased for at least six months or more. The bad news is that the risk of relapse is distressingly high.

Fortunately, we have more good news — you can do quite a bit to reduce the risk of relapse, and if you should fall back into melancholy, you have a good chance of beating back your depression once again.

Determining what's going on

In Chapter 3, we discuss the fact that, with depression, progress always proceeds in an uneven fashion with many ups and downs along the way. In fact, we can't remember working with anyone who progressed without ever making the slightest slip. Furthermore, everyone has bad moods and rotten days from time to time. So how can you tell if what you're experiencing represents a true relapse?

When you experience a full-blown relapse of depression, you have clear signs of one of the types of depression we discuss in detail in Chapter 2 following a period of six or more depression-free months. If your symptoms are mild and don't meet the criteria for depression spelled out in Chapter 2, you've encountered one of depression's early warning signs — something to take seriously, but not an actual relapse. To deal with early warning signs, try the suggestions we provide in the "Preparing a Prevention Plan" section later in this chapter. On the other hand, if you're in the middle of a relapse, read the "Reining In Relapse when It Occurs" section, which you can also find later in this chapter.

Laying out relapse rates

So, just how high is the risk of depression relapse? Well, in part, the answer depends on whether your depression was treated with medication or therapy.

If you discontinue medication after your depression lets up, your chances of relapse exceed 50 percent over the next year or two. Your odds appear somewhat better if you received cognitive therapy either alone, or in conjunction with or following antidepressant medication. Interpersonal therapy (we discuss elements of this therapy in Chapters 13 and 14) has also shown some promise in reducing relapse. Your odds of reducing the risk of relapse further improve if you also receive behavior therapy, such as problem solving (see Chapter 12) or mindfulness techniques (see Chapter 18).

The therapies we chose for this book have been selected in part for their potential to reduce relapse. Combining them gives you particularly robust tools for reducing your risks.

Although many treatment avenues lessen the chance of relapse, your risk of relapse is considerably higher if you stop treatment before your symptoms of depression have virtually vanished. In other words, your chances of experiencing a relapse increase if you stop treatment before you are truly back to a full, non-depressed condition. Don't stop treatment until you have six months or more of normal energy, appetite, sleep, and enjoyment of activities.

Getting personal about your risks

In addition to the relapse factors we outline in the "Laying out relapse rates" section earlier in the chapter, one other intriguing, possible factor is emerging. New evidence suggests a surprising problem that may increase the likelihood of a recurrence of your depression.

You can take our "Relapse Quiz" in Table 17-1 to get an idea of whether this risk for relapse pertains to you. For each question, rate your extent of agreement on a scale of 1 to 7. Use 1 if you *completely disagree,* 2 if you mostly disagree, 3 if you disagree a little, 4 if you neither agree nor disagree, 5 if you agree a little, 6 if you mostly agree, and 7 if you *completely agree* with the question.

Table 17-1	Relapse Quiz
Question	**Rating of Agreement or Disagreement**
I will sacrifice my own needs in order to please other people.	1 2 3 4 5 6 7
I feel I must have the approval of others if I'm going to be happy.	1 2 3 4 5 6 7
I know I can control depression if it strikes.	1 2 3 4 5 6 7
There's nothing I can do to deal with depression.	1 2 3 4 5 6 7
When I feel sad, I'm sure that my view of life is realistic.	1 2 3 4 5 6 7
When I'm depressed, I absolutely know that my thoughts and emotions don't accurately reflect what's going on.	1 2 3 4 5 6 7
I'm the cause of my own depression.	1 2 3 4 5 6 7
I get depressed when I mess up.	1 2 3 4 5 6 7

You score this quiz a little differently than most self-tests. You don't add or subtract any of the scores. Rather, the more items you either *completely agree* or *completely disagree* with, as indicated by a rating of 1 or 7, the higher your odds of relapse.

We know that it sounds strange to hear that your relapse risk rises if you *completely agree* with items such as:

- ✓ I know I can control depression if it strikes.
- ✓ When I'm depressed, I absolutely know that my thoughts and emotions don't accurately reflect what's going on.

And we also know that having an increased risk of relapse sounds strange if you *completely disagree* with items such as:

- ✓ I feel I must have the approval of others if I'm going to be happy.
- ✓ When I feel sad, I'm sure that my view of life is realistic.

Why wouldn't we want you to totally believe that you can control your depression when it strikes? And if you're sad, wouldn't we want you to completely believe that you're viewing life and events unrealistically? Well, sort of, but hold on a moment.

In Part II, we detail how cognitive therapy helps people to appraise them-selves and their world *realistically.* If you've ever experienced a bout of serious depression, absolutely and completely controlling your depression when it strikes probably doesn't sound all that realistic. It may be more reasonable to say that you have *some* confidence in your ability to control your emotions, but not total confidence. You may even be able to say that you have *quite a lot* of confidence, but not *complete* confidence. Stating that you don't believe you need other people's approval to be happy may also be realistic. But isn't it likely that you could have a little doubt?

Idealistic, overly optimistic thinking just may set you up for relapse. In Chapter 7, we explain that viewing yourself as superior to other people can put you at risk for disappointment and depression. Similarly, Pollyannaish thinking can do the same.

Our relapse quiz isn't a scientific test, so don't worry excessively if you respond with quite a few 1's or 7's. However, research by Dr. John Teasdale and colleagues does suggest that you want to avoid thinking in absolutist, extreme terms. Also, if you've never been depressed, this quiz has no relevance to whether you may develop depression in the future. Because you've never lived in the pit of depression, it's probably more reasonable for you to have more complete confidence in the views you hold about yourself and the world.

Preparing a Prevention Plan

If you completely ignore the real possibility of your depression returning, relapse may very well lie around the corner ready to jump out and snare you. But you can do a lot to minimize the dangers of a recurrence. We now review the strategies you have available for preventing relapse.

Sustaining success

When depression finally loosens its grip, most people feel like stopping treatment. And we don't blame them for feeling that way. All treatments of depression (including self-help) require time, energy, and at least a little money.

Given the various challenges that treatment presents, why put in any more effort than you have to — especially when you're feeling good again? Well, we'll tell you: Because the risk of relapse is unacceptably high if you stop prematurely, especially when you factor in the debilitating nature of depression.

Most professionals advocate treating depression until the symptoms completely subside, not just until they're partially resolved. Furthermore, therapists typically recommend continuing treatment for at least a few months following the full remission of depression — a return to normal energy, concentration, appetite, sleep, and enjoyment of life's activities.

The suggestion to continue treatment is based on the idea that attaining a thorough mastery of new skills, behaviors, and ways of thinking is the best approach. Newly acquired, fledgling skills won't hold up in the face of the inevitable adversities of life. The skills you acquire need drill and repetition. In order to hold up under pressure, they need to be "over-learned."

Continue practicing the strategies that first alleviated your depression until you feel you've completely mastered them. In addition, you may want to try something different (such as behavior therapy in Part III or relationship therapy in Part IV) and rehearse those new skills. If you haven't yet tackled thought therapy (see Part II), we strongly urge you to do so because thought therapy not only defeats depression, it also helps prevent relapse.

The more skills you master for handling depression, the less likely you are to experience relapse in the future. Continuing either psychotherapy or self-help for some months beyond the alleviation of your depression can help keep relapse at bay.

Even if you choose to treat your depression with medication only, we suggest that you continue taking the medication for at least 6 to 12 months after your depression fully subsides. Doing so will reduce your chances of relapse somewhat, although we highly recommend trying some type of psychotherapy, such as thought therapy (see Part II), in addition to the medication. Alternatively, some folks with a history of recurrent depressions find that continuing to take antidepressant medication for a lifetime provides them with reasonable protection against relapse. (See Chapter 15 for more information about medications.)

Monitoring the signs

In Chapter 2, we review the myriad of ways that depression affects your thoughts, behavior, body, and relationships. If you've worked on beating your depression, you no doubt know what depression looks like for you. We suggest that you observe yourself and the symptoms discussed in the following exercise from time to time.

Conduct a "Depression Review" at least once a week. Select a convenient time and pencil your Depression Review in your calendar. We recommend conducting this review for at least a year after the depression lifts. In your Depression Review, ask yourself these questions:

✔ Have I been having gloomy, dark thoughts?

✔ Have I started avoiding people or situations that make me feel uncomfortable?

✔ What is my mood on a 1 (extremely depressed) to 100 (completely happy) point scale? Has my mood dropped from its usual rating by more than 10 points and remained lower for more than a day or two?

✔ Am I having any noticeable problems with my appetite, sleep, or energy?

✔ Have I been down on myself more than usual?

✔ Have I been more irritable than usual?

✔ Have I had an increase in guilty feelings?

✔ Am I having problems with concentration?

If you answer yes to one or more of the questions above, pay attention! This list contains the early warning signs of an impending depression. Of course, anyone can experience a few gloomy thoughts, a little guilt, and difficulty concentrating without sliding into a full-blown depression. However, we recommend taking these warning signs seriously by reinitiating some form of treatment, or possibly self-help efforts if your symptoms are mild.

Using a fire drill

No one knows when a fire will start. That's why school children everywhere periodically engage in fire drills. These drills prepare them for exactly what to do when fire breaks out.

A "Fire Drill" for depression involves vividly imagining potential adversities or hardships. Then you ask yourself how you might cope with them. Finally, you imagine yourself coping in a productive manner.

We're guessing that you're not a psychic, so you can't predict which adversities you may encounter in the future or when those hardships may appear. However, you probably do know what types of events have given you trouble in the past, as well as what you fear about the future. Rather than pretend that the entire remainder of your life will be nothing but roses, we suggest that you make up a list of worrisome scenarios.

On your list, include anything that you believe could actually happen to you and that you fear could overwhelm your capacity to cope. A few possibilities include

✔ Embarrassment

✔ Failing to meet a deadline

✔ Financial reversals

✔ Illness

✔ Injury

✔ Losing a loved one

✔ Rejection

Next, take your list and select one item. Imagine that event happening and finding a way to cope with the adversity. When you perform a Fire Drill, use the questions in this list to help you come up with ideas on how to cope:

✔ How would someone else cope with this situation?

✔ Have I dealt with something like this in the past? How did I do it?

✔ How much will this event affect my life a year after it occurs?

✔ Is this event as awful as I'm making it out to be?

✔ Are there any intriguing, creative ways of dealing with this challenge?

People often dread future possibilities because they assume they'll be unable to cope with them. However, when you face fears head-on, more often than not, you find you can cut them down to size. That's why you should conduct a Fire Drill on each and every item on your list of worrisome scenarios.

Ryan recovered from his bout with depression about a month ago. He feels much better, but he realizes that he needs to consider the issue of relapse seriously. Thus, he monitors his early warning signs of depression (see the preceding "Monitoring the signs" section) and realizes that he's starting to avoid certain people and situations. He knows that, in the past, he's been highly sensitive to embarrassment and rejection.

So he chooses to use the Fire Drill with this issue. He vividly imagines asking Brooke (a girl he's attracted to) out on a date and getting turned down in a hurtful way. Then he answers the coping questions as follows:

✔ **How would someone else cope with this situation?** "Actually, I bet this happens to people all the time. The key is to accept the rejection, ask myself if there's anything I can learn from it, and move on. It's not like the rejection will be pasted on my forehead for everyone to see."

✔ **Have I ever dealt with something like this in the past? How did I do it?** "Yeah, I've been turned down before, and I got through it. I didn't like it, but I dealt with it."

✔ **How much will this event affect my life a year after it occurs?** "If you put in that way, I guess not much at all."

✔ **Is this event as awful as I'm making it out to be?** "No. I guess I tell myself that it's awful and that it means I'm a total reject, but just having those thoughts doesn't make them true."

✔ **Are there any intriguing, creative ways of dealing with this challenge?** "Maybe I could try out that new speed-dating service where you meet something like 20 people in an hour. I may meet somebody interesting, and even if I don't, maybe I can learn to deal with rejection better by going straight at it."

Ryan's Fire Drill helps him realize that his ability to cope with feared situations is greater than he has allowed himself to believe. He then imagines getting turned down and dealing with the rejection many times. After he realizes that he can deal with this problem, he asks Brooke out.

The Fire Drill strategy works best if you first read about thought therapy, also known as cognitive therapy, in Part II. Thought therapy helps you understand how to tackle difficult events with more reasonable ways of thinking. When you perform a Fire Drill, you get extra practice using this type of thinking.

All too often, people who suffer from depression also struggle with excessive anxiety and worry about future events. And for many, anxiety appears to predate the emergence of depression. If you suffer from anxiety along with your depression, we recommend that you read our other *For Dummies* book, *Overcoming Anxiety For Dummies* (Wiley Publishing, Inc.), or *The Anxiety and Phobia Workbook* by Edmund Bourne (New Harbinger Publications). Additional work on your anxiety will help you make better use of the Fire Drill technique as well as help insulate you against recurrent depressions.

Reaching for well-being

If you work hard on overcoming depression and search diligently for solutions, the odds greatly favor a positive outcome. In other words, you stand a good chance of defeating your depression. But why stop there?

You may no longer feel depressed, but have you achieved a solid sense of well-being? If not, Dr. Giovanni Fava at the University of Bologna, Italy, investigated strategies that may not only prevent relapse but improve life satisfaction, as well. We review three of his techniques.

Chapters 18 and 19 contain additional information for increasing your overall sense of well-being. These chapters can help you further enhance your resilience and ability to repel relapse.

Tracking your well-being

Some individuals report that they rarely feel a true sense of satisfaction or well-being even when they're not depressed. However, when asked to closely track their well-being, they usually discover that certain types of situations and events do create greater satisfaction than others do. This discovery often inspires them to increase their involvement in gratifying activities.

Take some time to ponder the activities that feel satisfying to you. Write them down in a notebook. Then record the thoughts you have in response to those events as well as how much satisfaction they give you. Rate the intensity of your satisfaction on a scale of 0 to 100. You can use this "Satisfaction Tracker" to help you discover the activities that improve your sense of well-being. (See Table 17-2 for an example.) Then you can use that information to increase those activities, thereby increasing your overall satisfaction.

Alec no longer feels depressed, but he doesn't feel like he enjoys very many things. His therapist suggests that he use a Satisfaction Tracker to get a better idea of what kinds of situations increase his sense of well-being. Table 17-2 shows what Alec discovers when he records the intensity of the satisfaction he experiences when he participates in specific events.

Table 17-2	Alec's Satisfaction Tracker	
Situation	*Satisfying Thoughts*	*Satisfaction Intensity (On a Scale of 0 to 100)*
Taking the dog to the dog park.	I love watching my dog run!	60
Going to a party.	I like talking with a couple of my friends.	40
Showing off my new car to Linda.	I think she might like me.	35
Waxing my new car.	I feel great when I take good care of things.	65
Having lunch with Larry.	I like catching up on things with him.	70
Cleaning out the garage.	It feels good to do things I've been putting off.	65

Alec discovers that a few more things than he thought lead him to feeling satisfied. Clearly, he enjoys taking out his dog and making headway with certain types of chores. He also likes catching up with Larry. He decides to take on at least one satisfying chore, go out to lunch with a friend, and take his dog to the park every week. But Alec also observes that his satisfaction isn't as high as he would have expected on two items — going to a party and showing off his new car. This discovery leads to the next strategy for enhancing your well-being.

Cutting off the well-being interrupters

If you start tracking your satisfying situations as Alec did in Table 17-2, you're likely to discover that some of your satisfactions aren't as terrific as others. When that's the case, take a look at your thoughts regarding the event. First, consider any thoughts you have that involve feeling good about the event. Then ask yourself if you have any thoughts that interrupt that sense of satisfaction. We call those thoughts "satisfaction interrupters" — any thought that takes away from your enjoyment of a positive activity.

For example, **Annette** tracks her satisfying activities as Alec did in Table 17-2. She then chooses a couple of these events that didn't feel as satisfying as she might have expected. Table 17-3 shows the nature of her satisfaction interrupters.

Table 17-3	Annette's Satisfaction Interrupters	
Event	*Satisfying Thought*	*Satisfaction-Interrupting Thoughts*
Volunteering at the homeless shelter.	I like contributing something to society.	But then I thought that I really should be working on my school project: I'll never get it done.
Going to a party.	I think Kyle might like me.	Then I thought that he probably has a girl friend and he's just being polite.

See how Annette's interrupting thoughts managed to deflate her sense of well-being and satisfaction? If you're not feeling as satisfied by events as you think you should be, try tracking your satisfaction interrupters like Annette did. Then ask yourself the following questions about those deviously disruptive thoughts:

✔ What evidence do I have that either supports or refutes my satisfaction-interrupting thoughts?

✔ If a friend of mine told me that he or she had this interrupting thought, would I think that it sounded reasonable or merely self-defeating on my friend's part?

✔ Do I have experiences in my life that may refute this interrupting thought?

✔ Is this interrupting thought distorted in any way?

✔ Can I reflect on a satisfaction-interrupting thought that may be more accurate and help me feel better?

When Annette subjects her satisfaction-interrupting thoughts to these questions, she's able to generate a more satisfying alternative. You too will likely discover that subjecting your satisfaction interrupters to scrutiny pays off. When you answer the preceding questions, you'll likely be able to dispute those interrupting thoughts and come up with more satisfying perspectives. We recommend keeping track of this information in a personal notebook.

The strategy of challenging satisfaction-interrupting thoughts may look familiar to you if you read Part II, which talks about thought therapy. In Part II, you find many more strategies for tackling problematic thinking. The main difference here is that you track *satisfying* events rather than disturbing, depressing ones, and then you record which thoughts *interfere* with that satisfaction.

Changing your lifestyle

A third useful strategy for increasing your overall sense of well-being and decreasing the likelihood of relapse lies in taking a good look at your lifestyle. Ask yourself these "Lifestyle Analysis" questions:

✔ Am I spending my time doing things that make me feel good, or do I merely numb myself by doing things like watching excessive television or drinking too much?

✔ Am I working longer hours than necessary?

✔ Am I obsessing over driven, self-imposed standards of perfectionism that cause unnecessary pressure for me?

✔ Do I take reasonable vacation times and breaks?

✔ Do I engage in a reasonable amount of recreation?

✔ Are there things I have always wanted to do that I haven't gotten around to doing? If so, what are they, and why am I not doing them?

Take time out to examine your life. Think about whether the way you spend your time reflects your priorities. If it doesn't, consider allocating your time differently. If you feel trapped and unable to make these changes, read Chapter 12. You may discover a creative way of escaping the trap set by your mind.

Reining in Relapse When It Occurs

Sometimes depression returns despite enormous efforts to fend it off. What do you do in this case? First, you need to know what a true relapse looks like. (To find out what a true relapse looks like, check out the "Determining what's going on" section, earlier in this chapter.) Then if you determine that you may be experiencing a relapse, you have to take some steps to deal with it.

The very first step in dealing with relapse is to seek professional help. If you've never seen a therapist or psychiatrist before, make sure that you see one, because self-help alone won't suffice when dealing with recurrent depressions. If you've seen a professional before, don't conclude that a relapse means professional help is useless.

If therapy seemed to help before, then more therapy will likely prove quite beneficial. If you previously tried therapy and it didn't help, you need further treatment — perhaps with a different therapist (see Chapter 4 for info on finding the right therapist).

If you haven't tried medication, you may want to consider it. If medication worked before and you stopped, you may want to restart medication or add therapy to your arsenal. Recurrent depressions are one indication that long-term medication may be in order.

The very worst thing you can do when you experience a relapse is to think of it as a catastrophe and assume that it means you have failed or your condition is uniquely hopeless. You have to understand that depression is a formidable foe with numerous causes, including genetics, trauma, and unknown factors. Professionals don't believe that depression reoccurs because of personal weakness, a lack of moral fiber, or any other fault that resides within a person. Although it may not be pleasant to face this foe again, you can defeat depression.

The vast majority of depression relapses can be treated successfully. You have many treatment avenues to explore.

Chapter 18

Confronting Depression with Mindfulness

*B*eing aware of the present moment is the goal of mindfulness. In a mindful state, you're aware, engaged, connected, and nonjudgmental. Mindfulness is a central aspect of Buddhist teachings, but you don't need to practice Buddhism to benefit from mindfulness.

You may be wondering what mindfulness is doing in a book about depression. Fortunately we have an answer to your question: Recently, Drs. Zindel Segal, J. Mark Williams, and John Teasdale investigated the use of mindfulness for preventing relapse with depression. When they added mindfulness to cognitive therapy (see Part II for information about cognitive therapy), they found that adding mindfulness cut the relapse rate by almost half among patients who had three or more previous episodes of depression.

In this chapter, we try to help you become more mindful. To start you on the path toward mindfulness, we demonstrate the difference between *you* and *your mind.* Then we show you the clutter that clogs up your mind and how to clean it out. Finally, you can discover how to apply mindfulness to your day-to-day life. Doing so can both decrease depression and help prevent depression from making an unwelcome return. So, read this chapter if you continue to have some depressive symptoms or if you wish to keep depression at bay.

Drawing the Line Between You and Your Mind

The human mind is *a thinking machine*. Your mind continuously uses language to form judgments, evaluations, and analyses of yourself and the world. Language (like the written word) is uniquely human. If you don't think so, e-mail a three-toed sloth and see what kind of response you get.

But human minds tend to make too many judgments and evaluations. These judgments become your sense of reality. And when the mind is depressed, these judgments can be overwhelmingly negative. Believing that you *are* the same thing as those negative evaluations and thoughts becomes too easy. So, as important as your mind is, in this section, we want you to realize that *you* are something more than your mind.

Okay, maybe we're getting a little deep here, but bear with us. Take a few moments to reminisce about yourself as a child. Choose any age you can recall. What was your life like? What did you feel? What did you do? What did you like and dislike? Where did you live?

Do you have an image of yourself as a child; are you able to see yourself? If so, you probably can't remember a lot about your thoughts back then. When people try to remember themselves as a child, they usually recall their lives. The *you* in your memory consists more of your experiences — what you did and how you felt — than the thoughts running through your mind.

Another way to see the difference between you and your mind is the following experiment: Sit still for a few moments and listen for a thought to come into your mind. Perhaps it will come instantly or it may take a little while. When your mind generates that thought, listen. *You* are the one listening. *You* aren't the same thing as your mind and your thoughts.

The *you* that isn't your mind is the part of you that observes, experiences, breathes, and lives without judgment and analysis. It's funny that the term mindfulness was coined to describe this state of awareness *without* thoughts and judgment. We think that the term *mindlessness* is far more descriptive. But alas, we succumb to convention in this chapter and stick with the term mindfulness.

Losing Your Mind

It's payday and I don't have enough to cover the bills. I guess I'm a failure. Here I am 35 years old, and I still don't make enough money. What's wrong with me? My life sucks.

Look at that gray hair. God, I look old. I'm an out of shape mess. People must look at me and think I'm a loser.

Have you ever heard thoughts like these run through your mind? The mind never stops. It produces this steady stream of evaluations and judgments throughout your waking day. And this chatter sometimes even creeps into your dreams. If you're like most folks, you've probably had at least a few dreams where you feel unprepared, embarrassed, or humiliated.

Mindfulness is about seeing the difference between you and your mind. In this section, we show you how to stop viewing thoughts as facts and start viewing them merely as mind chatter. We give you some tools to shake up your conviction that negative, self-evaluative thoughts are true. And we also show you how the mind keeps you out of the present by feeling guilty about the past or worrying about the future.

Thinking about negative thoughts as facts

When we sat down to write this morning, we felt pretty good because we had what we thought was a great way to introduce a particular concept. But we soon realized that we both completely forgot what the idea was about. "That's okay," we said, "we'll just look through our notes and find it." No such luck. We then had a slew of negative thoughts (see Chapters 5 and 6 for more on negative thoughts):

✔ How could we forget something like this?

✔ Are we getting early dementia?

✔ How could we be so stupid as to not make a note and file the idea?

✔ We're completely stuck and can't come up with another idea.

You may guess that our moods sank like a stone dropped into a lake. But that didn't happen. Instead, we took our dogs for a walk and noticed what a wonderful day it was. We observed the unbridled joy of our dogs as they sniffed every bush, barked at the birds, and watered a few choice spots.

How did we remain in a good mood and enjoy the walk? Although it's taken us a while, we view our thoughts less seriously than we used to — *thoughts are just thoughts, not facts.* By letting go and not dwelling on our negative thinking, we simply came up with another idea for presenting the issue.

All too often, the human mind responds to thoughts as though they truly reflect reality. Think of cutting into a fresh lemon with a sharp knife. Bring the lemon to your lips and squeeze out a little juice. Are you salivating? If so, your mind is responding to these words and associated images almost as though they were actually a real lemon. Nothing wrong with that.

However, if you believe that all your negative thoughts are somehow as real and solid as this book you're holding, you're probably setting yourself up for some mental anguish. In Part II, we discuss in detail how frequently thoughts contain distortions. In this chapter, we ask you to take these ideas further and to view thoughts merely as thoughts. Psychologist Steven Hayes goes so far as to call your mind's incessant stream of thoughts *mind chatter*. In the sections that follow, we have some ideas for dealing with this mind chatter in ways that can help you start taking these thoughts less seriously.

Thanking your mind!

When you hear negative, self-downing thoughts rambling through your mind, thank your mind for developing such an interesting idea! In case you're wondering, we recommend you carry out this strategy with a significant dose of sarcasm directed at your mind — remember, you aren't your mind. You can also tell your mind how creative it's being. Take a look at some responses you can make when you hear your mind chattering away:

> **Your mind's thought:** I am such a jerk!
>
> **You:** Thank you, mind, for that lovely thought!
>
> **Your mind's thought:** I'll never find someone to love.
>
> **You:** Excellent job, mind! Thanks!
>
> **Your mind's thought:** I'm hopeless.
>
> **You:** Very good. How in the world do you come up with these ideas, mind?
>
> **Your mind's thought:** I can't stand this feeling!
>
> **You:** Thank you, mind, for making my day that much more enjoyable!

Getting the idea? Try this technique each and every time you hear your negative mind chatter. You do have a choice. You can decide to take all this jabbering seriously, or you can hear your mind's drivel and dismiss it.

All minds generate a certain amount of negative chatter. You aren't unique in this respect. When you're depressed, you no doubt fall into the trap of listening to this jabbering as though it has true relevance to your worth as a human being. Understand that this chatter need not be taken seriously. Mastering this skill takes time; be patient.

Playing with your mind's thoughts

One of our favorite strategies for dealing with negative, self-downing thinking is to play with it. You can change the meaning of your thoughts and your response to them if you get playful. We have a number of ideas you may want to try.

Write down all your negative thoughts for a day. Then sing those thoughts to yourself over and over again. That's right, sing them. You can use them as substitute lyrics to a popular tune or make up your own song. Somehow these negative thoughts don't have the same meaning when you sing. Or say them out loud in a highly distorted voice. We particularly like using a Donald Duck voice. Buying into negative chatter is more difficult when you hear it coming from Donald Duck!

If you have a truly trusted partner, you can do what we do with our mind chatter. We say our negative thoughts out loud and let the other one of us amplify the chatter. We speak in an obviously silly, sarcastic tone. The dialogue goes something like this:

> **Dr. Elliott:** What I wrote today felt like junk. Who will ever want to read this stuff?

> **Dr. Smith:** That's right! You never write anything interesting at all. You may as well quit right now!

> **Dr. Elliott:** You're right, I think I will quit! Perhaps I should find different work to do.

> **Dr. Smith:** Well, that would be a good idea, but who would ever hire you?

Obviously, this exchange is meant to be a good natured, light hearted exercise. If you try it, and it doesn't feel that way, don't do it anymore. This technique only works if you and your partner fully trust each other and completely understand the nature of mind chatter as well as the value of approaching it whimsically. If you're so lucky, it can even be kind of fun!

Next, consider making a demonstration for yourself about the impotence of your mind's thoughts. People so often act as though all thoughts have power and meaning, as though thoughts alone directly cause events. We have an exercise that you can use to convince yourself otherwise. It's a bit similar to an exercise we present in Chapter 10, but worth repeating in this section. (If someone happens to be reading this book to you because you're unable to read, construct a similar scenario that reaffirms your power to defeat your mind's chatter.)

1. Declare out loud, "I can't read."

2. Say it louder, "I can't read!"

3. Now, shout, "I really, can't read!"

4. One more time, "Truly, there is no way that I can read."

5. Now, realize that you read each of these statements in order to say them.

Thoughts have no power that you don't give to them.

If you're still struggling to view your mind's stream of incessant judging thoughts as mere chatter, we have another idea for you to try. Wherever you are right now, survey your environment. If you're outside, look at the sky and the entire landscape. If inside, closely observe all the details of the room you're in. Now, evaluate every single aspect of what's around you negatively. Everything. It isn't that hard to do, is it?

The human mind is trained to evaluate everything. And it can do so negatively at the snap of a finger. But does that make the evaluation correct? Of course not! Especially when judging the self, the mind easily slips into automatic negativity.

We have one more suggestion for dealing with your mind's thoughts and negative self-judgments. When you hear these thoughts, try imagining them written on a large leaf. Then see that leaf gently float down a stream. In other words, practice playing with these thoughts as something outside yourself. Observe them. Watch them float. See how they swirl and dance as they go by. Let them go. Meditate in this manner for 10 to 20 minutes. Simply sit and relax. Put each thought on a leaf and watch it float, one after another.

The bottom line: We suggest that you form a new relationship with your thoughts. Back away and just observe the thoughts (with the exception of occasional warnings of clear and present danger, which you'll want to act upon). At most consider your thoughts as lightly-held possibilities, rather than statements of fact.

Resisting what is

Everyone wants to feel good. And that's perfectly natural and human. In addition, some pop psychology books even make the claim that all you have to do is grab onto happiness and never let go. Never feel bad again!

So what does the mind do when it confronts a negative experience or thought? It resists. The mind tells you that you absolutely *must not* feel this way. Avoid, deny, and suppress all negativity! Refuse to accept what is.

Unfortunately, denying negativity causes a problem: The more you absolutely must not have or feel something, the more certainly you'll have it. Thus more often than not:

- ✔ If you can't stand the idea of feeling anxious, you'll feel anxious.
- ✔ If you can't tolerate any sadness, you're headed for depression.
- ✔ The more you absolutely must not fail, the more likely you are to fail.

There's nothing wrong with a few bad feelings and outcomes. It's often the struggle to suppress these feelings that intensifies and magnifies them to the point that they overwhelm. In fact, psychologists have studied what happens when people with depression attempt to suppress all negative thoughts. You guessed it; they experience more negative thoughts.

Psychologist Steven Hayes has said that depression is what you end up feeling when you desperately try not to feel anything unpleasant. He suggests that you make a little room for bad feelings; open up a small space for them. Literally accept and invite the bad feelings to stay a while.

Dr. Hayes related a story of a little boy who had troubling, recurrent nightmares of monsters. The boy so much wanted not to have these nightmares. Dr. Hayes told him that instead of trying to rid himself of the monsters, he should keep a small box under his bed where they could stay. He told the boy that the monsters had nowhere else to go and needed a little space of their own. Soon the monsters no longer disturbed the boy's sleep.

Living anytime but now

Only humans have a deep appreciation of the past. Only humans can see far into the future. Sometimes that ability can be both useful and pleasant. But too often the mind keeps you waiting to live your life in the future or bogs you down in past regrets. This is unfortunate because some pretty unpleasant feelings can come from living in the past or the future. For example, dread, worry, concern, stress, anxiety, and hopelessness all bloom from focusing on thoughts about the future. On the other hand, guilt, resentment, revenge, self-hate, and sadness mushroom from dwelling on the past.

In this section, we show you how the mind messes you up with two kinds of illusions about the future; then we discuss what it does with the past to ruin your present. When you see how living in the past and the future mess you up, we hope you see the value of living in the present.

Waiting to be happy

How often have you thought that you'll be happy *when*

- You finish writing the book you've been working on.
- You can buy that dream home.
- You retire.

✔ You finish your degree.

✔ You finally meet someone.

✔ You can afford to buy that new car.

Thus, you find yourself continually engaged in a series of unsatisfying struggles to arrive at a happy spot. Perhaps you work excessive hours or choose a career that pays more, but that you find less agreeable than another lower-paying occupation. You set goals, but after you achieve them, the mind comes up with another goal promising even greater ultimate happiness. So you sacrifice again to seek this new objective. The repeated seduction of a promised future happiness manages to ruin present moment after present moment.

Projecting images of an intolerable future

The depressed mind has another trick to play on you regarding the future: The mind tells you that nothing but bleak, foreboding events lie ahead. And the mind makes you believe that these distant occurrences will prove intolerable.

Janet, a PhD student in sociology, battles a low level depression for more than a year. She's finished her coursework; only her dissertation stands in the way of completing her degree. Only? A dissertation is a very large body of work. She must exhaustively review a huge literature base. Then she must design a study, send the study for numerous reviews with her doctoral committee, finally obtain approval for her study proposal from the committee, conduct the study, analyze the results, and write the entire project up.

Her mind focuses on horrific images of the mounds of work that lie ahead. These images cause a motivational meltdown. Janet has no idea how she'll move forward. But Janet eventually digs down deep and starts to work.

When she finally completes her dissertation, Janet looks back and comes to a profound realization: She couldn't recall one single moment of working on her dissertation that actually felt horrible or insufferable. Not one. And quite a few times, the work felt surprisingly positive.

Embracing victimhood from the past

We feel that understanding the origins of your negative thinking has a certain value. For example, you can appreciate that your responses to events often have more to do with events from the past than with what has just happened to you. Understanding that difference may help you to reinterpret the current reality in a more useful way. You may wish to read Chapters 3 and 7 for more information about this way of thinking about events.

However, don't allow your mind to become overly attached to tragedies from the past. If you do, your mind may focus on all the outrageous injustices that you encountered in your life. Soon you could find yourself turning into a victim that resents and blames others for all that has happened to you previously. In essence you could *define* yourself in terms of your past. Chapter 3 discusses the seductiveness of victim thinking as well as ways out of that mind set.

Finding guilt in the past

The mind also can lead you to judge yourself today based on your past. If you fall for this trick, you'll likely make these judgments harshly and immerse yourself in guilt and self-loathing. Do you know anyone who wouldn't love to redo many decisions and actions from the past?

Of course if you went back in time, knowing what you know today, you would do many things differently. But you didn't know then what you know now. Besides, you can't change the past. The past is useful for one thing and one thing only — as a guide for making changes. You make those changes *now* — in the present.

Our dogs don't live in the past, but they usually seem to learn from it. Eventually anyway. We came home a couple of months ago to an entire house of feathers. Feathers in the living room, feathers in the master bedroom, feathers in the bathrooms, feathers in the kitchen, feathers everywhere. A down-filled comforter no longer existed.

And our two dogs couldn't have looked guiltier if they tried. They truly appeared ashamed as we yelled at them. But how long do you think it took them to recover from their transgression and guilt? About three minutes. We're pretty sure they felt bad about what they'd done. And we're equally sure they didn't spend the next few days berating themselves with self-loathing thoughts. In fact, only moments later they ran around happily as if nothing had happened.

The next time you mess up, try feeling guilty like a dog. Feel bad for a little while, then drop the matter. Prolonged pounding on yourself will do nothing to enhance your life. It will merely ruin your present in addition to your past.

Living Mindfully

If you read the previous sections of this chapter, you'll be more prepared to live your life mindfully. Mindful living largely consists of two practices — acceptance and connecting with experience.

When life deals you a hand of cards, acceptance keeps you in the game. When you discover acceptance, you don't judge yourself as a good or bad player, you just play. And you view the dealer as neutral, neither good nor bad.

Connecting with experience also requires that you stay in the game. You don't spend time lamenting about previous hands or worrying about future games. If your hand is good, you play it out with pleasure. However, when you're dealt a poor hand, you do the best you can. You don't throw your cards down in disgust and walk away. Perhaps you may draw better cards, or not. Connecting embraces whatever deal you get.

Acquiring acceptance

Acceptance is a willingness to cope with whatever comes your way, including a certain degree of sadness. Acceptance is the opposite of rejection and resistance. In order to become accepting, you must give up judging and evaluating yourself, others, and events. That's because judgments and evaluations lead to rejection and unpleasantness.

Acceptance may be a rather strange concept for you. Your mind probably has been long trained to fight and resist anything and everything that feels unpleasant. To do the opposite seems downright illogical, self-defeating, and dangerous. Virtually unthinkable.

How could we possibly write an entire book about ridding yourself of depression and now suggest that you consider accepting depression? Do we *want* you to be depressed? Are we suggesting you *resign* yourself to depression? Quite the contrary.

Your mind may be telling you right now, "These ideas are crazy! You can't possibly accept feeling depressed! Don't listen to this garbage!" Try to hang with us a while.

Psychologists are discovering something that Buddhist monks have known for many centuries is apparently quite true: Acceptance actually provides a key toward peace and harmony. Accepting your current state of affairs may seem like the wrong thing to do, yet it has great value:

 ✔ **Acceptance permits you to walk away from the struggle.** Imagine you're playing tug of war with your depression. You fight your depression with all your might and throw everything you have at it. Inexplicably, your depression only deepens. Yet, this tug of war is no game. Depression is like a 12-foot tall, 800-pound monster. And in-between the two of you lies a huge gaping canyon with no visible bottom. Every time you pull harder on your end of the rope, the depression monster pulls even harder. You feel yourself gradually being pulled into the hole. You feel hopeless. Then you have a novel idea. You drop your end of the rope. The monster falls on his butt. And you walk away from the struggle.

Acceptance involves walking away from the war. That's because, as we say earlier in this chapter in the "Limiting resistance to what is" section, the more you absolutely and totally must not have something like anxiety or depression, the more likely you'll end up with what you're trying to avoid.

✔ **Acceptance of where you are now often helps you discover a better path.** Imagine that you're out driving in a blizzard at night. You're ten miles from home and your car slides into a snow bank. You push on the accelerator and the wheels spin. You accelerate more and they merely spin faster. You're completely and totally stuck. You fear you may die if not rescued soon. So, paralyzed with fear, you accelerate even more and the tires start to smoke.

Then you collect yourself for a few moments. You remember that the way out of such spots is not by stomping on the gas pedal. So you gently accelerate and when the wheels begin to spin, you let up. The car rocks back a little and then you apply a little pressure to the accelerator. You get into a rhythm. Slowly but surely the car makes bigger swings to and fro. Eventually you move on.

In essence, you escaped your predicament by *accepting* the idea of dealing with where you are for a little while (stuck), allowing yourself to rock backwards (not where you want to go), and only then gently moving forward a little. Working on depression is something like extricating yourself from a snow bank.

Now that you have a sense of what acceptance is about, we have two strategies for incorporating acceptance into your life.

Figuring out the skills of acceptance requires practice and time. *Any* gains you make can improve your life. Acceptance isn't about judging how accepting you manage to become. Accept where you are; move ahead gradually as you're able.

Accepting without judging

First, we suggest that you consider the value of nonjudgmental acceptance of yourself. If you want to evaluate or judge something, judge the consequences of your actions rather than your "self." By the way, this is the same advice psychologists give to parents about raising their kids. They say, "Judge the child's behavior as bad or undesirable, but don't label the child as 'bad.'" If you don't like something you've done, appreciate the lesson you can gain by looking at the undesired consequences of your actions. Don't judge your entire self.

You probably don't judge others nearly as harshly as you do yourself. You enjoy your friends and acquaintances for who they are as a total package. Try to do the same for yourself.

Living as if no one will know

Imagine if no one would ever know about any of the important things you do in your life. No one would know about your achievements, your accomplishments, or failures. No one to judge you at all. Not yourself or anyone else.

After you have this idea fixed in your head, ask yourself what you would do differently if no one would ever know about your successes or failures. Would you make any changes in the way you live your life? If so, you've been dancing to the tune played by the judgments of others. Try living for yourself.

Connecting with experience

As you begin to find acceptance (see the "Acquiring acceptance" section) you'll be prepared to experience life grounded in the present. Connecting with present-moment experience is rather foreign to many people. Staying connected with now takes practice. However, even small steps in this direction can provide you with important respite and peace.

Don't forget; few people in this world currently know how to mindfully accept what is. Today's world bombards you with countless pressures and distractions. In the face of all these distracters, give yourself time to acquire these skills. Be nonjudgmental about your attempts. Your mind will generate disrupting thoughts as inevitably as the sun rises and sets each day. You can acquire this skill more easily if you appreciate each accomplishment and accept each and every disruption.

Living like a dog

Relatively few moment-to-moment experiences feel terrible. Obviously, there are a few horrific events in life, but most of what upsets people is the small stuff. And thoughts can all too easily remove you from your actual experience and cause you to focus on *mind manufactured,* awful, horrible, or unpleasant feelings.

We like to break up our writing days with exercise. And Charles never feels as grounded and at peace as when he takes our dogs on a long jog three or four times each week. He heads out the door and in just a few minutes makes it to the West Mesa overlooking Albuquerque. You can see the entire city laid out at the footstep of a majestic mountain range. The view is stunning and you can see many miles out to the horizon.

The mesa is laced with dirt roads and gullies created by occasional downpours that blow through the otherwise parched land. Rabbits routinely dart across the running path. And once in a while, you can spot a coyote in the distance. Charles connects with the experience by noticing the rhythm of his running, the obvious joy the dogs exhibit, the quiet, and the (usually) gentle breezes.

Because he runs a long way, sometimes predicting a sudden downpour is impossible. The first few times rain started to drizzle, Charles cursed his fate and picked up the pace to return home as quickly as possible. But frequently Charles got soaked before he arrived home, and he felt distressed at his soaked condition. After all, everyone knows it's awful to get drenched in the rain.

But he noticed that the dogs never seemed to mind the rain. They occasionally shook off the excess water and continued to enjoy the run as much as ever. Charles wondered how they could continue to connect with their experience unfazed and undaunted. Then it hit him. Their minds are unfettered by thoughts of how awful it is to get soaked. They merely connect with their joyful experience, nothing else.

And could he not do the same? Yes. He then realized that the sensation of the rain feels not much different from his usual morning shower. What does "getting soaked" matter? The experience of running in the beautiful setting, rain notwithstanding, felt wonderful if he let the thoughts go and simply existed.

Self-absorption

Research by psychologists Dr. Susan Nolen-Hoeksema and Dr. Rick Ingram have implicated the role of self-absorption in a range of emotional disorders, including depression. They have found that the more one increases a focus on one's self, the more negative feelings intensify. Sometimes those with depression obsess about their thoughts and feelings in an understandable attempt to gain some kind of "insight." However, it appears that this practice may cause more harm than benefit. Furthermore, much of this self-focus involves judging and evaluating the self, often negatively. The techniques involved with both cognitive therapy discussed in Part II and mindfulness discussed in this chapter ultimately result in lessened self-focus. Although our exercises require you to look at aspects of yourself, the likely result at the end of the day is that you'll end up engaged in far less focus on self-evaluation.

Of course, you could wonder, but what about lightning, wouldn't that be dangerous and indicate a need for action? Yes, that's one way thoughts can be useful.

On the occasions that thoughts alert you to real, legitimate danger, you need to listen to them. However, all too often, thoughts send out false messages that don't involve realistic assessment of potential harm.

You can take the same approach that Charles did with many of the activities in your life. When thoughts magnify the awfulness of what you're going through right now, try disengaging from your thoughts. Merely connect with the actual experience, not with what you're making the experience out to be in your mind.

Connecting with the present

When you find yourself dwelling on regrets from the past or worries about the future, try out the "Connecting with the Present" exercise. We suggest you practice this exercise frequently — perhaps for 10 or 15 minutes a day for a couple of weeks. Over time, you'll discover that your ability to stay with the moment increases. This exercise teaches you how to observe your thoughts *mindfully*. Try not to get upset if troubling or distracting thoughts interfere with this exercise. But if those thoughts enter your mind, merely notice them without judging whether you're doing the exercise correctly.

- Focus on each moment that comes to you.

- Study all the sensations in your body, including touch, sights, sounds, and smell.

- You'll probably notice thoughts coming into your mind. Notice if these concern the future or the past. If so, just notice the thoughts. Then return to your body's sensations. Focus on your breathing as it goes in your nose, into your lungs, and out again.

- Notice the rhythm of your breathing.

- No doubt more thoughts will enter your mind. Remember, *thoughts are just thoughts.*

- Return to your breathing. Notice how good the air feels.

- If you have sad or anxious feelings, notice where you feel them in your body. Does your chest feel tight or is your stomach churning? Stay with those sensations.

- If you have thoughts about your feelings, notice how interesting it is that the mind tries to evaluate everything. Notice those thoughts and let them drift. Return to the present moment in your body.

- If more thoughts come, notice the *you* observing those thoughts in the present moment.

✔ Return to your breathing. Notice how nice and rhythmic it feels.

✔ If you hear sounds, try not to judge them. For example, if you hear a loud boom box from the outside, just notice the sounds as sounds. Not good or bad. Pick out the rhythm or the notes and let yourself hear them. If the phone rings, do the same, but don't answer it right now.

✔ Notice what you see at the back of your eyelids when you close your eyes. See the interesting patterns and forms that come and go.

✔ Once again notice your breathing for a while.

If you have trouble with this approach to dealing with your thoughts, you may wish to read or re-read Part II, which will help you appreciate how entrenched mind habits don't reflect reality. The techniques of cognitive therapy in Part II have been shown to help people rework these thoughts in a useful way. After you've accomplished that task, the strategies in this chapter may help you further improve your relationship with your thoughts.

As you start exploring the idea of viewing your thoughts as something to observe rather than statements of fact, you'll no doubt slip into old habits fairly frequently. Thus, you'll sometimes discover that you've been listening to your thoughts too seriously. At those times, be careful not to engage in negative thoughts about your negative thoughts. Realize that forming a new relationship with your thoughts takes time. The goal is a slow progression toward connecting more directly with experience rather than your thoughts.

Connecting mindfully even with the mundane

The mind has such an interesting way of turning everyday, mundane tasks into things to avoid. Perhaps you find yourself waiting in line at the local price club with 15 carts standing between you and the cashier. Do you ever hear thoughts rambling through your head such as:

✔ This is terrible; I have so much to do today.

✔ Why did I come here on such a crowded day, am I stupid or what?

✔ I'll never get everything done today.

✔ I can't stand waiting in line.

✔ Why don't they have more lines?

✔ This line isn't even moving.

✔ I should have chosen that line; at least it's getting somewhere.

✔ Oh no, the light is blinking; they have to get someone else to check a price. I'll *never* get through this line.

✔ This line must have the slowest cashier in the world.

✔ I hate this!

Sound familiar? Those are the sounds of a mind resisting what is. And what do you suppose all those thoughts do to the person hearing them? Most likely they stir up considerable tension, anxiety, and angst. And how futile, because what is, is. Simple as that.

As an alternative to resisting what is, consider "Accepting What Is" the next time you're somewhere or doing something that your mind tries to tell you is unacceptable. Take the often annoying task of waiting in a very long line, for example. It's a great chance to practice Accepting What Is:

- ✔ Notice your breathing.
- ✔ Feel the air go in your nostrils, down into your lungs, and out again.
- ✔ Notice the rhythm of your breathing.
- ✔ Notice how your feet feel in contact with the floor.
- ✔ Notice the sounds around you. Try not to judge them. Rather, hear the loud, sharp noises, the soft sounds, the background hum, and the unexpected disruptions.
- ✔ Notice the people around you without judgment. See what they look like. Notice what they do.
- ✔ If thoughts start to enter your head about things you must do, notice how interesting those thoughts are and let them drift by. Then refocus on now.
- ✔ Notice your breathing once more. Feel the air.
- ✔ Notice any smells wafting by. Again, don't judge them as good or bad.
- ✔ Don't suppress thoughts; just notice them as they may try to interfere with your attempt to experience and accept what is.

How many commonplace chores and tasks do you resist? Perhaps, doing the dishes, mowing the lawn, vacuuming, picking up the house, or shopping? You can probably come up with a pretty good list if you think about the things you put off.

For example, Charles recalls resisting trips to the library during graduate school days long ago. He would procrastinate until he *had* to go to the library if he wanted to finish a paper by the due date. His mind somehow convinced him that he absolutely hated library work. Odd thing though; almost every time he spent a few hours in the library, he discovered that he actually enjoyed the work he did there.

The more you resist what is, the more you will store up negative feelings and tension.

Try approaching the tasks of life mindfully. At first, many thoughts expressing current irritation, future apprehensions, or past regrets will inevitably attempt to interrupt and disrupt your attempts to connect with what is. Slowly but surely, with practice, you'll begin to notice those interrupting thoughts as just passing thoughts. As you do, you'll find that most everyday tasks no longer elicit the same avoidance and upset in you.

Enhancing pleasure mindfully

The depressed mind manages also to rob you of small pleasures by generating thoughts about the future or the past. For example, how many times have you sat down to consume a meal and finished without even tasting your food? That happens when thoughts race through your mind. Generally, you're going over thoughts that dwell on the future or the past.

The next time you engage in what seems like ought to be a pleasurable activity (almost any activity will do), try to approach it mindfully. For example, if you sit down to eat a meal, do so with the "Mindful Eating" strategy as follows:

- ✔ Notice your food sitting on your plate; observe the shapes, colors, smells, and textures.
- ✔ Take a small bite of food and bring it to your nose.
- ✔ Smell the food for a few moments.
- ✔ Touch the food first with your lips and then your tongue.
- ✔ Put the food in your mouth, but wait a moment before you chew.
- ✔ Feel the texture of your food as it sits on your tongue.
- ✔ Chew ever so slowly.
- ✔ Notice how your food feels and tastes on different parts of your tongue.
- ✔ Swallow your food and notice the taste and texture as it slides down your throat.
- ✔ Continue consuming your meal in this manner.

Consider making a habit out of mindful eating. You're likely to experience enhanced pleasure if you do. If troubling thoughts start to interfere, deal with them in the same manner as we've suggested in several sections of this chapter — notice that these thoughts are just thoughts and return your focus to your eating when you're able to do so. You will likely experience an additional benefit by feeling more relaxed when you eat. You may even lose a little weight, because slower eating allows the brain to detect feelings of fullness.

Thoughts are just thoughts . . .

Chapter 19

Pursuing Happiness Through Positive Psychology

In This Chapter

▶ Realizing that happiness is a good thing

▶ Avoiding seductive, illusory paths to happiness

▶ Building a foundation for real happiness

Donald inherited a popular neighborhood grocery store from his Dad. His father, who had always been a happy man, derived considerable pleasure from providing "beyond the call of duty" service to his friends and neighbors. Donald had always seen his father as out of touch with the times, and he couldn't wait to expand the business. In just ten years, Donald started ten new stores across the city and amassed considerable personal wealth.

However, Donald grew the business so rapidly that, when huge grocery chains moved into town, he didn't have the resources to compete effectively. Donald was forced into bankruptcy. He then fell into a deep depression. Antidepressant medication (see Chapter 15 for more information) brought him out of his depression, and a year later he established a successful dry-cleaning business. Nevertheless, Donald felt that something was missing in his life. Although he was no longer depressed, he felt empty and lacking in purpose.

As 20th century drew to a close, the field of psychology gave birth to a new discipline that addresses problems like Donald's. Dr. Martin Seligman and colleagues dubbed this new movement *positive psychology*. They spawned this fledgling endeavor out of concern that psychology had for too long focused almost all its attention on fixing what goes wrong in people's lives with little regard for fostering and enhancing positive emotions and outcomes. In a short time, psychologists have discovered much about what people can do to achieve genuine happiness.

In this chapter, we review key concepts from the field of positive psychology. Hopefully you've reached the point where depression doesn't dominate your life. But we want you to feel better than merely "not depressed." And in discovering how to reach for happiness, we hope that your depression will be less likely to reoccur.

You'll benefit from this chapter the most if you've already emerged from depression. A number of the ideas contained in this chapter won't seem particularly workable to someone in the throes of a major depression. Please first consider reading other chapters (such as 5, 6, and 7) and/or seeking professional help to alleviate your depression prior to seriously looking at achieving true happiness.

Hunting Down Happiness

Everyone wants to be happy, right? Not exactly. Some people feel that they don't deserve happiness. Others view happiness as a frivolous pursuit, essentially a waste of time. And finally, some people both desire and pursue happiness, yet fail to find it. We now explain why, for many folks, happiness all too often remains out of reach.

Making the case for being happy

Perhaps you feel that you don't deserve to be happy. If so, you're likely someone who experiences guilt and self-blame rather often. If that description fits you, we suggest reading or rereading Chapters 3, 5, 6, and 7 carefully. You may need further work on certain core change-blocking beliefs or habitual ways of thinking before you embark on a quest for happiness.

On the other hand, maybe you feel as deserving of happiness as anyone else, but you view happiness as flippant foolishness. This perspective is often the result of the messages parents convey to their children. Some children are told that work is the one and only valuable activity in life, and that any other undertaking merely diverts attention from what's important.

The information gathered from a growing pile of studies stands in stark contradiction to the dreary idea that happiness is irresponsible and wasteful. Today we know that happy people

- ✔ Live longer
- ✔ Are more creative
- ✔ Have lower blood pressure

✔ Have more active immune systems

✔ Have more empathy for others

✔ Make more money

✔ Are more productive

So, even if work is your primary concern in life, it appears that happiness makes you work more efficiently and productively. Happiness is also good for your health and your overall sense of well-being, and it likely enables you to live longer. It's hard to argue with something so good for you, isn't it?

Looking for happiness in all the wrong places

Many advertisers, booksellers, drug dealers, cult leaders, pornography peddlers, and workshop gurus have something in common. What can it be? To one degree or another, they offer shortcuts and quick-fixes to happiness and well-being. More than a few people must be buying the messages from these quick-fix happiness traffickers — just take a look at the sales of cars, appliances, clothing, workshop tickets, and even drugs today when compared to 40 or 50 years ago.

Has any of this consumption and wealth increased the happiness of the public? Nope, not in the slightest. The number of people who declare themselves "very happy" actually *declined* over the last 40 years (from 35 percent to 33 percent), while personal income (adjusted for inflation) doubled. At the same time, the divorce rate doubled, suicide among young people tripled, and violent crime quadrupled. Dr. Martin Seligman estimates that, among the affluent countries in the world, depression now occurs at levels that are as much as ten times greater than they were in 1960.

You may find it hard to believe, but numerous studies have conclusively demonstrated that for most people money fails to improve happiness. If you're not in a state of extreme poverty, money has almost no correlation with reported happiness — you're as likely to be happy if you just have enough money to get by as you are if you have piles of cash you don't know what to do with.

So if money doesn't pave the road toward happiness, what does? According to the popular ideas on the subject, the factors that breed happiness include

✔ Power

✔ Health

✔ Education

> ✔ Good looks
>
> ✔ Youth
>
> ✔ Good climate

Guess what? Like money, not one of the issues on the previous list has been found to be a particularly strong predictor of happiness and well-being. Yet many people devote much of their lives in pursuit of these very things, convinced that their quest will lead to happiness. They don't realize that they're chasing highly seductive illusions.

Being healthy doesn't even guarantee happiness. Don't get us wrong; extremely disabling illnesses of long duration do seem to detract from happiness. But studies have shown that, within fairly broad limits, not even poor health hampers happiness.

So if all these rather indisputably desired, sought-after items don't lead to happiness, what does? Though no one knows all the answers, the field of positive psychology is beginning to unearth some interesting possibilities. We devote the remainder of this chapter to some of those possibilities and urge you to consider each of them carefully.

Getting on the Right Path to Real Happiness

The steep road to happiness contains no shortcuts. Thus, you may wonder why, in Chapter 11, we advocate indulging in so-called healthy pleasures. Some of our suggestions include short-lived enjoyments such as drinking tea or coffee, eating chocolate, taking a hot bath or shower, playing games, going to a movie, and smelling fresh flowers.

We make those suggestions because people typically avoid anything pleasurable when they become depressed. Temporary, sensory delights don't lead to genuine, long-lasting happiness, but they can kick-start your efforts to climb out of depression. In the following sections, we set aside the tea and chocolate and discuss what leads to lasting well-being.

Gathering gratitude

Gratitude. We bet that you wouldn't put gratitude at the top of your list if we asked you to compile your ideas about possible foundations for happiness.

By *gratitude* we mean an appreciation or thankfulness for the good things that have either happened to you or been bestowed on you by others.

Most of the world's major religions extol the values and virtues of gratitude. And numerous literary references suggest that gratitude may increase a sense of well-being, happiness, and contentment. However, does consciously focusing on feeling grateful lead to happiness?

Studying the effects of gratitude

A colleague of ours volunteered to counsel two different couples who lost their homes and most of their possessions to a terrible fire. The first couple focused on the horror of their loss and the magnitude of the work they faced. Insurance claims, government bureaucracies, and rebuilding seemed almost overwhelming. They felt depressed and hopeless.

The other couple had a different take on what happened. They definitely felt a certain amount of sadness and despair, but they also talked about feeling grateful that their family emerged healthy and intact. And they were deeply appreciative of all the help bestowed on them by relatives, friends, neighbors, and even complete strangers.

Both couples received fairly similar acts of kindness and assistance from others. However, the second couple experienced more gratitude. Not surprisingly, they suffered far less emotional pain than the first couple.

We also have some clinical-type proof of the positive effects of gratitude. Researchers, Dr. Robert Emmons and Dr. Michael McCullough, conducted a series of studies that suggest that gratitude does indeed lead to an increased sense of well-being. During these studies, several groups of participants were asked to list items for which they feel *grateful.* These items, which could be large or small, included waking up this morning, performing an act of generosity, or even being able to listen to a favorite musical group. Other groups were asked to list neutral happenings, ways in which they felt others were less fortunate than themselves, and the hassles they experienced during the day.

Overall, the results of the studies were rather striking and impressive. Dr. Emmons and Dr. McCullough found that asking participants to focus on events for which they felt grateful caused a number of interesting changes (when compared to the groups that were asked to track different types of happenings). In general, the groups that focused on gratitude

- ✔ Had more positive feelings
- ✔ Helped other people with their problems more frequently
- ✔ Had less negative feelings (in one study)

> ✔ Slept longer
>
> ✔ Had better quality sleep
>
> ✔ Felt more connected to other people
>
> ✔ Were more optimistic
>
> ✔ Exercised more, even though no one had asked them to do so (in one study)
>
> ✔ Reported fewer health complaints (in one study)

These results are particularly amazing given that the groups that focused on gratitude weren't led to expect any particular benefits. Furthermore, these groups tracked their blessings for a relatively short period of time, ranging from a couple of weeks to a couple of months. In addition, people who knew the participants in the gratitude groups reported that they were able to tell that the participants felt better about their lives.

Putting gratitude to work for you

We recommend that you consider tracking what makes you feel grateful as a way to improve your sense of well-being. We call this strategy the "Gratitude Tracker." Perform the following tasks each day for the next month or two:

> ✔ Write down *five* things that make you feel grateful. Review your entire day, and consider both small and large events.
>
> ✔ Reflect a few moments on how appreciative you feel about each item on your list.

That's it. This exercise only requires about five minutes of your time each day. But we believe that you can use the Gratitude Tracker to start you on the way toward "counting your blessings" as a regular part of your life. The benefits you derive may very well surprise you.

In down, negative times, you may feel as though you have nothing to feel grateful about. However, even during those negative times, we urge you to ponder and reflect awhile. You'll likely find a few small things to feel grateful about. If, on the other hand, you're so depressed that you find this exercise impossible to do, please work on your depression before going back to this exercise.

Dr. Martin Seligman suggests another emotionally powerful way of expressing gratitude. He found that the groups of college students who tried this idea typically reported feeling wonderful after carrying it out. We call his strategy the "Testimonial Exercise." This exercise is simple and straightforward:

1. **Think of someone in your life who has made a positive difference for you.**

   This person shouldn't be a recent romance or someone you'd hope to gain something from.

2. **Write a single page testimonial or tribute to that person.**

   Fully express your feelings, gratitude, and appreciation.

3. **Review your testimonial carefully and rewrite it until it reflects your true feelings about the person.**

4. **Arrange a time to visit that person (don't just call), but don't reveal the reason for your visit other than wanting to chat or touch base.**

5. **Bring a copy of your testimonial in laminated form.**

   You can go to a copy store to get it laminated. Trust us, the person will likely want to hold on to your testimonial for a long while.

6. **Read your tribute to the person with feeling, eye contact, and expression.**

7. **Don't rush the person to react.**

8. **Spend a little time reminiscing with the person.**

We'll be surprised if you don't feel pretty good after you carry this exercise out. Bring gratitude into your life. We think appreciation just may help buffer you against future episodes of depression.

Helping others

We believe that a connection exists between *altruism* (unselfish concern for others) and the ability to feel gratitude. Support for this idea can be found in the study we discuss in the "Studying the effects of gratitude" section, earlier in this chapter. An increase in gratitude led study participants to help others more often. We suspect that the reverse may hold as well — that an increase in altruism may lead to an increase in gratitude.

Thus, we suggest that you look for ways to help others. You may wonder how to go about doing this. It isn't that hard after you begin thinking of ideas, but here's a short list to get you started:

✔ Find a kid in your neighborhood who needs tutoring, or volunteer to help with a literacy program.

✔ Volunteer to read stories to kids at the hospital.

✔ Offer to help an elderly neighbor with some chores.

✔ Spend a day picking up trash somewhere other than your own neighborhood.

✔ Take cans of food to a local food bank.

We won't give you a long list, because we believe that half the fun of performing this exercise is coming up with ideas. You may also want to check out the Random Acts of Kindness Foundation on the Internet at www. actsofkindness.org.

If you tend toward cynicism, you may think that people can't truly have unselfish concern for others because, ultimately, the person acting altruistically expects to obtain benefits. Well, we choose not to argue with this idea. We believe that benefits do indeed flow both ways. We're not suggesting that you perform kind acts in anticipation of actual personal gain; that wouldn't be in the spirit of this suggestion. However, we think that you'll derive a considerably more enduring sense of pleasure from altruistic activities than from temporary pleasures such as eating a nice meal or watching your favorite television show. Give altruism a try and see for yourself.

Finding flow

Momentary pleasures won't help you find enduring happiness. Yet it seems that society has gravitated more and more in the direction of cheap, quick-fix approaches to finding happiness. At the same time, we don't recommend that you abandon all small pleasures.

Rather, we suggest searching for engaging challenges. Dr. Mihaly Csikszentmihalyi (don't worry; we have no more idea of how to pronounce his name than you do) describes these challenges as something that cause you to feel a sense of what he calls *flow*. When you're in a state of flow, you typically find yourself completely absorbed in the activity you're engaged in (so much so, that you lose a sense of time). These are the activities that you want never to end and that engage you so powerfully that your involvement feels utterly effortless, even if the pursuit is physically strenuous.

You may have to search to find activities that give you this sense of total engagement and flow, but you're likely to discover great value in searching for and finding such completely captivating challenges. Look back on your life and ask yourself what types of activities may have engaged you in the ways we're describing. You'll likely find something if you reflect for awhile. If you don't, search for ideas in hobbies you currently enjoy.

For some people, certain sports like running or tennis do the trick. For others, a particular hobby like painting, gourmet cooking, dancing, or reading a book presents new and stimulating ideas. We sometimes find that writing puts us in a state of flow. Some days we write for hours and barely realize that the clock has moved.

Activities that stimulate flow require a considerable amount of effort — more than is required by temporary pleasures like watching television, going to movies, or snacking on delightful junk food. Unlike transient delights and amusements, activities that put you in a state of flow require you to hold off gratification for awhile. But at the end of the day, you'll very likely find rich rewards in making the effort.

Most of these fully engaging challenges have the potential to produce failure experiences before and after they become inherently rewarding. In most cases, we think that you'll find these transient failures worth the effort. However, if you're in the throes of a depression, we don't particularly recommend that you start trying to find flow experiences. Recover from your depression first, and then turn your attention to finding activities that produce flow.

Focusing on strengths

We want you to feel better than okay. In order to do that, you'll need to focus on your personal strong points, rather than beat yourself up over your flaws. If you're still in the throes of depression, you'll probably need to work through other parts of this book (especially Part II) to enable you to let go of your negative focus. But if you have emerged from depression, read on.

Building a definition

What do we mean by strengths? We'll start off by telling you what we don't mean. We don't mean attributes that are largely inherited: Appearance, athletic skill, height, and a great singing voice are features about yourself to appreciate and feel grateful for.

Think about it. You may enjoy hearing a friend sing, but that's not likely why you value that person as a friend. Similarly, you may enjoy watching your children develop as athletes, but we suspect that their athletic skill has little to do with why you love them. When you think about what makes a person invaluable to you, don't you think more about that individual's fundamental human characteristics?

Strengths are really the virtues, attributes, and characteristics that you value in others. Strengths involve a person's core character. The following list provides examples of important strengths, at least some of which you no doubt possess.

Appreciation of beauty/aesthetics	Joy in learning
Compassion	Kindness
Curiosity	Loyalty
Dependability	Listening skills
Empathy	Loving
Generosity	Perseverance
Helpfulness	Sense of humor
Honesty	Trustworthiness

Exercising your strengths

We suggest that you review our list of 16 sample strengths. Ponder which of these strengths capture your personal strong points. Although few people can lay claim to having all these positive attributes in abundance, we also believe that almost no one comes up lacking in all these areas.

By identifying, appreciating, and building on your strengths, you can find value in yourself and increase your sense of well-being. Start by observing your strengths. Identify the personal strengths you value the most in the previous list, such as honesty, sense of humor, and listening skills. Or perhaps you can think of a few strengths not listed. Then, over the next few weeks, you can work on our "Appreciating Strengths Strategy." Get out a notebook and take notes on your strengths.

1. **Notice each time you use one of your personal strengths.**

2. **Notice the type of occasion that allows you to express your strength.**

3. **Observe how you feel when you employ that strength.**

4. **Appreciate how that strength enhances your life.**

5. **Mentally pat yourself on the back for having that strength.**

We hope that, as you try out our Appreciating Strengths Strategy, you'll feel a sense of gratitude for your strengths. Next, we suggest building on your strengths and exercising them often. Look for opportunities to use your strengths at work, home, and play.

Anna cleans houses for a living. She struggles to get through each day and views her work as something she must do to survive, nothing more. Though she's not depressed, her life is dull and lacking in purpose.

By contrast, **Jenna** also cleans houses, but she creates meaning from her work by focusing on ways to express her personal strengths of appreciating aesthetics, kindness, and helpfulness. Jenna approaches her work from the standpoint of how she can "beautify" the homes she works in, not merely clean them. She carefully arranges items in aesthetically pleasing ways; she doesn't just dust them off. She also looks for any opportunity to make her clients' lives easier. Thus, she readily reorganizes pantries and occasionally runs errands without being asked.

Cynics may think that Jenna is merely "sucking up." And indeed she is in far greater demand as a house cleaner than Anna. However, she truly finds joy in expressing her personal strengths through her work. Jenna frequently enters a state of flow, and her work enhances her sense of well-being.

Given the opportunity, choose work that will maximize your personal strengths. However, no matter what type of work you do, you can find ways to express your strengths and build on them if you try hard enough. And remember that work is just one part of life. Take the opportunity to discover, apply, and build on your strengths in every aspect of your life.

For more information about ways to build on your strengths, we recommend reading *Authentic Happiness: Using the New Positive Psychology to Realize Your Potential for Lasting Fulfillment,* by Martin E. P. Seligman (Free Press).

Rejecting the quick fix

Self-restraint, self-discipline, moderation, self-denial, temperance, self-control — these terms don't exactly conjure up images of joy and happiness. In fact, they may even sound downright dreary. Yet the fact remains that self-control will lead you toward happiness more certainly and directly than any quick-fix approach.

Unfortunately, we live in a world that increasingly delivers promises of instant happiness and good feelings. Though we see a role for medications when it comes to treating certain types of depression (see Chapter 15), some advertisements seem to suggest that you should pop pills the moment a bad feeling arises. Other ads condition you to believe that instant happiness will come if you drive the right car or own the best sound equipment available. And instant solutions are offered for every conceivable hassle, from preparing meals to the "horror" of having to wait in line for a rental car.

In addition, books, videotapes, and workshop gurus tell everyone that they should feel good about themselves all the time. And if you don't, they suggest simplistic solutions like merely repeating positive, yet silly self-affirmations over and over every day. Guess what:

 ✔ Quick fixes don't work.

 ✔ No one is happy all the time.

 ✔ The more you expect instant gratification, the more miserable you're going to be.

Psychologists have even found that the ability to exercise self-control and delay gratification is highly predictive of ultimate adjustment and well-being from childhood through adulthood. Although self-control is arguably best figured out in childhood, the good news is that you can increase your self-control at any time.

Moderation and self-control appear to be valuable for a number of reasons:

 ✔ Many of the most-satisfying goals require considerable patience and work in order to obtain them.

 ✔ When you shower yourself with indulgences, they lose much of their appeal. Psychologists call this phenomena *satiation*. In other words, too much of a good thing ends up feeling less enjoyable.

 ✔ As we discuss in Chapter 7, when you have an inflated view of yourself, thinking you're better than others, you may end up causing problems. For example, if you allow yourself to feel superior to other people, others will more likely reject you.

The remarkable value of waiting

Psychologist Walter Mischel and his colleagues conducted a fascinating study that was reported in the *Journal of Personality and Social Psychology.* They had a group of 4-year-olds come into a room one at a time. A single marshmallow was placed on one part of a table in the corner of the room, while two marshmallows were placed on another part of the table. The researchers told each child, "If you wait until I come back by myself, then you can have this one [pointing to two marshmallows]. If you don't want to wait, ring this bell and bring me back. But if you ring the bell, you can only have one marshmallow."

Some of the kids couldn't wait, so they rang the bell. Others managed to delay their urges for instant gratification and hang in there for both marshmallows. The researchers followed these kids for ten years. Incredibly, they found that the kids who displayed the most self-control were better than the other kids at getting along with others, performed better academically, were better at coping with stress, and had fewer personal problems. These kids were also more self-reliant, skillful, trustworthy, and eager to discover. Since this initial study, researchers have verified these findings with different types of self-control tasks and with many groups of children of varying ages and from various walks of life.

Thus, we advocate moderation as a realistic path toward sustainable happiness. Money, alcohol, drugs, and self-indulgence represent seductive illusions. If you focus your efforts on quick fixes, you'll find yourself disappointed time and time again.

Finding forgiveness

Of all the paths toward happiness, figuring out how to forgive may be the most difficult. When people have been wronged, it can be so tempting to hold a grudge and desperately desire revenge (whether it is ever acted upon or not). And why not? After all, if you did nothing to deserve the injustice, don't you deserve to at least have a *desire* for retribution? Absolutely. You completely deserve to have those feelings!

Unfortunately, those feelings will cost you. Quite a lot, actually. Holding onto feelings of rage and revenge will likely make you feel like a victim. Chapter 3 discusses the harmful effects of feeling like a victim, which include increased anger and a sense of helplessness. We suggest that you read Chapter 3 to discover ideas on how not to feel like a victim.

More importantly, figuring out to forgive is likely to enhance your sense of well-being. Several studies have shown that the more you cling to your resentments and grievances, the less happy and satisfied with life you're likely to be. But how in the world can you find forgiveness if you've been egregiously wronged?

A few horrific things can happen to people, such as sexual abuse or violence, that you may not be able to forgive. In such cases, it's probably more important to accept one's self and attempt to let go of thoughts of revenge than to actually find forgiveness.

As we say earlier, finding forgiveness is no easy task. However, you can do it. We recommend the following steps for conducting what we call a "Revenge Reanalysis and Forgiveness Technique." See what this process can do for you. We understand that the concept may seem foreign to you at first, but we believe that you're likely to discover surprising benefits after exploring the idea.

1. **Remember the wrong in the most dispassionate, nonjudgmental terms possible. Imagine the happening in your mind and try to avoid feelings of rage, retribution, or sorrow as best you can.**

   Play the tape of your memory many times until your feelings dissipate at least a little.

2. **Search for some understanding of the perpetrator's perspective.**

   This step may be particularly difficult. You may find it useful to realize that people typically hurt others when they feel threatened, fearful, or anxious. Sometimes they perceive a need to defend their honor or self-esteem, even though their perceptions may be misguided. Consider the possibility that many offenders don't understand the hurtfulness of their actions. Some offenders may also feel the need to attack to enhance a self-image that was destroyed by a horrific childhood.

3. **Form an image of yourself in your mind as someone who copes well, rather than as someone who's a victim. Think of yourself as someone with strength and fortitude who can rise above adversity and forgive.**

4. **If thoughts of revenge come into your mind, remind yourself that revenge and retribution will harm you at least as much as the offender, and arguably even more so.**

   Even the thoughts and feelings of revenge inflict damage on your emotional soul — and hurt your body by kicking off a flood of harmful stress hormones that raise blood pressure and may eventually cause damage to your organs.

5. **Dig down deep and forgive.**

   If you can forgive the offender publicly, that's even better. Perhaps you can write a letter of forgiveness. At least write the forgiveness down and then talk about it with others. Give your forgiveness with as much altruism as you can muster, without any regard for yourself.

When memories of the wrongful act reoccur, go through the forgiveness process again. Don't expect saintly perfection from yourself. Every step you make in the direction of finding forgiveness helps you.

Searching for meaning and purpose

People find meaning and purpose in life in quite diverse ways. Finding meaning and purpose generally involves reaching out and relating to concepts that feel larger, more enduring, and of greater significance than yourself. Of course, religion and spirituality stand as the most prominent methods for finding meaning, and the largest number of people likely employs them.

If you're not very spiritually inclined, you can still infuse meaning into your life. Ask yourself what you want your life to be about. What do you want your legacy to be to the world? Consider the following exercise we call the "Eulogy in Advance."

1. **Sit back and relax for a few moments. Take a few slow, deep breaths.**

2. **Reflect on your life for awhile. Don't dwell on past regrets.**

3. **Ask yourself what you want people to say and think of you at your own funeral. What do you want friends, loved ones, or others to remember about your life?**

4. **Consider what you can do with the rest of your life to infuse it with the meaning you want to leave the world.**

Very few people write such a eulogy extolling their appearance, the money they've made, the long hours they worked at the office, or the power they wielded over others. Most people choose to emphasize their strengths of character (such as those listed earlier in this chapter, in the section "Focusing on Strengths").

No matter what your age, you can devote at least a portion of your life to enhancing its meaning. These purposes don't need to be monumental. You may choose to

✔ Be a kind person.

✔ Help others.

✔ Advance knowledge in some way.

✔ Do something positive for the environment.

✔ Be kind to animals.

✔ Teach and pass knowledge on to the younger generation.

✔ Forgive yourself and others.

✔ Express gratitude.

You can fill your life with meaning in any number of ways. All you need to do is connect and contribute to something (almost anything) that feels larger than yourself. Whether you have a day, a year, or decades left on this planet, you *can* make a difference.

Part VII
The Part of Tens

The 5th Wave   By Rich Tennant

"Remember, we're here to cheer him up, but don't be obvious."

In this part . . .

It wouldn't be a *For Dummies* book without the Part of Tens. Here's where you can find our depression-related top ten lists. We present ten quick ways of getting out of a bad mood. And if you're reading this book because a child, friend, or significant other suffers from depression, we offer tips. Discover how to prevent depression in your kids, as well as what to do if they should get depressed. Finally, you can see how to respond to a friend or loved one who is depressed.

Chapter 20

Ten Ways Out of a Bad Mood

*B*ad mood or depression — what's the difference? Bad moods are typi-cally unpleasant but short emotional states. Depression drags on for weeks, or in some cases, far longer.

And after you're over your depression, you'll still encounter occasional bad moods. Nonetheless, realizing that bad moods aren't intolerable and that you can do something about them may help prevent a longer-lasting negative spiral. So, in order to keep your bad moods from spiraling into a depression, this chapter gives you some tips for handling the blues.

Chomping on Chocolate

Various types of food reputedly affect moods. People probably turn to chocolate as frequently as they do any of the other mood-altering foods. A host of the substances found in chocolate have been cited as responsible for its mood-lifting effects. However, some researchers believe that chocolate, like most especially palatable foods, alters mood primarily by causing a release of endorphins, the brain's opiates (see Chapter 10 for more on endorphins). If you find that chocolate works for you, indulge a little when a bad mood sets in.

If you're a chocoholic, and you feel pronounced guilt when you indulge in chocolate, this isn't the food for you when you feel low. Guilt will only deepen your funk. As with all things, moderation is the key.

Doing Something Nice

Take a page from Chapter 19 on positive psychology. Doing something nice for someone else is one of the best ways we can think of to extricate yourself from a bad mood. It helps you refocus your attention away from what put you in the bad mood and onto other people in a positive way. And your improved mood is likely to last a lot longer than it will with other nice, quick-fix pleasures like chocolate.

Getting a Lift from Exercise

Exercise has the potential to lift you out of a bad mood. Of course, when you're in such a mood, you probably don't *feel* like exercising. But just because you don't feel like exercising, that doesn't mean that you can't do it.

Short-circuit your negative thinking about exercising and just move your body toward doing something active. Getting yourself moving is half the battle. When you get over that hurdle, your momentum will carry you forward.

Take a long walk, jog, lift some weights, follow the instructions on a yoga videotape, or do whatever form of exercise you prefer. Exercise releases endorphins, improves your health, and helps you feel a sense of accomplishment. For more information about the benefits of exercise, see Chapter 10.

Singing Yourself into a Better Mood

If you like to sing, try it when you feel low. Belt your favorite song out at the top of your lungs. There's something about singing that's almost diametrically opposed to feeling down. Of course, we do recommend an upbeat tune rather than the blues.

Putting your negative thoughts into a whimsical song can also be useful. If you're in a lousy mood, you probably have some negative thinking running through your head (see Chapters 5, 6, and 7 for more information about this type of thinking). Listen to those thoughts and write them down. Then use those thoughts as the lyrics to a popular song. Somehow your negative thinking loses some of its meaning when you sing your thoughts in a silly song.

Calling a Long-Lost Friend

If you're like most people, you have friends that you haven't connected with in a while. If you want to feel good, call one of these friends. Don't wait and talk yourself out of it. Just do it.

Besides, research shows that social connections can help with all kinds of ills, including bad moods. So even if you don't have a long-lost friend, call any friend at all. Talking things out may help. And reconnecting feels good.

Dancing to a Different Beat

Do you like to dance? If so, you just may be able to dance your way to a better mood. Dancing, much like exercise, releases endorphins (see Chapter 10 for more info about endorphins). If you pick the right upbeat song to dance to, the music alone may pull you into a better mood.

If you don't have a partner, you can just dance by yourself in the privacy of your home. You can dance in a serious way, or you can create a giddy, whimsical dance (the wilder and crazier the better!).

Soaking the Blues Away

Many people find that a long, hot bath helps soothe the body and mind. A hot tub makes a good alternative. Often, when people end up in a bad mood, doing something soothing doesn't quite "feel" right. Nevertheless, trust us on this idea. Just do it.

Petting Your Way to a Better Mood

If you're in a bad mood, try spending some time with your pet. Don't have one? Consider getting one. Really! Studies are demonstrating that pets actually help people feel better, and they may even improve your health. If we want a good laugh, all we have to do is play with our dogs. Sometimes just looking at them makes us laugh.

Why would petting a dog help your health and mood? No one knows for sure. However, pets help you shift the focus from yourself and your problems to something positive — perhaps even something warm and affectionate. Many studies have shown that self-absorption deepens depression and bad moods, while shifting attention outside of yourself helps improve your condition.

Taking a Hike

Again, we can't exactly say why, but spending time in the outdoors seems to do a much better job of brightening moods than does staying inside. In the winter, it may be the natural light that helps, because the sun emits a far brighter light than you can get inside. And bright light appears to alleviate seasonal affective disorder, or SAD (see Chapters 2 and 16 for more information).

However, the outdoors may just lift moods because it puts people into contact with nature. We don't know of specific studies that suggest that nature improves moods, but we do know that almost all our clients report feeling better when they spend time outside of their homes. When you get out there, appreciate what you see.

Mellowing Through Mindfulness

You may be able to get out of a bad mood by accepting that bad moods are an inevitable part of life! Sound confusing? Actually, the idea isn't that complicated. When you catastrophize about bad moods, they intensify. When you accept them as unpleasant but inevitable, they lose some of their grip on your psyche. If this notion still seems confusing, you may want to read Chapter 18.

You may also want to consider connecting with the present rather than pondering awful thoughts about the past or future. The following exercise can help you refocus your thoughts on the present.

1. **Notice the rhythm of your breathing.**

2. **Feel the air as it passes through your nostrils and into your lungs.**

3. **Notice how good the air feels.**

4. Notice how your body feels. Focus only on your bodily sensations.

5. Return to the rhythm of your breathing.

6. Feel where your body touches the surface on which you're sitting, standing, or lying.

7. Notice how nice the air feels.

8. Continue noticing these various sensations for five or ten minutes.

When you connect with the present, you let go of negative thoughts about the future or past. The "now" is usually far more tolerable than your mind's worries about the future or concerns with the past.

Chapter 21

Ten Ways to Help Kids With Depression

● ●

In This Chapter

▶ Preventing depression before it starts

▶ Recognizing depression in kids

▶ Dealing with depression if it shows up

● ●

Depression has reached close-to-epidemic levels among our youth. The causes of depression in the young are the same as they are for adults — biology and genetics, trauma, loss, stress, chronic family conflict, and so on. (See Chapter 2 for more about depression's causes.) Of course, the ideal solution is to prevent depression from occurring in the first place.

This chapter provides tips for preventing depression in kids. We also discuss what to do if your child, or a child you care about, becomes depressed, because not all depressions can be prevented, even despite your best efforts.

Finding Fun

Kids flourish when they feel engaged, involved, and interested in what they're doing. Explore activities and hobbies together until your child finds an interest that she can be good at and enjoy. You may have to try many different activities, such as dance, drama, swimming, stamp or coin collecting, tennis, computers, art, soccer, or horseback riding. The goal is to find a hobby that your child both enjoys and feels reasonably competent at performing.

Then make sure that she participates frequently. Getting your child involved in an engaging activity can help prevent depression, because it gives her something to look forward to and helps her develop social support.

Doling Out Discipline

Many parents are reluctant to discipline their kids. They fear that they'll upset their children and make them feel bad. These parents worry that disciplining their children will turn their kids away from them. They want to be best friends with their children. But parenting isn't about being your child's best friend.

Care enough to discipline your child. Psychologists know that self-control and the ability to tolerate frustration are the two most important skills to learn in childhood. Armed with these skills, kids can face whatever life deals them. Children can't learn self-control unless their parents give them clear rules and consequences. Children need self-control so that they can live up to these rules, and consequences provide an incentive for learning this self-control.

Disciplining children can be hard work. So sometimes it may be tempting to ignore bad behavior. But your children are counting on you. When kids misbehave, take the opportunity to teach an important lesson. Children who learn self-control are far less likely to become depressed.

Giving Feedback

When your child goofs up, criticize the behavior, not your child. Never call a child "stupid" or "bad." Such negative labeling paves the way for the emergence of depression down the road. As an alternative, you can label the behavior "bad." For example, "stealing is bad," or "hitting your sister is wrong." When you apply such labels to your child's entire self, you risk instilling negative self-views that are difficult to alter.

Climbing Every Mountain

Give your child the opportunity to accomplish something difficult. Children learn self-confidence by mastering tough tasks. Help your child enter a race (you can train together), learn how to canoe, or master a piano concerto. During the learning process, your child will no doubt experience frustration and fatigue. Encourage him to persevere.

Life isn't easy. Children who learn how to work hard carry that quality into adulthood. As a result, they're much more likely to be able to bravely tackle life's problems, including depression.

Revving Up Responsibilities

Many parents find it easier to do household chores themselves rather than beg and nag the kids to help out. That's a mistake. Children need to feel connected and useful. Participating in family responsibilities helps kids develop character.

When kids are allowed to take without giving, they begin to feel special — perhaps too special. Laziness at home may work with some moms or dads, but when kids venture out into the real world, others view that sense of specialness and entitlement as simply a case of being spoiled rotten. The resulting rejection may trigger depression.

Talking and Listening

No matter what, you need to make it safe for your children to talk. What do we mean by "make it safe"? First, listen without interrupting. Let your children tell their stories. Next, don't judge or criticize their feelings. The following example illustrates both the wrong way and the right way to listen:

> **Breanna** tells her mother: "No one likes me. Everyone thinks I'm stupid. I feel horrible. I don't want to go to school anymore."
>
> Her mother could respond with, "Don't be ridiculous. You have no reason to feel horrible. You have lots of friends. And don't think for a second that you're going to get away with not going to school!"
>
> But a better response would be, "It sounds like you're feeling down. What happened?"

The better response didn't judge and encouraged more talking. Notice how the first response stopped the conversation cold. Your kids will only talk with you if they feel listened to and understood. Even if you don't agree with what they say, at least let them say what's on their minds.

Recognizing Depression

When children have depression, they experience symptoms that are similar to those experienced by adults. They feel sad, lose interest in things that were previously interesting, have trouble concentrating, and have low self-esteem. (See Chapter 2 for more on the signs and symptoms of depression.)

On the other hand, children may differ from adults in that their moods may vary more over the course of a day. Depressed children are often irritable and moody. The early warning signs of depression in children can include

- Ditching school
- Drop in grades
- Excessive reactions to criticism or rejection
- Loss of interest in usual activities
- Risky behavior, such as taking drugs or reckless driving
- Vague physical complaints, such as headaches and stomachaches
- Withdrawal from friends

Don't ignore such signs of depression in your kids. Depression is a serious problem, and it isn't a normal part of childhood. In fact, suicide is the third leading cause of death in people between the ages of 10 and 24.

Looking Under Rocks

Depression stems from multiple sources. If your child exhibits signs of depression, exploring all possible causes is important. Although depression does have genetic and biological underpinnings, some kind of outside stress often contributes to it.

Many parents blame themselves for their kids' depression. Self-blame and guilt won't help your child. But family life may play a role in depression. Be willing to look at that possibility and get help if you find any indication that your family life is negatively affecting your child.

Children spend much of their lives outside of the home. Some possible causes of depression include

- Bullying at school
- Emotional, physical, or sexual abuse (unknown to the family)
- Social rejection
- Unidentified academic problems, such as learning disabilities
- Unidentified health problems

If your child is depressed, carefully explore all possible contributing factors. Treating the depression without understanding the causes may prevent the treatment from working. For example, if your child is depressed due to bully-ing at school, giving an antidepressant medication won't address the problem.

Getting Help

If you think that your child is depressed, get help. Depression in children can be treated with many of the same tools that help adults — therapy and anti-depressant medications. Be prepared to take an active part in the treatment. Don't feel guilty or embarrassed about taking your child for help. If you get treatment early for your child's depression, you may prevent your child from experiencing repeated depressions later in life. See Chapter 4 for advice on how to find the right help.

Loving No Matter What

Part of being a child involves testing the limits. Kids act out, disobey, dress weird, and act out with stupid, childlike behaviors. What would adolescence be without a little rebellion? Some kids go to extremes by shoplifting, using drugs, and shocking their parents with numerous body piercings and tattoos.

Parents typically feel angry and outraged at these excessive behaviors. However, you have to make an important distinction between reacting to unacceptable behavior with feelings and consequences versus total rejection and rage. You need to let your kids know that, no matter what, you love them. That doesn't mean that you can't express displeasure or disappointment. Temper condemnation with concern. Care and love walk hand in hand with discipline.

Chapter 22

Ten Ways to Help a Friend or Lover with Depression

. . . .

In This Chapter

▶ Being a friend — not a counselor

▶ Realizing your loved one's depression isn't personal

▶ Viewing time as an ally

. . . .

*N*othing's much more distressing than seeing someone you love suffer from depression. You care, and you want to help. But most people don't know where to start. This chapter gives you ten ideas for how you can help someone you care about with depression.

Recognizing Depression

You must recognize that your loved one is depressed before you can do anything to help. Of course, you can read the formal diagnosis of depression in Chapter 2 if you want to see an entire list of symptoms. But we don't exactly suggest that you give your friend a diagnosis — that's a task only for professionals.

However, perhaps you've noticed lately that your loved one is acting differently, displaying behaviors such as:

✔ Changes in appetite or sleep

✔ Disinterest in previously enjoyable activities

✔ Increased irritability

✔ Lower energy and fatigue

- Lower mood than usual
- Problems concentrating or making decisions
- Self-disparaging talk

If your loved one has more than a couple of these symptoms, she may very well be depressed. As we said, don't make the diagnosis yourself. However, you can gently ask about the possibility of depression, and perhaps urge your partner to check out this possibility with a counselor or the family doctor.

If seeing a counselor or doctor feels too threatening to your loved one, the Internet has screening resources. See the Appendix for a list of these and other resources. National Depression Screening Day usually falls in October. You can check out this program at www.mentalhealthscreening.org/ depression.htm. In addition, this Web site has screening tools you can use at any time of the year.

The Internet contains an incredible amount of useful information. However, it can't replace professional help. Furthermore, some sites are more reliable than others. We provide you with the Web addresses of some high-quality Web sites in the Appendix.

Referring for Help

One of the more useful actions you can take is to encourage your loved one to get help. You can start by recommending *Depression For Dummies* — just be sure you point out that you're not suggesting that your friend is a dummy in a negative sense! In addition, you can suggest a visit with the family doctor. Finally, if your loved one agrees to see a therapist and doesn't get around to doing so, offer to help find one. Read Chapter 4 for ideas on how to go about finding a good therapist.

Although you can be helpful to someone you know who has depression, you can't solve the problem. You can't be responsible for the depression or even for insuring that the people you care about get help. You can facilitate help, and that's as far as you can go.

Listening Without Solving

More than anything else, realize that it's truly not up to you to cure your loved one of depression. Even if you're a counselor, physician, or psychologist, you can't treat someone you care deeply about. Friends may not have the necessary objectivity and perspective needed for effective treatment. Your friend needs you to be someone who will listen, not treat or solve the problem.

Therefore, you should provide a sounding board. Listen with empathy and concern. You may want to express that you've had similar feelings at times in the past, if that's truly the case. If you listen carefully, you'll no doubt find yourself tempted to talk your loved one out of the quagmire of depression. Don't give in to that temptation; such attempts will likely be met with resistance and possibly a worsening of symptoms.

Your loved one needs a sympathetic ear; professionals are the only people who can actually intervene therapeutically.

Taking Care of Yourself

Helping someone you care about who's depressed can drain you of energy and resources. Listening to tales of woe and misery isn't always easy. We advise that you connect, listen, and empathize to the extent that you can. But don't let yourself sink into the throes of depression in the process.

Thus, attending to your own needs is important. Continue to live your life and seek sources of enjoyment. Connect with friends and keep balance in your life. If you invest too much of yourself in helping your loved one, you can easily lose the capacity to help, and you risk falling into your own depression.

Holding Criticism at Bay

If your loved one is depressed, the last thing you need to do is criticize. Nonetheless, you may find yourself tempted to do so when you hear some of the things a person who's depressed may say. For example, your friend may say something like, "I'm no good to anyone anymore."

Upon hearing something like that, you may find yourself blurting out, "That's ridiculous! Why would you ever say something so stupid?"

Try to use empathy instead. Perhaps say, "I know you feel that way. I don't really agree with you, but it must feel awful to have that thought."

In addition, people with depression may bait you to criticize them. Due to the increased irritability, they may criticize you more than usual, and you may feel tempted to defend yourself. Try to resist defending your ego and realize that the criticism is probably due more to depression than anything else.

Depersonalizing Depression

When someone you love is depressed, it's rather easy to think that the depression is the result of something you've done, or that somehow it's your fault. Please realize that depression has many causes — genetics, biological factors, certain diseases or drugs, childhood events, culture, and so on. (See Chapter 2 for more information.)

That's not to say that your relationship with your loved one has nothing to do with the depression. In fact, it may. Being open to the idea of working on your relationship is a good idea — perhaps through counseling, if that seems appropriate. And consider reading and implementing the ideas presented in Chapter 14. But blaming yourself for your partner's depression won't help. And in most cases, other causes play a far greater role.

Finding Patience

When you're dealing with a case of serious, major depression (see Chapter 2 for more information about the various types of depression), you need to understand that treatment takes time. Even antidepressant medication typically requires a few weeks to start working. Furthermore, some depressions require a considerable search for the right medication, which may take many months.

Psychotherapy also takes time to work. An average case may show some improvement within two to three months, but many cases require a longer period of time. As with medications, sometimes the first therapist doesn't work out, and your loved one may need to search for another mental health professional to receive the right type of help. (See Chapter 4 for information about finding help for depression.)

Avoid falling into the trap of thinking that your loved one actually *wants* to feel depressed. We truly believe that no one wants to feel depressed. Sometimes a person with depression can act somewhat irrationally or in self-defeating ways, but that doesn't mean that the depression is actually desired.

Try not to lose patience. You may want to consult a therapist yourself if you find the task of getting your loved one to go to a therapist to be too difficult.

Remembering to Care

When people become depressed, they need the care and concern of loved ones more than ever. Unfortunately, people with depression sometimes push others away. Thus, it may seem that they prefer to be alone and isolated.

Don't believe it. Whether your efforts seem appreciated or not, continue to do caring things for someone who's depressed. Send a card or flowers. In addition, look for small caring things you can do. We provide an entire list of nice things you can do for someone in Chapter 14.

Providing Encouragement and Remaining Hopeful

Feeling hopeless isn't unusual for a depressed person. In fact, hopelessness is one of the more common symptoms of depression. Nonetheless, the vast majority of depressed people do manage to improve a great deal.

If you listen too long to what someone with depression says, it can be very easy to start believing in the hopelessness you're hearing. The fact is, many people with depression can present you with an amazing array of evidence concerning the awfulness and hopelessness of their lives. However, you need to understand that depressed minds generate thoughts that are almost always distorted in major ways. Thus, the "evidence" they give you probably isn't accurate. Check out Chapters 5, 6, and 7 for detailed information about how depression inevitably distorts thinking.

When you understand how depressed minds can distort the hopelessness of a situation, it becomes easier to remain encouraging. Your loved one with depression doesn't want you to give up, whether it seems that way or not. Remain hopeful and encouraging.

Exhorting Exercise

As we tell you earlier in this chapter, you can't be a therapist for someone you care about who has depression. That's true without question. Although there is one rather therapeutic thing you can do: Consider encouraging your loved one to find some type of exercise. Ideally, you should also participate.

Activity has a positive effect on depression. The more active you are, the better. See Chapter 10 for more about the effects of exercise on depression.

 Although encouraging someone who's depressed to exercise is a good idea, don't push the idea too hard. Some people, especially those with severe depression, simply can't get themselves cranked up to exercise. Pushing hard to get someone to exercise isn't worth harming your relationship.

Appendix

Resources for You

● ●

*H*ere we provide some additional resources for helping you find out more about depression and how to defeat it. In addition, we give you resources for other emotional issues, such as anxiety and relationship problems, that sometimes contribute to depression. Many other excellent books and Web sites that we have no doubt overlooked are available. In dealing with most any emotional problem, reading more than one book is often a good idea.

Self-Help Books

Here's a list of self-help books we recommend:

- *Authentic Happiness: Using the New Positive Psychology to Realize Your Potential for Lasting Fulfillment,* by Martin E. P. Seligman (Free Press)

- *Changing For Good: The Revolutionary Program that Explains the Six Stages of Change and Teaches You How to Free Yourself From Bad Habits,* by James O. Prochaska, John C. Norcross, and Carlo C. DiClemente (William Morrow & Co., Inc.)

- *Choosing to Live: How to Defeat Suicide Through Cognitive Therapy,* by Thomas E. Ellis and Cory F. Newman (New Harbinger Publications)

- *Cognitive Therapy of Depression,* by Aaron T. Beck, A. John Rush, Brian F. Shaw, and Gary Emery (Guilford Press)

- *Feeling Better, Getting Better, Staying Better: Profound Self-Help Therapy for Your Emotions,* by Albert Ellis (Impact Publishers, Inc.)

- *Full Catastrophe Living: Using the Wisdom of Your Body and Mind to Face Stress, Pain, and Illness,* by Jon Kabat-Zinn (Delta)

- *Interpersonal Psychotherapy of Depression,* by Gerald L. Klerman, Myrna M. Weissman, Bruce J. Rounsaville, and Eve S. Chevron (Basic Books)

- *Love is Never Enough: How Couples Can Overcome Misunderstandings, Resolve Conflicts, and Solve Relationship Problems Through Cognitive Therapy,* by Aaron T. Beck (HarperCollins)

- *Mind Over Mood: Change How You Feel by Changing The Way You Think,* by Dennis Greenberger and Christine A. Padesky (Guildford Press)

- *Mindful Recovery: A Spiritual Path to Healing from Addiction,* by Thomas Bien and Beverly Bien (Wiley Publishing, Inc.)

- *Mindfulness-Based Cognitive Therapy for Depression: A New Approach to Preventing Relapse,* by Zindel V. Segal, J. Mark G. Williams, and John D. Teasdale (Guilford Press)

- *Overcoming Anxiety For Dummies,* by Charles H. Elliott and Laura L. Smith (Wiley Publishing, Inc.)

- *Self-Coaching: How to Heal Anxiety and Depression,* by Joseph J. Luciani (Wiley Publishing, Inc.)

- *The Anxiety & Phobia Workbook,* by Edmund J. Bourne (New Harbinger Publications, Inc.)

- *The Feeling Good Handbook,* by David D. Burns (Plume)

- *The Noonday Demon: An Atlas of Depression,* by Andrew Solomon (Touchstone Books)

- *The Power of Now: A Guide to Spiritual Enlightenment,* by Eckhart Tolle (New World Library)

- *The Seven Principles for Making Marriage Work,* by John M. Gottman and Nan Silverman (Three Rivers Press)

- *Why Can't I Get What I Want? How to Stop Making the Same Old Mistakes and Start Living a Life You Can Love,* by Charles H. Elliott and Maureen Kirby Lassen (Davies-Black Publishing)

- *Your Perfect Right,* by Robert Alberti and Michael Emmons (Impact Publishers, Inc.)

Resources to Help Children

We recommend the following books for helping your child overcome depression:

- *Hollow Kids: Recapturing the Soul of a Generation Lost to the Self-Esteem Myth,* by Laura L. Smith and Charles H. Elliott (Prima Publishing)

- *Keys to Parenting Your Anxious Child,* by Katharina Manassis (Barrons Educational Series)

- *SOS Help for Parents,* by Lynn Clark (Parents Press)

- *The Optimistic Child: Proven Program to Safeguard Children from Depression and Build Lifelong Resistance,* by Martin E. P. Seligman (Perennial)

> ✔ *Why Can't I Be the Parent I Want to Be? End Old Patterns and Enjoy Your Children,* by Charles H. Elliott and Laura L. Smith (New Harbinger Publications, Inc.)

Helpful Web Sites

If you type the word *depression* into a search engine, you get access to an endless stream of possible resources. You need to beware, though, because the Internet is filled with clever advertisements and gimmicks. Be especially cautious about official sounding organizations that heavily promote expensive materials. And don't believe absurd promises of quick, instant cures for depression.

Many Web forums host chat rooms for people who have depression and other related emotional problems. Feel free to access them for support. At the same time, realize that you have no idea who you're talking to when you join a Web forum. The other people in the forum may be uneducated about depression or, even worse, trying to take advantage of a person in distress.

Here's a list of some legitimate Web sites that don't sell snake oil but do provide excellent information about depression and related emotional issues.

- ✔ **The American Psychiatric Association** (www.psych.org/public_info) provides information about depression and other mental disorders.

- ✔ **The American Psychological Association** (www.apa.org/pubinfo) provides information about the treatment of, as well as interesting facts about, depression and other emotional disorders.

- ✔ **The Anxiety Disorders Association of America** (www.adaa.org) lists self-help groups across the United States. It also displays a variety of anxiety screening tools for self-assessment. On their site, you can find an online newsletter and a message board. Because anxiety sometimes accompanies depression, you may want to check this site out.

- ✔ **National Alliance for the Mentally Ill** (www.nami.org) is a wonderful organization that serves as an advocate for people and families affected by mental disorders. Information is available about the causes, prevalence, and treatments of mental disorders that affect children and adults.

- ✔ **The National Association of School Psychologists** (www.nasponline.org) maintains information, or "fact sheets," for parents and teachers.

- ✔ **National Center for Complementary and Alternative Medicine** (www.nccam.nih.gov) is a government-sponsored site designed to provide information about alternative treatments for depression and other disorders. Most of the advice on this site is based upon research (unlike other sites about alternative treatments).

✔ **National Foundation for Depressive Illness** (www.depression.org) is a nonprofit group established to provide information about affective disorders.

✔ **National Institute of Mental Health** (www.nimh.nih.gov) reports on research about a wide variety of mental health issues. They also have an array of educational materials on depression. They provide resources for researchers and practitioners in the field.

✔ **WebMD** (www.webmd.com) provides a vast array of information about both physical and mental health issues, including information about psychological treatments, drug therapy, and prevention.

Index

• *H* •

• *I* •

FOR DUMMIES®

A world of resources to help you grow

TRAVEL

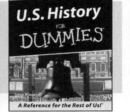

Italy
FOR DUMMIES
A Travel Guide for the Rest of Us!
0-7645-5453-0

Hawaii
FOR DUMMIES
A Travel Guide for the Rest of Us!
0-7645-5438-7

Walt Disney World & Orlando
FOR DUMMIES
A Travel Guide for the Rest of Us!
0-7645-5444-1

Also available:

America's National Parks For Dummies
(0-7645-6204-5)

Caribbean For Dummies
(0-7645-5445-X)

Cruise Vacations For Dummies 2003
(0-7645-5459-X)

Europe For Dummies
(0-7645-5456-5)

Ireland For Dummies
(0-7645-6199-5)

France For Dummies
(0-7645-6292-4)

Las Vegas For Dummies
(0-7645-5448-4)

London For Dummies
(0-7645-5416-6)

Mexico's Beach Resorts For Dummies
(0-7645-6262-2)

Paris For Dummies
(0-7645-5494-8)

RV Vacations For Dummies
(0-7645-5443-3)

EDUCATION & TEST PREPARATION

Spanish
FOR DUMMIES
A Reference for the Rest of Us!
0-7645-5194-9

Algebra
FOR DUMMIES
A Reference for the Rest of Us!
0-7645-5325-9

U.S. History
FOR DUMMIES
A Reference for the Rest of Us!
0-7645-5249-X

Also available:

The ACT For Dummies
(0-7645-5210-4)

Chemistry For Dummies
(0-7645-5430-1)

English Grammar For Dummies
(0-7645-5322-4)

French For Dummies
(0-7645-5193-0)

GMAT For Dummies
(0-7645-5251-1)

Inglés Para Dummies
(0-7645-5427-1)

Italian For Dummies
(0-7645-5196-5)

Research Papers For Dummies
(0-7645-5426-3)

SAT I For Dummies
(0-7645-5472-7)

U.S. History For Dummies
(0-7645-5249-X)

World History For Dummies
(0-7645-5242-2)

HEALTH, SELF-HELP & SPIRITUALITY

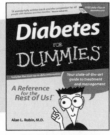

Diabetes
FOR DUMMIES
A Reference for the Rest of Us!
0-7645-5154-X

Sex
FOR DUMMIES
A Reference for the Rest of Us!
0-7645-5302-X

Parenting
FOR DUMMIES
A Reference for the Rest of Us!
0-7645-5418-2

Also available:

The Bible For Dummies
(0-7645-5296-1)

Controlling Cholesterol For Dummies
(0-7645-5440-9)

Dating For Dummies
(0-7645-5072-1)

Dieting For Dummies
(0-7645-5126-4)

High Blood Pressure For Dummies
(0-7645-5424-7)

Judaism For Dummies
(0-7645-5299-6)

Menopause For Dummies
(0-7645-5458-1)

Nutrition For Dummies
(0-7645-5180-9)

Potty Training For Dummies
(0-7645-5417-4)

Pregnancy For Dummies
(0-7645-5074-8)

Rekindling Romance For Dummies
(0-7645-5303-8)

Religion For Dummies
(0-7645-5264-3)

FOR DUMMIES®

Plain-English solutions for everyday challenges

OME & BUSINESS COMPUTER BASICS

0-7645-0838-5

0-7645-1663-9

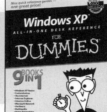

0-7645-1548-9

Also available:

Excel 2002 All-in-One Desk Reference For Dummies (0-7645-1794-5)

Office XP 9-in-1 Desk Reference For Dummies (0-7645-0819-9)

PCs All-in-One Desk Reference For Dummies (0-7645-0791-5)

Troubleshooting Your PC For Dummies (0-7645-1669-8)

Upgrading & Fixing PCs For Dummies (0-7645-1665-5)

Windows XP For Dummies (0-7645-0893-8)

Windows XP For Dummies Quick Reference (0-7645-0897-0)

Word 2002 For Dummies (0-7645-0839-3)

ITERNET & DIGITAL MEDIA

0-7645-0894-6   **0-7645-1642-6**   **0-7645-1664-7**

Also available:

CD and DVD Recording For Dummies (0-7645-1627-2)

Digital Photography All-in-One Desk Reference For Dummies (0-7645-1800-3)

eBay For Dummies (0-7645-1642-6)

Genealogy Online For Dummies (0-7645-0807-5)

Internet All-in-One Desk Reference For Dummies (0-7645-1659-0)

Internet For Dummies Quick Reference (0-7645-1645-0)

Internet Privacy For Dummies (0-7645-0846-6)

Paint Shop Pro For Dummies (0-7645-2440-2)

Photo Retouching & Restoration For Dummies (0-7645-1662-0)

Photoshop Elements For Dummies (0-7645-1675-2)

Scanners For Dummies (0-7645-0783-4)

Get smart! Visit www.dummies.com

- **Find listings of even more Dummies titles**
- **Browse online articles, excerpts, and how-to's**
- **Sign up for daily or weekly e-mail tips**
- **Check out Dummies fitness videos and other products**
- **Order from our online bookstore**

Available wherever books are sold. Go to www.dummies.com or call 1-877-762-2974 to order direct

FOR DUMMIES

Helping you expand your horizons and realize your potential

GRAPHICS & WEB SITE DEVELOPMENT

Photoshop 7 For Dummies
0-7645-1651-5

Creating Web Pages For Dummies
0-7645-1643-4

Macromedia Flash MX For Dummies
0-7645-0895-4

Also available:

Adobe Acrobat 5 PDF For Dummies
(0-7645-1652-3)

ASP.NET For Dummies
(0-7645-0866-0)

ColdFusion MX For Dummies
(0-7645-1672-8)

Dreamweaver MX For Dummies
(0-7645-1630-2)

FrontPage 2002 For Dummies
(0-7645-0821-0)

HTML 4 For Dummies
(0-7645-0723-0)

Illustrator 10 For Dummies
(0-7645-3636-2)

PowerPoint 2002 For Dummies
(0-7645-0817-2)

Web Design For Dummies
(0-7645-0823-7)

PROGRAMMING & DATABASES

C++ For Dummies
0-7645-0746-X

Visual Studio .NET All-in-One Desk Reference For Dummies
0-7645-1626-4

XML For Dummies
0-7645-1657-4

Also available:

Access 2002 For Dummies
(0-7645-0818-0)

Beginning Programming For Dummies
(0-7645-0835-0)

Crystal Reports 9 For Dummies
(0-7645-1641-8)

Java & XML For Dummies
(0-7645-1658-2)

Java 2 For Dummies
(0-7645-0765-6)

JavaScript For Dummies
(0-7645-0633-1)

Oracle9i For Dummies
(0-7645-0880-6)

Perl For Dummies
(0-7645-0776-1)

PHP and MySQL For Dummies
(0-7645-1650-7)

SQL For Dummies
(0-7645-0737-0)

Visual Basic .NET For Dummies
(0-7645-0867-9)

LINUX, NETWORKING & CERTIFICATION

Red Hat Linux 7.3 For Dummies
0-7645-1545-4

TCP/IP For Dummies
0-7645-1760-0

Networking For Dummies
0-7645-0772-9

Also available:

A+ Certification For Dummies
(0-7645-0812-1)

CCNP All-in-One Certification For Dummies
(0-7645-1648-5)

Cisco Networking For Dummies
(0-7645-1668-X)

CISSP For Dummies
(0-7645-1670-1)

CIW Foundations For Dummies
(0-7645-1635-3)

Firewalls For Dummies
(0-7645-0884-9)

Home Networking For Dummies
(0-7645-0857-1)

Red Hat Linux All-in-One Desk Reference For Dummies
(0-7645-2442-9)

UNIX For Dummies
(0-7645-0419-3)

Available wherever books are sold.
Go to www.dummies.com or call 1-877-762-2974 to order direct

WILEY